SQUARING UP

SQUARING UP

Policy Strategies to Raise Women's Incomes in the United States

EDITED BY MARY C. KING

Ann Arbor
THE UNIVERSITY OF MICHIGAN PRESS

2004   2003   2002   2001   4   3   2   I

A CIP catalog record for this book is available from the British Library.

Library of Congress Cataloging-in-Publication Data

Squaring up : policy strategies to raise women's incomes in the United
    States / edited by Mary C. King.
        p.   cm.
    Includes index.
    ISBN 0-472-09747-4 — ISBN 0-472-06747-8 (pbk.)
        I. Wages—Women—United States.   2. Pay equity—United States.   3.
    Sex discrimination in employment—United States.   I. Title: Policy
    strategies to raise women's incomes in the United States.   II. King,
    Mary C. 1956–
    HD6061.2.U6 S72   2001
    331.4'2153'0973—dc21   00-012729

To Rosa, Rio, and Clifford

Contents

Acknowledgments

First, I would like to thank the chapter authors, who all contributed such excellent work. Second, I'm very grateful to my editor, Ellen McCarthy, who supported this project from the beginning, coached me through the process of making it happen, and recruited very constructive reviewers. Third, I thank Clifford Lehman, Catherine Weinberger, Deborah Figart, and Johanna Brenner, who read and critiqued my contributions, strengthening them in all cases. Fourth, I'd like to thank my parents, Alan and Carolyn King, who have always encouraged me. And finally, I'd like to thank Clifford Lehman, my partner in all things, who helped me think through every aspect of this book from its inception.

Why We Need Policies to Raise Women's Incomes

Mary C. King

When a cigarette company targeting women in the 1970s used the slogan, "You've come a long way, baby!" many women used to mutter in response, "Yeah, we've a long way to go!" And that is still true.

American women have made progress. In the last one hundred years American women gained the ability to vote, serve on juries, own property including their own wages, acquire legal custody of their children, work in jobs other than domestic service—and smoke in public, for what that's worth—but women still lag far behind men in terms of political, economic, and social power. One of the most important ways in which American women have yet to achieve equality with men is in incomes. In fact in 1997, the average woman had only a bit more than half the income of an average man, as shown in figure 1.1.[1] Mostly due to women's rising relative pay, women's incomes have risen considerably from the lowest point in the last fifty years, 1965, when women's incomes were only 30.3 percent of men's.[2]

Many people assume that women's incomes nearly equal men's, on average, because they keep hearing news of women's rising wages. And the hourly earnings of women who work full-time are now four-fifths of men's. However, compared with men, women more often work part-time; may work fewer hours even when they work full-time; do not earn as much in overtime or bonuses; do not get as much pension income; receive less in Social Security, unemployment insurance, and veteran's benefits; do not earn as much from property or savings; and are con-

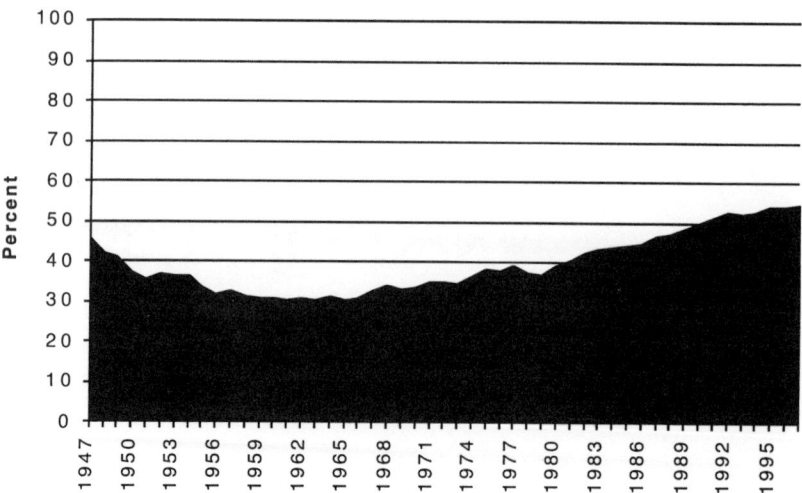

FIG. I.I. Women's incomes as a percentage of men's incomes. (From U.S. Bureau of the Census 1998.)

sidered responsible for much more unpaid work, such as child care, elder care, and housework.

However, low incomes for women are not like the weather, an unalterable fact of life. Our own recent history shows us that women's relative incomes can change considerably, and international comparisons demonstrate that women's incomes can be much closer to men's than they currently are here in the United States. The reason the gap between women's and men's incomes and poverty rates is much smaller in many other countries than it is here in the United States is because other countries implement policies that directly improve women's relative status.[3]

The objective of this book is to assess several potential policy changes that could raise women's incomes in the United States. The chapter authors, most of them economists, are experts in their fields who base their evaluation of potential policy strategies on years of research. Their work, combined here, is a formidable challenge to the prevailing notion that American women cannot expect much more from the economy than they already get. What is required are policy changes.

Why Are Women's Incomes Low?

Several factors combine to keep women's incomes low. The first and most important is that women are socially assigned most of the unpaid but time consuming and necessary work of child rearing, housework, and care of the sick and elderly. Social scientists often call this work "reproductive labor," distinguishing it from "productive labor," which produces goods and services for sale. Although men have started to do more child rearing and housework than in the past, much unpaid work is still socially designated "women's work." Women spend twenty-eight hours a week on these tasks as compared with men, who average sixteen hours a week, even when yard, home, and automobile maintenance are included (Schor 1991, 36). These figures are for the entire adult population; clearly the subset of women with children at home is spending many more hours than the average in reproductive labor.

Child rearing and housework are widely regarded as private activities chosen by parents for their own personal fulfillment, almost in the way we think of hobbies. However, child rearing is one of the most fundamental and essential tasks of any society. After we assure our own survival today, the next most important human function is to sustain ourselves into the future. Barbara Bergmann (1996) has written about the French, who provide parents with paid parental leaves, subsidized child care, and national health care as patriotic measures, to ensure that children will be able to sustain their national culture. At a minimum, we are utterly dependent upon parents to raise the labor force of the future. Few of us will be able to retire if we cannot count on Social Security, payments that will be funded by today's children when they become taxpayers. None of us will be economically secure if today's children are not productive in the future.

When parents divorce, women usually assume most of the responsibility of child rearing, both financial and otherwise. Child-support payments generally cover only a small part of the cost of child rearing, even when fathers earn high incomes.[4] When fathers cannot or will not pay, the U.S. government does not fill the gap. This is not the case in many other industrialized countries, where custodial parents are paid child allowances for each child, the government guarantees the payment of child support, and welfare payments are adequate to keep single-parent families out of poverty.[5]

Some women completely or periodically forego the opportunity to earn money when they stay home—full-time or part-time—to care for children or, increasingly, ailing parents and spouses (Rimer 1999). Other women work for pay but earn less because of their disproportionate caretaking responsibilities. Many more women than men work part-time so that they can care for their children. The hourly pay for part-time work is usually substantially lower than it is for the same work done full-time, and fringe benefits are rare.

Women are further penalized for spending time "out of the labor force" by our social safety net programs, which are not nearly as effective at keeping women out of poverty as men. Men get much more from Social Security and unemployment insurance than do women, as benefits are tied to earnings and time in the paid labor force. Further, programs like Social Security and unemployment insurance are seen as an entitlement to someone temporarily down on his or her luck or having earned the right to retire with dignity. The programs that serve women, particularly welfare, are seen as charity, are stigmatizing, are available only after people are completely impoverished, and are funded at levels that keep their recipients far below the poverty line (Pearce 1990).

Even when women are employed full-time, the jobs in which they are concentrated pay significantly less than "men's jobs." The majority of women still work in just a few occupations, particularly in clerical and service positions, where most of the other people in the same job are also women. Although women have moved into a wider variety of jobs than previously since the 1970s, occupational segregation by gender remains substantial. More than half of all women or men would have to change jobs in order for women and men to be identically distributed among occupations (Reskin 1994; King 1992).

"Women's jobs" continue to pay far less than jobs held by men that require comparable amounts of education, training, responsibility, and effort (Figart and Lapidus 1995). Women's jobs are often described as unskilled, while apparently comparable men's jobs are seen as semiskilled. For instance, seamstresses and electronic assemblers are thought of as unskilled, while auto mechanics and assemblers are considered semiskilled. Jobs that require skills perceived as feminine, such as nurturing, are particularly poorly paid; very few jobs pay less than child care, no matter how much education and training the workers have (England et al. 1994). It appears that work women have historically done is devalued in the marketplace and that work slips in value when women replace men in an occupation, as is seen in the case of teachers, clerical workers, and bank tellers, among others.[6]

Women also earn less than men because of direct sex discrimination on the job. When women and men are in the same occupation, women are not hired as often by the better paying firms.[7] Women are still frequently paid less than men at the same rank in the same occupation and are disproportionately bypassed for promotion, even in "women's jobs" like nursing and clerical work. Most hiring and promotion decisions are subjective, and managers continue to believe that men are more capable than are women.[8] Indeed women have made much more progress in the professions, where it is possible to gain educational credentials attesting to one's qualification for a particular job, than they have in management, where subjective assessments are far more important (King 1992).

The Consequences of Women's Low Incomes

The consequences of women's low incomes are serious. Perhaps the worst is the oppressive poverty experienced by too many women and their children. Diana Pearce coined the phrase "the feminization of poverty" to describe the phenomenon that she was among the first to point out, that the population of the poor in the United States was becoming more and more female.[9] Poverty became "feminized" when indexing Social Security payments to inflation lowered poverty rates among men over sixty-five to just over half the rate of the general population and among women over sixty-five to the same rate as that of the general population in 1997 (U.S. Bureau of the Census 1998b). The number of single mothers has increased so much in recent years that they now make up a large proportion of the poor, although poverty rates among single mothers have fallen considerably since the late 1950s.

Single mothers and their children suffer by far the highest rates of poverty in the United States. When exacerbated by race discrimination or disability, single mothers' poverty rates are staggering. In 1997, 13.3 percent of the population had incomes that fell at or below the official poverty line, but of "female headed households" with children under eighteen, 41 percent were poor. Of black single mothers, 47 percent were poor, and of Latina single mothers, 54 percent were poor (U.S. Bureau of the Census 1998b).

To be poor in this country too often means no escape from hunger, poor housing, immobility, inadequate medical care, inferior schooling, and dangerous neighborhoods. Women raising children on their own are having a hard time providing themselves and their children with a decent standard of living, despite the fact that the vast majority of single mothers have at least a high school education.

Another result of women' low incomes is a lack of bargaining power in relationships with men. Women's perception that they cannot support their children keeps too many women tied to partners who think that their wives and girlfriends "owe" them housework, child rearing, sex, and obedience. Although we may think of the distribution of work and resources among family members as determined by nature, evolving tradition, or need, researchers have found that money matters. On average, the higher the proportion of the family income brought in by the woman, the more money is spent on her needs and those of the children and the more housework is done by the man (Lundberg, Pollak, and Wales 1994; Goldscheider and Waite 1991).

Financial constraints limit women. Women have less ability to provide for themselves and others than similarly qualified men. Women have less ability to choose to divorce or remain unmarried than men. Women are less able to take advantage of educational and cultural opportunities than are men. Women have less ability to influence the world around them than do men.

Women's low incomes are both a symptom and a cause of gender inequity. Women have low incomes because women's lives and women's work are not as valued as are men's, and women's low incomes make it difficult for women to gain the training to be perceived as valuable, the purchasing power to be perceived as an important market, and the disposable income to make political donations on a scale that provides access to the political process.

It is no secret that money plays a hugely important role in U.S. politics, in determining who will be viable candidates and what sort of legislation will be enacted. After the 1998 elections, women constituted just 56 of 435 members of the U.S. House of Representatives, 9 of the 100 U.S. senators, 2 of 50 state governors, and 22 percent of state legislators.[10] United Nations' data on the proportion of women in the parliaments of different nations show the United States to be well back in the pack, behind even many developing countries. In fact we have a smaller proportion of women in our federal legislature than the world average.[11] Until quite recently, women have not had the financial clout to aggressively promote an agenda that would improve women's lives. The results are clear in the failure of the U.S. government to devote resources to child care, paid parental leave, women's health, enforcement of our antidiscrimination legislation, or any of a host of other issues of particular interest to women and their families.

Gender is clearly an important determinant of income in this country, yet few people would say that individual men *should* have far more control than women over economic resources. In our society, control over money means control over decision making, within families, within businesses, and within government.

Policies for Raising Women's Incomes

The policy options discussed in this book fall into three categories: those intended to lessen the impact of women's child rearing role on women's incomes throughout their lives, those that aim to raise the wages in "women's jobs," and those that examine ways to move women into higher-paying fields. These represent a selection of policies that deal with the institutions that keep women's incomes low, rather than individual discriminatory behavior, and that are of particular relevance for women at the middle or low end of the income spectrum currently. However, the chapter authors have striven to incorporate strategies beneficial to all women, educated and less educated; white, African American, Latina, Native American, and Asian American; married and single; mothers and nonmothers.

Reducing the Negative Impact of Child Rearing on
Women's Incomes

In chapter 2, Randy Albelda and Chris Tilly argue that welfare policy is important to all women for three reasons. Welfare is the primary social safety net for a woman with children; pushing women off welfare creates more competition and lower wages for "women's" jobs; and welfare policies are a barometer of the social valuation of women, especially of mothers. This chapter demonstrates why the outcome of current welfare reforms will be unsatisfactory and outlines policies that the authors believe would work better. It concludes with a program designed to go beyond the kinds of welfare reform presently being implemented, to create the possibility that all women and children—and men—would live decently.

In chapter 3, Barbara Bergmann notes that nearly two-thirds of mothers with children under the age of six are members of the paid workforce. The high cost of child care—especially of high-quality child care—means (i) that low- and middle-income families with children have a very hard time covering basic expenses and (ii) that the majority of children are not in care that is as good as it should be. Bergmann shows that single mothers really struggle; in 1998, a woman paying for two children enrolled in good child care had to earn $38,000 a year to be above the poverty line for a family of three that the National Academy of Sciences has developed as an improvement upon the one used by the U.S. Census Bureau. Few single mothers earn this much. Bergmann argues that we should both subsidize and better regulate child care.

Women provide the preponderance of unpaid labor for parenting, at the expense of their current and future earnings. In chapter 4, Nancy Folbre takes on the question of whether we, as a nation, should "support and reward parents for the time, energy, and money they put into raising the next generation." She answers that we should, because parents are creating the nation's most important economic resource, human capability. While considering how much support society should provide parents, what form that support should take, and who should pay to increase support for parents, Folbre also details our current programs, concluding that they are "complicated, inadequate and inconsistent."

Elderly women are twice as likely to be poor as are elderly men. The reasons for this are that very few elderly women have held jobs that provide them with pensions and that Social Security is designed to best support people who have worked for pay their entire lives at wages higher than many women earn. Further, women often outlive their husbands, after having substantially drawn down their savings to care for an ailing spouse. In chapter 5, Lois Shaw and Catherine Hill review the inequities in our current Social Security program, the problems with recent proposals to reform Social Security, and policy proposals to make elderly women far more secure.

Raising the Pay for "Women's Jobs"

Adult women comprise the single largest group of workers in minimum wage and near minimum wage jobs, due to their overrepresentation in retail and service work particularly. Consequently minimum wage policy truly is a "women's issue." In chapter 6, Deborah Figart reviews the evidence on the impact of minimum wage increases on unemployment, inflation, economic inequality, and poverty, with particular focus on women. She also describes the recent progress of living wage campaigns, a grassroots political movement to raise wages, often by working for local legislation to require any firm with a city contract to pay a "living wage" to all employees.

Researchers have shown that women remain concentrated in jobs dominated by women and that the pay for jobs with comparable requirements goes down as the proportion of women in the job goes up. It is this devaluation of women's jobs that pay equity advocates aim to end. Margaret Hallock was at the center of the comparable worth campaign of public sector workers in the state of Oregon, huge numbers of whom are clerical workers. Now executive director of the University of Oregon's Labor and Education Research Center, she is well positioned to appraise the costs and effectiveness of pay equity as a strategy to raise women's incomes. In chapter 7, Hallock assesses the problems and potential of pay equity efforts not only in Oregon but for the United States and Canada as well.

Membership in a union raises the pay of those on the bottom rungs of the wage structure relative to those at the top and tends to reduce wage differences by sex and race. In chapter 8, Peter Donohue relates the story of a group of small town nurses who successfully negotiated a much improved contract for themselves. With Donohue's assistance as a consultant provided by their union, the nurses identified the issues they felt most strongly about and then developed a bargaining strategy that included taking more control of the bargaining process, researching their hospital's financial situation, learning how to work with the press, and mobilizing their relationships with co-workers and neighbors to build a community campaign.

Moving Women into Higher-Paying Work

The policy of affirmative action was designed to promote the employment and advancement of women and members of ethnic minority groups into positions in which they are underrepresented. How well have these policies worked for women? In chapter 9, Lee Badgett and Jeannette Lim outline the history of affirmative action policy and the evidence—both quantative and qualitative—on its impact on women. They conclude that affirmative action has aided women but that better enforcement is necessary for major gains.

As Barbara Byrd points out in chapter 10, moving women into the skilled trades looks as though it ought to be a great strategy for raising women's incomes. Most jobs in the skilled trades provide relatively high earnings and the ability to work anywhere in the country, while apprenticeship programs require only a high school education, a driver's license, and physical fitness. Yet men are still 98 percent of skilled construction workers. Byrd's chapter includes data on women's representation in the trades, a discussion of the barriers to women in the trades, and a review of several efforts to reduce these barriers.

The math-intensive professions, such as engineering, also remain male dominated, and women in these occupations tend to earn more than women in many other fields. In chapter 11, Catherine Weinberger evaluates the potential of improving women's mathematical education as a strategy to raise women's incomes, examining separately the situations of women with high school educations, women with college educations and nontechnical majors, and women with college educations in relatively math-intensive majors.

The policies considered in each of the following chapters represent starting points for people interested in raising women's incomes in the United States. The final chapter of this book summarizes the lessons of the previous chapters and evaluates the potential of each strategy to mobilize a political coalition capable of successfully implementing it. Policies to raise women's incomes can appeal to people across the American political spectrum. We can implement a package of policies that allows women to choose to follow different courses in their lives, as best fit each individual's values and interests, and still be economically secure. The combined message of the following chapters is that we can raise women's incomes in the United States and that we should.

Notes

1. These figures include income from all sources, including wages, pensions, government benefits, interest income, child support, and alimony (U.S. Bureau of the Census 1998a).

2. According to the U.S. Department of Labor Women's Bureau, women's hourly earnings rose from 64 percent of men's in 1979 to 80 percent of men's in 1992, where they stalled through the remainder of the 1990s. (The U.S. Department of Labor Women's Bureau is a good source of data on women's earnings and occupational distributions, available on the web at <http://www.dol.gov/dol/wb/>.) Unfortunately, about 70 percent of the improvement in women's earnings relative to those of men over the 1980s and 1990s resulted from the loss of well-paying male jobs in manufacturing, so that men's wages were falling faster than were women's

over this period. This is documented in Mishel, Bernstein, and Schmitt (1999, 134–35).

3. The earnings gap between men and women who work full-time is smaller in a number of countries in Western and Eastern Europe, Scandinavia, Australia, and New Zealand. See the *OECD in Figures,* available on the web at <http://www.oecd.org//publications/figures/INDEX.HTM>. Another good source of international data is the United Nations Development Programme (1995).

4. See, for example, Garfinkel (1994).

5. See Smeeding (1992) and McFate, Smeeding, and Rainwater (1995).

6. See, for example, Strober and Arnold (1987); Kim (1989).

7. For instance, waitresses are particularly concentrated in restaurants where tips are lower. For office occupations, see Blau (1977).

8. See, for instance, Hartmann (1987).

9. Some commentators have bristled at this term, pointing out that the poor continue to disproportionately include men of color.

10. Center for the American Woman and Politics, Eagleton Institute of Politics, Rutgers University. Press release on general election results, updated November 25, 1998. <http://www.rci.rutgers.edu/~cawp/98electpress.html>.

11. See the United Nations Development Programme, *Human Development Report 1998,* available on the web at <http://www.undp.org/undp/hdro/98.htm.>

References

Bergmann, Barbara R. 1996. *Saving Our Children from Poverty: What the United States Can Learn from France.* New York: Russell Sage Foundation.

Blau, Francine D. 1977. *Equal Pay in the Office.* Lexington, MA: Lexington Press.

England, Paula, Melissa S. Herbert, Barbara Stanek-Kilbourne, Lori L. Reid, and Lori McCreary Megdal. 1994. "The Gendered Valuation of Occupations and Skills: Earnings in 1980 Census Occupations." *Social Forces* 73, no. 1:65–99.

Figart, Deborah M., and June Lapidus. 1995. "A Gender Analysis of Labor Market Policies for the Working Poor." *Feminist Economics* 1, no. 3:60–81.

Garfinkel, Irwin. 1994. "The Child Support Revolution." *American Economic Review* 84, no. 2:81–85.

Goldscheider, Frances K., and Linda J. Waite. 1991. *New Families, No Families?* Berkeley, CA: University of California Press.

Hartmann, Heidi. 1987. "Internal Labor Markets and Gender: A Case Study of Promotion." In *Gender in the Workplace,* edited by Clair Brown and Joseph Pechman, 59–92. Washington, DC: Brookings Institution.

Kim, Marlene. 1989. "Gender Bias in Compensation Structures: A Case Study of Its Historical Basis and Persistence." *Journal of Social Issues* 45, no. 4:39–49.

King, Mary C. 1992. "The Evolution of Occupational Segregation by Race and Gender, 1940 to 1988." *Monthly Labor Review* 115, no. 4:30–37.

Lundberg, S. J., R. A. Pollak, and T. J. Wales. 1994. "Do Husbands and Wives Pool Their Resources? Evidence from the U.K. Child Benefit." Discussion paper 94–06, Institute for Economic Research, University of Washington.

McFate, Katherine, Timothy Smeeding, and Lee Rainwater. 1995. "Markets and States: Poverty Trends and Transfer System Effectiveness in the 1980s." In

Poverty, Inequality and the Future of Social Policy: Western States in the New World Order, edited by Katherine McFate, Roger Lawson, and William Julius Wilson, 29–66. New York: Russell Sage Foundation.

Mishel, Lawrence, Jared Bernstein, and John Schmitt. 1999. *The State of Working America, 1996–97.* Armonk, NY: M. E. Sharpe.

Pearce, Diana. 1990. "Welfare Is Not for Women: Why the War on Poverty Cannot Conquer the Feminization of Poverty." In *Women, the State, and Welfare,* edited by Linda Gordon, 265–79. Madison, WI: University of Wisconsin Press.

Reskin, Barbara F. 1994. "Segregating Workers: Occupational Segregation by Race, Ethnicity, and Sex." *Industrial Relations Research Association Series, Proceedings of the Forty-sixth Annual Meeting.*

Rimer, Sara. 1999. "Study Details Sacrifices in Caring for Elderly Kin." *New York Times,* November 27.

Schor, Juliet. 1991. *The Overworked American: The Unexpected Decline of Leisure.* New York: Basic Books.

Smeeding, Timothy. 1992. "Why the U.S. Antipoverty System Doesn't Work Very Well." *Challenge,* January/February.

Strober, Myra H., and Carolyn L. Arnold. 1987. "The Dynamics of Occupational Segregation among Bank Tellers." In *Gender in the Workplace,* edited by Clair Brown and Joseph Pechman, 107–48. Washington, DC: Brookings Institution.

United Nations Development Programme. 1995. *Human Development Report, 1995: Gender and Human Development.* New York: Oxford University Press.

U.S. Bureau of the Census. 1998a. *Measuring Fifty Years of Economic Change Using the March Current Population Survey.* Current Population Reports, P60–203. Washington, DC: Government Printing Office.

———. 1998b. *Poverty in the United States: 1997.* Prepared by Joseph Dalaker and Mary Naifeh. Current Population Reports P60–201. Washington, DC: Government Printing Office.

PART I

Reducing the Negative Impact of Child Rearing on Women's Incomes

Moving beyond "Get a Job": What Real Welfare Reform Would Look Like

RANDY ALBELDA AND CHRIS TILLY

Welfare Reform Is a Women's Issue

In 1997, women comprised two-thirds of all adults who were poor. While the people in female headed households with children represented 14 percent of the total U.S. population they were 40 percent of all poor people. And while figures like these make it easy to see why poverty is a women's issue, we argue that how the government provides income to poor single mothers and their children matters to *all* women for three important reasons.

First, and most immediate, the level of welfare payments and the regulations on welfare receipt make up the "safety net" for any woman with a child. Single-mother families constitute 76 percent of all families receiving welfare.[1] If, as a woman, you find yourself supporting a family on your own—for whatever reason—you have a two in five chance of being poor but only a one in five chance of receiving welfare. What are your chances of ending up as a single mother? Currently, one woman in six is a single mother. Even many middle-class women are only a divorce, a layoff notice, or a pregnancy away from poverty.

Second, each time welfare benefits are slashed, eligibility rules tightened, or workfare requirements added, more desperate women flood the workforce. While most welfare recipients have limited education and skills, and consequently compete at the low end of the labor market, this competition has a ripple effect that reaches up to higher-skill jobs as well. At each level of the labor market, workers feel competitive pressure from those just a little below. Moreover, because women still earn only three-quarters as much as their male counterparts, more of them are concentrated close to the bottom of the wage hierarchy. Like the minimum wage or restrictions on child labor laws, decent welfare provisions not only protect the recipients themselves but shield other workers from rock-bottom competition.

Third, a bit more abstract but perhaps even more important, welfare policies indicate what the political and economic system thinks of women's work—all women's work, not just that of poor women. Welfare is designed to provide the income supplements mothers need when they lack male income. States determine the level of welfare benefits, and the range is immense. In 1998, the median welfare payment for a family of three was $388, 34 percent of the poverty line—and almost sure to fall farther. Even adding in the cash value of food stamps, welfare leaves families below the poverty level. In 1998, the value of welfare and food stamps combined for a family of three in New York—the state with the highest welfare benefit—was $928, and in Mississippi—the state with the lowest benefit—it was $441.[2] In the median state, the combined package was worth 62 percent of the poverty line. Considering families who would have been poor without government assistance, welfare payments only lift one single-mother family in ten above the poverty line—but government aid (mainly Social Security) to families headed by someone over sixty-five boosts three-quarters out of poverty. By keeping welfare payments so low, our political system ratifies an economic system that pays women far less than men and does not value (in terms of income) the work of caring for families.

But if welfare policy gives an indication of how much our society values women's work, we are clearly moving backward in this valuation. In 1996, Congress overhauled its welfare program AFDC (Aid to Families with Dependent Children), a program for low-income families in effect in the United States from 1935 to 1996, and established a block grant called TANF (Temporary Assistance for Needy Families). The federal changes mirror changes proposed and adopted earlier by many states. TANF, and before it AFDC, is what is generally referred to as "welfare." It, and its state counterparts, primarily serve low-income families headed by women. The main components of the welfare reforms at both the federal and state levels are to replace government assistance with earnings, discourage certain behaviors through reductions in assistance, and limit the time any family can receive cash assistance. Together the changes present a forceful message to women receiving welfare: Get a Job—Any Job—and Get It Now!

This chapter discusses why current welfare policies are ineffective, outlines a set of welfare reforms that we think would work, and proposes a much broader set of reforms that go beyond welfare—ones needed to implement a strategy that promotes paid work and a decent standard of living for all families, especially those that include children.

Mean, Lean, and Ineffective: Why Current Policy Won't Work

AFDC did not work—but not for the reasons most commonly heard. Conservative authors and politicians argued that the program encouraged dependency and irresponsibility, but these criticisms are wide of the mark. In reality, welfare did not work because the program refused to address the real issues facing single-mother families. What are these issues? American women's wages are simply not enough to support a family. Being a parent requires both time in unpaid activities and money to meet one's family's needs. Furthermore, families come in all shapes and sizes: for example, the welfare program did a poor job of helping parents of disabled children, mothers fleeing domestic abuse, or parents in high-crime neighborhoods where keeping a close eye on children is critical.

Instead of facing up to this reality, welfare "reform" in the 1990s got tougher and more intent on replacing public assistance with earnings. The expectation that women should work rather than receive public assistance is not new. It greatly shaped welfare policies of the early and mid-1980s when state policies aimed at enhancing employability spawned programs—with catchy names such as ET Choices (Employment and Training Choices [Massachusetts]), GAIN (Gaining Avenues to Independence [California]), and REACH (Realizing Economic Achievement [New Jersey])—that pushed women to get training and job hunt. For twenty years, the presumption has been that women—including single mothers—should and can do paid work and that paid work will provide economic independence.

Despite limited information on the success of states' programs, Congress reformed AFDC for the entire nation in the Family Support Act of 1988 to require states to provide education and training programs for work-eligible adult recipients through the Jobs Opportunity and Basic Skills (JOBS) program. By "work eligible," they meant adults whose children were three and older, though states had the option of pushing this down to children one year and older.

The state reforms of the 1990s took an even harder line than earlier state and federal changes, moving from enhancing employability to *requiring* work. State government reforms typically have included both carrots and sticks: allowing recipients to keep more of their cash benefits when they do waged work but also imposing mandatory work requirements with benefits and sanctioning recipients who do not comply with requirements. What was new in the 1990s was stepped-up rules with increased sanctions (reducing or eliminating welfare assistance) for not complying with rules, less substantive training and education, and tight limits on the length of time one person can obtain welfare. Many of the rules have harsh "behavior modification" implications. For instance, "family caps" withhold compensation for children born while the mother is receiving welfare—even though welfare recipients are less likely than other women to have another child. "Learnfare" reduces the grant if children miss school—even though average absenteeism rates for kids receiving welfare are comparable to those of other children. One can imagine the outcry if the dependent child tax deduction received by most middle-class Americans were made subject to restrictions such as these, but apparently telling poor women how to run their lives is politically acceptable.

Finally, the federal reform, passed in 1996, dismantled AFDC, which had guaranteed assistance to eligible families for as long as they needed it. Instead the new law gives states authority to define who is needy, provides a fixed budget regardless of the state of the economy, sets percentages of recipients who must be employed or placed in "workfare," and requires that federal welfare funds money not be spent on any adult for more than sixty months in his or her lifetime. The primary goal is to end welfare with "work," and while the new law gives states full authority, there is virtually no accountability. Since states are now free of federal oversight, they may attempt to spend as little as possible on public assistance—and some states are avidly pursuing that goal. Overall, these changes to welfare signal a low point in U.S. poverty policy. Neither the federal nor the state approaches hold much promise for significantly diminishing poverty; they amount to new ways to punish welfare recipients and bully them off the welfare rolls.

Why Can't "Work First" Work?

There are three basic reasons why this is a failed strategy. First, it ignores the fact that most mothers already work at taking care of their children. Raising children is work. It requires time, skills, and commitment. While we as a society do not place a monetary value on child rearing, it is work that is invaluable—and indeed essential to the survival of our society. (See chap. 1 for further discussion of this point.)

Second, many mothers are not "job ready." In order to successfully replace welfare with earnings, women need jobs that pay family-sustaining wages. But it is clear that the jobs held by women with children and low educational attainment typically do not pay enough to support the women and their families, due to sex segregation by occupation and the time demands of child care. Women need skills and confidence to secure decent jobs. Welfare reform does not promise to provide the skills or create the jobs. Further, in order to be able to get to work, mothers must have dependable child care, transportation, and elaborate backup plans for times when a child is sick or the car breaks down.

Third, the jobs available to welfare mothers are often not "mother ready." On the one hand many low-wage jobs—especially those in the service and retail sectors—do not work for single mothers. They often require workers to be at work at nontraditional hours and have frequent shift changes. This makes securing child care a nightmare. The jobs themselves can also be unstable. Banks, supermarkets, and hospitals—major employers of women—are industries that have gone through frequent ownership changes, generating job loss through downsizing and reorganization. On the other hand, single mothers are "fragile" workers. Juggling work and family is hard enough for two-parent families and far more difficult for single-mother families. Even a small crisis, such as a snow day or measles, can mean missing work. In the low-wage sector, missing work can mean losing a job. Employers want reliable workers as much as workers want reliable work—the combination of single mothers and low-wage work is not usually a very good match for either.

The best evidence that low-wage jobs cannot replace welfare is that most women on welfare already are engaged in low-wage work. Studies of former AFDC recipients found that three-fourths of women who received any AFDC over a twenty-four-month period in the late 1980s had some form of employment or were actively seeking employment during the time they received welfare (Spalter-Roth et al. 1995).[3] In fact, combining work with welfare is and always has been a vital strategy for low-income mothers.

For half of recipients who combine welfare and paid work, welfare substitutes for unemployment benefits, tiding over women who are just starting to look for work or are between jobs but have not built up enough continuous employment experience to qualify for unemployment benefits. About one-fifth of women who combine welfare and paid work earn so little money that they still qualify for welfare when they work, while another fifth use welfare temporarily as a form of disability insurance until they are well enough to work again or are able to obtain disability benefits.

Surveys and in-depth discussions with poor mothers suggest that welfare is a last resort, not an oasis. Not only are benefits extremely low, but the process of applying for and receiving welfare is itself often demeaning and dehumanizing. If there were viable options, many mothers would take them.

Long-term, continuous welfare recipients (the 12 percent of recipients who have not left the rolls five years after starting welfare) are mostly people who face serious employment barriers, such as very low education levels, little work experience, and significant health problems (Greenberg 1993). Researchers investigating this issue found that single mothers were much more likely to have health problems than other mothers (12 percent versus 4 percent). Among long-term recipients, 41 percent of those aged 45–60, and 20 percent of those aged 35–44, had disabilities or health problems that limited work (Wolfe and Hill 1993). Cutting off benefits for these women will not force them into the labor market. For many long-term recipients, but also even for many better-off recipients, time limitations without adequate child care, job availability, and wages are no more than a punitive measure.

Poor Results: The Impact of Welfare Reform

Program changes requiring paid work are moving women off the welfare rolls but are not necessarily moving them out of poverty. Between August 1996—when federal welfare reform was implemented—and December 1998 the welfare caseloads have plummeted by 37 percent from about 4.5 million families to under 3 million. The reductions are as high as 83 percent in Wyoming and 77 percent in Wisconsin (U.S. Department of Health and Human Services 1999). However, state evaluations of what has happened to women leaving the rolls indicate that there are good reasons to declare welfare reform a failure. In a recent publication summarizing seven of the most detailed follow-up studies done by the states, the General Accounting Office (GAO) found that substantial percentages (ranging from 19 to 30 percent) of those who left welfare are returning. Of those not returning, about two-thirds find employment. However, that employment is most often at low wages. Average quarterly earnings ranged from $3,786 in Washington State to $2,384 in Maryland. Making the heroic assumption that people work all year,[4] these earnings amount to $15,144 and $9,536 annually (U.S. General Accounting Office 1999). By way of comparison, the poverty line for a family of three in 1998 was $13,650.

A good example of what is going on can be found in Massachusetts. That state instituted a very rigid "work first" policy and has had a spectacular economy—with unemployment rates as low as they have been in twenty-five years—since welfare reform's implementation there in 1995. In April 1999—too late to be included in the GAO's report—the state released its first study on what has happened to recipients a year after they left welfare and found that 26.5 percent were employed at wages of over $250 a week; 26.5 percent were employed at wages at or below $250 a week, or poverty level wages; 18.6 percent of women were back on welfare and not employed; and 28.4 percent were not on welfare and not employed (Albelda 1999). In short, about one-quarter of those who left welfare were one year later working at nonpoverty wages—about the same results as under the old welfare program.

And while earnings for those with jobs may surpass the amount of cash families received under welfare they do not take into account the new costs of employment—especially child care and transportation—and the loss of food stamps and Medicaid, which are available only to people with very low incomes. Further, while welfare was stable, low-wage employment for mothers with young children is not, since people are frequently laid off or are fired for missing work.

Moreover, these rather poor findings are the best we can expect. The economy has been highly cooperative, with record low unemployment rates. None of the studies has been able to find more than 85 percent of their target samples of ex-recipients, and many believe that those missing from the sample are the worst off, since that group presumably includes people who have become homeless or had their phones cut off. Further, none of the GAO-reviewed studies included people who hit the time limits. Surely families forced off welfare because their "time is up" are likely to fare far worse than those who have left voluntarily.

Creating Real Welfare Reform

What might real welfare reform look like?

First and foremost, welfare reform should "do no harm." Its primary purpose should be to end poverty, not punish the poor or force them into the ranks of the working poor or worse. There are reforms to the current welfare system that would make life more bearable for those who currently do receive assistance as well as serve to improve recipients' economic status and chances of staying off welfare permanently.

The nine proposals we make are not new or unusual. Several of the provisions have already been proposed by some states, and a few are already in operation. They build on the results of decades of social science research in the United States, as well as the policy experiences of other countries, particularly in Europe. What distinguishes our list of reforms from the majority of those currently in place is that we emphasize positive incentives, a broadening of the scope of welfare, and standardizing a basic set of benefits and rules in the program across the states.

1. Establish a minimum benefit, then index it to inflation

Even before states were given free rein to fashion their welfare systems any way they see fit, welfare benefits were embarrassingly low. Cash benefits, even coupled with the food stamp program, are woefully inadequate to support a family. Table 2.1 lists the maximum level of cash benefits for a family of three in all fifty states and Washington, DC, in 1998 and 1987 (adjusted for inflation). There are two important things to notice. First, the benefit levels vary tremendously state by state. While there are certainly very different costs of living across the fifty states, living costs do not vary as much as benefits do. The second bit of important information conveyed in table 2.1 is how low benefits are and the degree to which states have allowed benefit levels to fall over the last ten years. In all but three states, welfare benefits dropped. The median state saw a decline of 22.7 percent, and over 60 percent of all the states let benefits slide 20 percent or more over the decade. By way of comparison, the average hourly earnings of workers have fallen by just under 1 percent over the same period. Low—and falling—benefits for families with children help explain why the U.S. child poverty rates are by far the highest among the sixteen wealthiest industrialized nations and why the average "poverty gap" (the amount the average poor U.S.

family falls below the poverty line) has grown by $1,000 over the past thirty years (Mishel, Bernstein, and Schmitt 1999).

In the United States, a national minimum wage sets a floor to what workers get; why not a comparable social wage floor to what a family gets when its adult members cannot work? Boosting benefits and establishing a benefit floor would go a long way toward improving the lives of poor women and children, but in order to maintain the value of that floor, it must be indexed to inflation. The main reason poverty rates for

TABLE 2.1. **Maximum Welfare Benefit Level for a Family of Three and Percentage Change for 50 States and Washington, DC, in 1987 and 1998 (in 1998 dollars)**

State	1987	1998	Percentage Change in Benefits 1987–98	State	1987	1998	Percentage Change in Benefits 1987–98
Alabama	169	164	–3.1	Montana	515	461	–10.5
Alaska	1,075	923	–14.1	Nebraska	502	364	–27.5
Arizona	420	347	–17.5	Nevada	466	348	–25.4
Arkansas	290	204	–29.6	New Hampshire	697	550	–21.1
California	908	565	–37.8	New Jersey	608	424	–30.3
Colorado	496	356	–28.3	New Mexico	379	489	29.1
Connecticut	738	636	–13.8	New York	713	577	–19.1
Delaware	458	338	–26.2	North Dakota	532	440	–17.3
District of Columbia	544	379	–30.3	North Carolina	372	272	–26.8
Florida	379	303	–20.0	Ohio	443	362	–18.4
Georgia	377	280	–25.8	Oklahoma	419	292	–30.3
Hawaii	705	570	–19.1	Oregon	445	460	3.4
Idaho	436	276	–36.7	Pennsylvania	524	421	–19.6
Illinois	491	377	–23.2	Rhode Island	687	554	–19.4
Indiana	413	288	–30.3	South Carolina	287	402	40.1
Iowa	547	426	–22.1	South Dakota	525	430	–18.1
Kansas	550	429	–21.9	Tennessee	228	185	–18.9
Kentucky	283	262	–7.3	Texas	264	188	–28.8
Louisiana	273	190	–30.3	Utah	540	451	–16.4
Maine	581	439	–24.5	Vermont	865	656	–24.2
Maryland	515	388	–24.7	Virginia	418	354	–15.2
Massachusetts	732	565	–22.8	Washington	706	546	–22.7
Michigan	646	459	–28.9	West Virginia	357	253	–29.2
Minnesota	763	532	–30.3	Wisconsin	742	628	–15.3
Mississippi	172	120	–30.3	Wyoming	517	340	–34.2
Missouri	405	292	–27.8				
Median state	502	388	–22.7				

Note: Benefits are adjusted using the Consumer Price Index for Urban Consumers (CPI-U) to 1998 dollars.

Sources: U.S. Department of Health and Human Services (1998b), 372; and Congressional Research Service (1998), 7–8.

people sixty-five years of age and older are much lower than children's poverty rates is that Social Security and Supplemental Security Income benefits have not eroded with inflation.

2. Standardize and expand program eligibility

States are now free to define eligibility as they please. The limited resources provided by the federal government and the fiscal constraints states face make it unlikely that many states will increase the number of poor families that are eligible. However, wider eligibility is only fair. Under the old AFDC system, poor children in families with two able-bodied adults were not eligible for AFDC if their parents worked more than one hundred hours a month or did not have a prior work history. Under TANF, all states were required to cover two-parent families, although the eligibility requirements were left to the states. Still, a smaller percentage of all families receiving TANF funds in 1998 (7.2 percent) were two-parent families than were before welfare reform in 1994 (8.3 percent) (U.S. Department of Health and Human Services 1994, 1998a). Yet in an economy in which many of the fastest growing jobs are those that pay wages close to minimum, more and more two-adult working families are poor. In 1997, for example, 10 percent of people in married-couple families with at least one worker and with a child under the age of six were poor (U.S. Bureau of the Census 1998b). All needy families with children should be eligible for cash assistance or in-kind benefits on the same basis, without regard to whether one or both parents are in the home and regardless of in which state they reside.

3. Make work pay

Welfare regulations have been slanted against earners. Under previous federal rules, after four months of paid work, AFDC benefits were reduced almost $1 for $1 earned, so that gaining a job reduced time with one's children without boosting income much. A welfare mother could retain her health-care benefits and received a child-care subsidy but was eligible for this assistance only for one year after her earnings made her ineligible for cash benefits. Under those rules, going to work for most women with children just did not pay. A $6-an-hour job at thirty hours a week is more than enough to push a woman off welfare—but not out of poverty. Yet, a woman with small children probably cannot work more than thirty hours a week. At $6 an hour—85 cents over the minimum wage—her yearly earnings are $9,360 before she pays for her new costs of going to work—Social Security tax, clothing, and transportation. The Earned Income Credit, a refundable federal income tax credit aimed at low-income families, and food stamps help boost total family income considerably, but even so this family will end up with income near the poverty line for a family of three. After a year, if this woman loses her health benefits and her child-care subsidy is gone, even the meager level of welfare benefits can begin to look good. At a minimum, she does not have to find day care for her children and knows that if one of them gets sick he or she is entitled to health care.

One way to make work pay is to reduce the earnings penalty for welfare recipients who find work. That way when welfare recipients do work, they get to keep their earnings as well as some portion of their benefits—until the family is well out of poverty. As of 1998, two-thirds of the states had reformed their welfare systems to help do that. States accomplish this differently, but in all cases, women with earnings get to keep more of them as they go to work. And if implemented well, this change seems to help. A recent study of four different programs that provide financial incentives to work found that generous incentives produce large increases in employment. Further, the more generous the incentives the more the programs helped move families out of poverty (Blank, Card, and Robbins 1999). Unfortunately, the sixty-month limit imposed by TANF might jeopardize this important work incentive, since making work pay prolongs the period during which families collect cash assistance.

4. Expand health-care, child-care, and transportation services

The biggest challenge faced by most women who receive welfare is not the challenge of getting off "the dole." The problem they face is staying off. Recidivism rates are very high, especially among women who leave welfare because of increased earnings rather than marriage. One important way to make work continue to pay—and not just for welfare mothers—is to assure health-care and child-care subsidies to all families for as long as a child needs care and to make sure everyone has the means to get to and from employment and home, as well as to child- and health-care providers.

One of the unintended impacts of welfare reform has been that the Medicaid rolls have dropped along with welfare rolls, even though poverty rates have stayed nearly the same. Families U.S.A. estimates that welfare reform resulted in 675,000 people losing their health-care coverage in 1997 alone (Families USA 1999). As people leave welfare they are losing their Medicaid, and for many it is not being replaced with work-based insurance. The new welfare law does continue the provision of transitional Medicaid for twelve months for families who leave welfare because of increased earnings. However the new rules are more complicated, and after six months states may require families to pay a premium and limit the scope of coverage, or families may lose their eligibility if their income exceeds 185 percent of the poverty line. Twelve states have extended medical assistance beyond the federally mandated twelve months, and several states are pursuing programs to extend coverage to low-income children and families regardless of welfare status. These directions are encouraging, but there is still no guarantee that every child—and his or her parents—in the United States has access to health care.

The new welfare law does not require states to provide assistance with child care when families leave welfare for employment, as AFDC did. Instead the federal government established a new Child Care and Development Fund block grant, and states can transfer up to 10 percent of their federal TANF funds into child care. The new welfare bill has left child-care standards, payment schedules, and eligibility totally to the states, resulting in a patchwork of programs. A 1998 GAO report on child-care expenditures under TANF in seven states found that all seven had increased the amount they spent on child care, but the percentage increase varied tremendously, from 2 percent in Maryland to 62 percent in Louisiana. However, beyond covering women on welfare who were employed or in work programs and needed child care, there was no consistent coverage among the states (U.S. General Accounting Office 1998). Some covered nonwelfare, "working poor" families, but some did not. Even with the increased spending on child care, the Urban Institute estimates that under the provisions of the block grant states will be able to cover child-care needs for fewer than half of all low-income families (Long and Clark 1997).

Obtaining a job and then securing child care mean nothing if a welfare mother cannot transport herself to them. Only 6 percent of welfare families own a car, and many live in areas not well served—if served at all—by public transportation systems (Kaplan 1998). Even for those who live in cities with good public transportation, the transportation problems are immense. For those who find jobs at nontraditional hours, public transportation is spotty. If the jobs women find are in the suburbs they are also out of luck because public transportation routes have been designed to bring suburbanites into the city, not city residents out to the suburbs.

Under AFDC rules, owning a car worth $1,500 made one ineligible for welfare. The new welfare bill leaves transportation issues to the states. Many states have raised their eligibility asset limit of cars to at least $5,000, and others have eliminated the asset limit entirely. Raising the asset limit alone will not solve acute transportation problems. One solution, which some states have begun to experiment with, is to provide low-interest loans to help poor families buy cars. But truly meeting these needs will require substantial expansion of public transportation systems. In the short run, this expansion could draw on existing vehicles, such as senior shuttles or Head Start vans, or contract with van or minibus services to fill the biggest gaps in the transit net: rural transit, reverse commutes, and off-hours commutes. In the long run, transit systems must be redesigned with the working poor in mind (Kaplan 1998).

5. Improve the child-support system

Legislation to track down "deadbeat dads" easily sails through legislatures and gets signed into law in state after state. Under the old law welfare recipients were allowed to keep only the first $50 a month ($600 a year!) from any child-support payments. The rest of the child support went to the state and federal governments to reimburse them for AFDC payments to the family. If the father did not pay on time, the mother did not even get $50. So while the state defrayed some of its costs, families depending on welfare were not much better off, and fathers had little incentive to pay. The new federal law does not even require that the first $50 go to the family! Under TANF, twenty-nine states have picked up this option, meaning that in those states a mother on welfare gets none of the child-support payments (Gallagher et al. 1998).

To make child support work for welfare recipients, at a minimum, the recipients should keep the entire amount of child support, without any reduction in benefits, until the family has a decent income. In addition, welfare mothers should be able to keep the child support even if it is paid late. The state should not benefit, and the children should not lose out, just because Dad does not pay on time.

The idea of child-support insurance also has merit. Under such a plan, the state would pay the family a guaranteed amount for child support. If the father pays more than the guaranteed amount, the family would get what he pays. But if he pays less, the state would make up the difference, up to the amount of the guarantee. This makes sense because the absent fathers from families receiving welfare are usually poor themselves, so the amount that can be gleaned directly from child support is quite limited.

California has authorized three child-support-assurance pilot projects, although none had been funded as of 1999. In March 1999, Montana passed child-support-assurance legislation that, while covering only a modest four hundred families a year, would assure single-parent families with income up to 150 percent of the poverty line, $200 a month for the first child, $100 for the second, and $65 for each additional child (Center for Law and Social Policy 1999).

An insurance plan could be a plus if it increases income, protects Medicaid and child-care eligibility, and guarantees support even if the state has not established a child-support order. Of course, child-support insurance does not help children whose fathers are dead, and it does not help children in two-parent families. Nevertheless, well-designed child-support insurance would be a first step toward a much needed child allowance—a guaranteed income for all children, which is an established policy in many other countries.

6. Education and training for jobs that pay a living wage

One important reason why welfare reform that pushes immediate employment and downplays training programs will do little to boost women's earnings is that it does not invest in the long-term—and more expensive—training required to place women in well-paying jobs. A five-year follow-up study of four state-initiated AFDC programs in the 1980s found only one in which higher earnings for women in training programs resulted from better-paying jobs, not merely from finding employment earlier. This was a program in Baltimore that encouraged women to find and train for higher-paying jobs, even if it meant staying on AFDC longer. And even that program was not able to reduce the number of those who are long-term recipients—women who typically have serious health, disability, or basic skill problems (Friedlander and Burtless 1995).

Because of the federal requirements that an ever-increasing percentage of welfare caseloads be in employment or unpaid work placements in order for states to receive their full allotment of the TANF block grant, states feel pressured to limit training and education to meet these work requirements. States are currently spending large amounts of money on training in response to the new welfare-to-work philosophy, but much of that is directed toward job search or quick-fix "job readiness" training, rather than the development of job skills.

About two-thirds of welfare recipients lack a high school diploma (Spalter-Roth et al. 1995). This means the education and training needs for the adults using welfare are deep and wide. Research on past education and training programs for welfare recipients provides useful, but discouraging, information about their effectiveness. Fewer than half of the basic education programs—ones targeted to women with low educational attainment—improved the earnings of participants when compared to a group with similar characteristics but not participating in programs. And of those that did improve wages, much of that improvement had to do with leaving welfare quickly, rather than resulting from higher wages (Pauly 1996).

One of the few bright spots in states' education and training record for AFDC mothers in the past had been access to postsecondary education, one of the best ways for single mothers to escape poverty. Unfortunately, states are now restricting this directly and indirectly, and the possibility of higher education may be completely lost with time limits or workfare requirements, because they do not exempt women in education and training programs. States who are vigorously pursuing "work first" welfare reform actually are reducing the amount of training and education welfare recipients can get. For example, in college-rich Massachusetts, welfare recipient enrollments in community colleges fell by more than 50 percent—far beyond the reduction in welfare rolls—only two years after the state passed its welfare reform. Pushing women out of college is not helping their earning power. In a study of students receiving welfare at Eastern Washington University in 1997, Thomas Karier found that those who had dropped out in 1998 (some because of the stricter requirements) had much lower average wages than those who had graduated: an average of $6.40 per hour for those who dropped out after their first year versus $11.00 an hour for those who graduated (Karier 2000).

7. *Comprehensive assessment for parents and children who receive welfare*

Most women resort to welfare not because they do not want to hold a job but because they cannot. While many simply lack child care, transportation, or training, others have much larger problems associated with a collapse in their family networks and support systems or depletion of their families' internal resources. Abusive home situations, depression and other mental health disorders, homelessness, chemical abuse, physical disabilities, and lack of coping skills are not uncommon among women seeking cash assistance. Poverty takes its toll on self-esteem and health. Further, being poor often makes even small problems harder to solve because of lack of financial resources. Most states' welfare efforts do not address these issues and in some cases can make them worse. Solutions become even more elusive when women are reluctant to reveal their problems for fear of losing their children to the foster care system. Time limits, workfare, mandatory training, and requirements to disclose paternity information might cause further harm to children and their mothers. Rather than this punitive barrage, support services linking recipients to psychological services, drug treatment programs, or housing assistance are a vital first step toward economic security.

One particularly powerful argument for better assessment is the high incidence of domestic violence among women who turn to public assistance. Men who physically and sexually abuse women or their children who currently receive public assistance often feel threatened by the economic control their partners would gain if they received income on their own through earnings. Such men often refuse to allow women and girls to work or even participate successfully in training programs or employment (Raphael 1996). Further, women who have experienced abuse are more likely to have used welfare discontinuously than other women. If abusive partners stalk women and their children, as is often the case, time limits may place undue time pressures on welfare recipients and force them into potentially dangerous situations. Helping women to escape domestic violence will take both flexible policies and a sensitive approach.

Currently, welfare offices are notoriously "user unfriendly." Changing the climate at the welfare office will be necessary to make any welfare reform work. Caseworkers could use the application process as an interactive exploration of the barriers that applicants face to finding stable employment. Intensive case management may not be financially feasible for most states, but certainly states could identify the highest-risk populations and begin there.

Assessment is crucial, especially as the welfare rolls thin and those left are the people with the most barriers to employment. Oregon has set up a screening mechanism for mental health problems, while Washington and Kansas have been developing ways to recognize learning disabilities. A few states are working on developing protocols for caseworkers to recognize signs of domestic violence. Utah, through intensive case management with qualified social workers, has been a leader in identifying and providing appropriate services for women with multiple barriers to employment (Kramer 1998).

8. State flexibility and monitoring

While the federal government needs to set a higher baseline standard of welfare support, states can and should be able to build on this standard and have sufficient flexibility to try different approaches to providing services and reforms, as suggested previously. The old waiver process, which required evaluation of any deviation from federal rules, should be reinstituted. It can assure that states provide a minimum level of benefits and services and at the same time can serve as an important way for states to share "best practices." A welfare system combining solid minimum guarantees, space for experimentation that recognizes the diverse needs of the welfare population, and fundamental respect for the work entailed in caring for children offers the best prospects for really reducing poverty.

9. End time limits

The new federal welfare bill limits the amount of time a family can receive welfare to a lifetime limit of sixty months in effect since July 1, 1997. Twenty states have limits that are shorter. States may exempt up to one-fifth of their caseloads from the time limit, and most states have exemptions for some families from their time limits based on factors like age of youngest child and physical ability of family members.

One of the popular arguments for time limits is that women who receive welfare get stuck in a "cycle of dependency." However, there is not much evidence for this assertion. In reality, the vast majority of women leave welfare within two years, but half of those end up returning. The median lifetime use of welfare, based on studies using 1980s data, is four years (Bane and Ellwood 1994). Since benefits levels are extremely low, most mothers would prefer to support themselves through other means but for a wide range of reasons—many discussed in this chapter—cannot.

Some argue that time limits provide welfare recipients with a needed "kick in the pants." But, given the nature of low-wage work, the work required to care for children without much income, and the lack of family or work supports, time limits will likely end up shoving many down a deep hole without much means to dig their way out. It is hard to predict what will happen when families hit their time limits, since to date few states' limits have arrived. For those that have, there is not yet information available about the impacts.

A few states have chosen not to have limits at all or to have them only in some cases: Michigan has no state-imposed time limit; Vermont and Illinois exempt single-parent families from time limits if the parent works at least twenty hours a week; and Arizona, California, and Rhode Island exempt all children from time limits.

Time limits work against efforts by states to make work pay. The limits will cut off families who are employed but earn too little to support themselves—the group that has long combined welfare and paid work. Meanwhile, the substantial minority of adults who are longtime welfare users almost always suffer multiple barriers to employment and need extensive services to help overcome these barriers. Time limits will not solve these problems and could even make them worse by pressuring parents to make poor choices.

Beyond Welfare Reform

The changes we propose here will not end poverty, wipe out gender inequality, or solve the tension between work and family; in that sense they are modest. But in the current, very constrained political context they are quite ambitious. They extend far beyond the parameters of most political discussions today, and to some they may seem like "pie in the sky." Yet, still they are not enough. To make real progress, we need to go beyond welfare reform. In the next section we present a seven-point program to help all working families and with it move toward less poverty and more gender equality.

It's Not Just Welfare:
Policies as If Families Really Mattered

What is needed—and not just for poor single mothers but for all families—is child-care reform, wage reforms, and job reforms. Here, in shorthand form, is an economic program that is antipoverty, pro-family, and pro-woman—unlike the current policies of the public and private sectors. Welfare as we knew it—income transfers to families in need—will still be necessary, but the need for welfare will be dramatically reduced if the government and employers begin recognizing that families and work need to coexist, not compete with each other.

Lest the checklist of policies that follows be dismissed as a frivolous feminist fantasy, we hasten to point out that the hard-nosed governments of Western Europe have adopted similar policy packages. *Family policy* is an unfamiliar term in the United States because our family-friendly public policies are so few and far between, but they form an integral and accepted part of European society. Most Western European nations offer universally available child care, extensive paid parental leaves, child and housing allowances to supplement the income of families with children, universal health coverage, and government-guaranteed child support for single parents. And these generous benefits do not prevent the countries from thriving economically: they provide a standard of living comparable to or in some cases higher than that of the United States, and their businesses compete successfully with U.S. corporations in many markets.

Family Policies for the United States

The costs of real welfare reform are high—but so are the costs of poverty, child neglect, and overwork. Under the current system, low-income families, women, and children disproportionately bear these costs. But that does not mean that the rest of society escapes them. Perhaps the most striking element of Europe's family policies is not any particular policy but rather the deeply held philosophy of "social solidarity," meaning that "children and young people belong to the entire community, not just to their individual families," in the words of researcher Katherine McFate (1991). Here are seven broad policy approaches that embody the notion of social solidarity. Since many of the topics we list here are discussed elsewhere in this book, we keep our discussion of these policies brief.

1. Financially support full-time child care

That means financially supporting women engaged in full-time child care or providing alternate sources of child care for those who work outside the home. High-quality, affordable child care should be available to all who need it. Even with child-care supports, families must be afforded the right to choose who does the work of child rearing. If we acknowledge the reality of children's needs and truly value families, then the important work of taking care of young children or relatives who cannot take care of themselves is at times best kept within the family. For families with only one adult, this will mean that paid employment will not be possible or even desirable at all times, requiring some form of cash assistance.

2. *Boost wages to a "living wage" level and make them fairer*

With earnings the main source of income for most families and the key alternative to government support, we cannot afford to leave so many adults stuck in low-wage employment. Between 1973 and 1998, the average hourly wage for nonsupervisory workers in the private sector slumped from $14.46 to $12.77 in 1998 dollars (U.S. Council of Economic Advisors 1998). For those who earn the lowest wages, work is no guarantee of escaping from poverty. In 1997, 10 percent of all poor persons sixteen and over worked full-time, year-round, and 42 percent of all poor people had some type of employment (U.S. Bureau of the Census 1998b). And job discrimination against people of color, non-English speakers, and women persists, lowering the wages of many in these groups.

There is no magic bullet that will solve the problems of low and unfair wage levels. But three measures could make a big difference. First, *mandate equal pay for comparable work.* "Equal pay for equal work" is an important principle, but with women and men segregated into different types of jobs (with very different pay levels!), it does not do enough to overcome gender inequality. Comparable worth, requiring equal pay for comparable work, could do a lot more to close the pay gender gap. (See chap. 7 for more on comparable worth strategies.) Economists Deborah Figart and June Lapidus estimated the effect of comparable worth, also called pay equity, on women's wages. They concluded that a comprehensive pay equity program would raise women's average hourly wage by 8.5 percent. The biggest effect would be at the bottom: while before comparable worth 25 percent of women would not earn enough to bring a family of three up to the poverty line, after comparable worth only 15 percent would fall short of this threshold (Figart and Lapidus 1995).

Second, *raise the minimum wage and expand requirements for a living wage.* Almost 60 percent of minimum-wage workers are women.

Further, women are more likely to stay in minimum-wage jobs over the course of their working lives. Between 1979 and 1995, the inflation-adjusted value of the minimum wage tumbled by 30 percent. In 1996, Congress increased the minimum wage from $4.25 an hour to $5.15, still leaving it far below its 1979 level of $6.29 (in 1997 dollars). Even at that higher level a minimum wage is still not a living wage; one definition of a living wage is one that will allow a full-time, year-round worker to bring a family of three up to their poverty threshold—$6.94 per hour in 1999. Community-labor coalitions have pressed city governments to require any business that contracts with the city to pay a living wage and have won such laws in over thirty cities and counties, including Baltimore, Boston, Houston, Los Angeles, and Milwaukee. (See chap. 6 for further discussion.) An important complement to increasing the minimum wage is expanding the Earned Income Credit (EIC).

Third, *level the playing field for labor unions.* While unions' diversity track record remains mixed, the most dynamic unions today are the ones that are aggressively recruiting and representing women and people of color. Unions raise wages most for the lowest paid, and that is good news for women and minority workers. But union coverage has shrunk from one-third of the workforce in the 1950s to less than one-sixth today. Businesses have discovered that they can run hardball union-busting campaigns—misleading, threatening, and even firing workers—and pay only minimal penalties, usually years later after the damage is done. To level this playing field, we need stronger laws protecting workers' right to unionize without fear of employer retaliation and to strike without fear of being immediately—and permanently—replaced. Union representation increases a woman's wage by an average of 20 percent compared to that of an otherwise identical woman without union coverage. Doubling the percentage of women unionized would be expected to push women's average wage 3 percent higher.[5] Every bit helps!

3. Tame the family budget-busters

Housing is the largest expense for most families, and paying for health care is a serious problem for those who do not get coverage from an employer or the government. The growth in housing and health-care costs is outrunning income, leaving increasing numbers of families behind.

Housing costs have grown faster than income since the early 1980s, leading to declining home ownership and rising rent-to-income ratios. The housing squeeze pinches low-income households hardest. Nearly one-fifth of all renters, but three-fifths of poor renters, spend more than half of their income on housing costs (Dreier and Atlas 1996; Daskal 1998). Whereas in 1970 there were more low-rent units than low-income renters, by 1995 the situation had dramatically reversed, and there were 4.4 million fewer affordable units than low-income renters (Daskal 1998). One predictable result has been growing homelessness: one careful 1992 estimate put the ranks of the homeless at 600,000 on any given night and 1.2 million over the course of a year (Burt 1992). Families with children are the fastest-growing group among the homeless.

A variety of approaches can help make housing more affordable, and the best strategy is to combine approaches. Rent vouchers and opportunities for affordable home ownership can assist many families, but we also need public housing as the housing of last resort. Low-income women—like any other group—have particular housing needs, and some nonprofit organizations have specifically targeted those needs. For example, the Women's Development Corporation (WDC) in Providence, Rhode Island, has developed 550 units of housing for low-income women. The Boston-based Women's Institute for Housing and Economic Development (WIHED), rather than developing housing itself, provides technical assistance to organizations providing housing for women and children. A partial list of WIHED projects highlights the diversity of women's situations: it includes housing for grandmothers raising their grandchildren, for Haitian American single mothers and their children, for teen mothers trying to piece their lives back together, for recovering substance abusers (many of whom are trying to regain custody of their children), for elderly women who have been homeless, and for younger formerly homeless women and their children. For each of these groups, the mix of common space uses, unit sizes and configurations, and on-site services is different. The creativity of groups like WDC and WIHED deserves support.

Health care is the other major family budget buster. The average family spent 18 percent of its income on health care in 1992, and the burden weighs most heavily on the poorest one-fifth of the population, who shelled out 23 percent of their income for medical care. Over 43 million people lacked health insurance in 1997, but even among those who were insured, many have trouble paying for health-care expenses: in a 1992 survey of people with private health insurance, one in six reported difficulty paying medical bills (Physicians for a National Health Program 1998; Rassell 1994).[6] Since 1960, health-care costs have increased by more than a factor of ten (U.S. Council of Economic Advisors 1998)!

After all the sound and fury over health-care reform in the last few years, the only federal reform so far is to guarantee people the right to continue health insurance coverage at their own expense after leaving a job. It is past time to get in step with the rest of the industrialized world and make health care a basic right. The other industrialized countries, which provide universal coverage through "single payer" plans, meaning that there is a single, government-controlled insurer for all, spend less per person on health care than the United States and have healthier populations![7]

4. Expand the safety net

Neither welfare recipients nor the general public are enthusiastic about welfare—to put it mildly. But cash assistance—whether as TANF or the old AFDC program—remains necessary as the ultimate safety net for families with children. However, expanding other parts of the social safety net could help reduce reliance on welfare. Two candidates for expansion are unemployment insurance and temporary disability insurance.

Unemployment insurance, established as part of the 1935 Social Security Act, offers compensation to unemployed workers based on their earnings while employed. Unfortunately, research by the Washington-based Institute for Women's Policy Research (IWPR) indicates that unemployment insurance is currently a fairly exclusive program (IWPR 1995a; Spalter-Roth, Hartmann, and Burr 1994). This is true even for men and for full-time workers, the traditional targets of the program: 74 percent of unemployed men, and 62 percent of unemployed full-time workers, do not meet eligibility requirements—including reasons for leaving a job, number of weeks worked, minimum pay requirements, and industry restrictions. But women and part-time workers are most often shut out: 80 percent of unemployed women, and 90 percent of unemployed part-time workers, fail to meet eligibility criteria for unemployment insurance. And although many welfare recipients cycle between welfare and work, only 11 percent of working welfare mothers draw on unemployment insurance—instead relying on welfare as a "poor woman's unemployment insurance."

What can be done? The Center for Law and Social Policy has suggested a variety of reforms that would enable unemployment insurance to help more people: widen eligibility, extend time limits, add a component covering temporary disability (including pregnancy and childbirth), and possibly even consolidate the unemployment insurance program with cash assistance for families with children that include an employable adult (Savner and Greenberg 1996). One positive step in this direction was President Clinton's adoption in 2000 of a regulation permitting states to extend unemployment insurance to cover parental leaves—though no state has yet implemented such an extension as of this writing.

Another option would be to strengthen and expand temporary disability insurance (TDI) systems. About one-quarter of women who leave their jobs do so because of family reasons such as pregnancy. The 1993 Family and Medical Leave Act (FMLA) guarantees twelve weeks of unpaid leave for childbirth and family illnesses or other emergencies. It helps, but the FMLA only covers about half of the workforce, those in businesses employing fifty or more. More important, few people can afford to take an unpaid leave. Creating a universal, paid family leave, as in all of the countries of Western Europe, would do far more to ease work-family tensions. This could be done by establishing a nationwide temporary disability insurance program—or simply by strengthening the FMLA—at relatively low cost. The Institute for Women's Policy Research estimated the monthly total cost per worker in ten states of current (or proposed) TDI benefits plus paid family leave benefits for care of a sick spouse, elderly parents, sick children, or newborns to range from $12.60 in Rhode Island to $17.70 per month in New Jersey (IWPR 1995b).

5. Provide affordable and available education and training for all

The United States boasts one of the best higher education systems in the world. But the U.S. education and training system stacks up far less well for the 75 percent of the workforce with less than a four-year college degree and worst of all for those who do not finish high school. Since the large majority of welfare recipients have no more than a high school diploma, they suffer from these shortcomings in the country's school-and-skill system—but so do many other groups, including displaced workers, older women reentering the workforce, and young people who do not follow the college track. And as the tuition costs of postsecondary education mount, the simple affordability of college has also become an issue.

The education and training system must be rebuilt from the bottom up. High school students in noncollege tracks need a curriculum that is richer and more linked to actual jobs—possibly adapting West European apprenticeship programs. The "second-chance" system for those who drop out of high school or who require retraining needs to be expanded and retooled. It would take in a much wider spectrum of people, recognizing that most, if not all, of the workforce requires retraining at some point, and would offer special supports, rather than segregation, for those with greater training needs. Over the last ten years, for every $100 worth of production taking place in the United States, the government spent 10¢ on training; the rate in Sweden was six times as great (Gibson and Hall 1993).

Finally, we need to broaden access to and the affordability of higher education. The combination of skyrocketing tuition plus a college requirement for a growing number of jobs adds up to a crisis. Tuition tax breaks help middle income families, but give no relief to poorer ones. One part of the solution is expanded student aid, including aid tied to national service and loans whose repayment schedule depends on actual postcollege earnings. Another part of the solution is bolstering public higher education, which is struggling across the country but continues to offer the best bargain in postsecondary schooling.

6. Promote community-based economic development

Private sector–driven development has left increasing numbers of people—and in some cases, entire neighborhoods or regions—stranded. But mistrust of government is at an all-time high. While government action is needed to set standards and redistribute resources, it is important to remember that there is a third option for economic development: community-based economic development, in which locally controlled nonprofits take the lead in providing employment opportunities, housing, training, and services.

Community economic development can take a wide variety of forms, such as supporting the creation of small businesses or producer cooperatives, investing in the revitalization of neighborhood commercial areas, or training community members for better jobs. Some community economic development organizations, such as Chicago's Women's Self-Employment Project and Los Angeles's Coalition of

Women's Economic Development, focus specifically on women. Community economic development's strengths are the flexibility, creativity, and accountability that community control brings, plus the fact that community action on economic development helps to build broader social and political cohesion. Its chief limitation is that even when a poor community pools its resources, those resources are still quite limited—and communities acting separately can do little to change the large structural forces and the market economy's "rules of the game" that powerfully shape their destinies. Despite these limitations, community-based strategies have made an important difference in many areas and deserve government support.

7. Secure funding with a fairer tax structure

Let's face up to the fact that wage earnings and child support from absent fathers are not going to be enough to pull single-mother families out of poverty. Some supplemental assistance in the form of child allowances, child-care subsidies, and transfers will be necessary to help with the costs of child rearing. The best way to share those costs is through government financing. The government gets its income from taxes and fees. Financing new government programs means raising taxes or cutting spending on other areas.

It may seem politically and economically infeasible to finance new programs when most states have shown little interest in these goals and the federal government is concerned with reducing its already large debt. However, the costs of our current system are already unacceptably high. Disproportionately women, children, and people of color bear the costs of child poverty and all its attendant problems. In fact, not funding the programs recommended here may be far more costly than funding them. Society will pay a price in policing, prisons, and health-care spending on poverty-fueled conditions, as well as foregone production from children who will grow up without the schooling and skills that would allow them to contribute fully to the economy.

To finance new programs, the United States needs a fairer tax system at the federal and state levels. This means overhauling the current tax structure so that those who can most afford to pay taxes do so. In the 1980s, the federal tax system cut taxes for the wealthiest and placed a larger share of the burden on middle- and low-income families. These changes, plus the large increases in Social Security contributions, have both reduced federal tax receipts and made lower-income families pay a higher percentage of their income to fund programs that typically offer them little, such as defense and "corporate welfare." In the states and localities, taxes are even less fair: states rely heavily on property and sales taxes that take a bigger chunk of low incomes than high ones. After federal tax deductions, total state and local taxes in 1995 claimed a nationwide average of 12.4 percent of the incomes of the poorest fifth of families of four but only 5.8 percent of the incomes of the richest 1 percent (Ettlinger et al. 1996). Graduated state income taxes—tax rates based on ability to pay, as at the federal level—would be a real step forward.

Surveys show that U.S. citizens would be willing to pay more taxes if the money goes to policies they believe in, such as Social Security or education. The programs proposed here have important economic and social benefits for everyone. To start with, they are likely to have handsome productivity payoffs. Providing a social floor for every U.S. citizen—including the right to health care, the right to child care and a child allowance, and the right to housing—will in fact improve the productivity of U.S. workers immensely. By helping workers to balance work and family, it will cut down on absenteeism and divided attention. More fundamentally, with an enhanced sense of economic security, U.S. workers will be more committed and productive on the job, as they were during and after World War II when the private and public sectors both offered stronger guarantees of economic well-being. Already, companies such as Xerox that have experimented with family-friendly policies have achieved large efficiency increases (Shellenbarger 1996). Think what we could accomplish if businesses, government, and communities worked together to strengthen economic security and help the most stressed families to balance workplace and family demands.

Conclusion: Moving beyond "Get a Job"

Welfare policies have their greatest impact on low-income women and their families. But welfare also forms a critical portion of the safety net undergirding the economic and social position of all women, and their children, in the United States. The punitive welfare reforms of the 1980s and 1990s have undermined that position considerably. Despite a few sensible reforms, the overall effect has been to push poor women off the welfare rolls, without lifting them out of poverty.

If we as a nation are serious about confronting women's and children's economic disadvantages, we will rebuild welfare from the bottom up—raising benefits, increasing other supports for poor women, and abandoning dead-end policies such as time limits. To substantially transform economic opportunities for low-income women, real welfare reform must be accompanied by a full package of family-friendly policies. The policies we propose will draw on, and reinforce, a society-wide sense of shared values and commitment to the work of raising all our children. These programs send a message: the work of raising and caring for children is important enough to be a social responsibility, not just an individual one.

Notes

This chapter is adapted from several chapters in *Glass Ceilings and Bottomless Pits: Women's Work, Women's Poverty*, by Randy Albelda and Chris Tilly (Boston: South End Press, 1997).

1. Calculated by the authors using the March 1998 Current Population Survey.

2. Benefits in New York apply to Suffolk County only; they are lower elsewhere in the state. Alaska and Hawaii have higher benefits but also have higher poverty income thresholds (Congressional Research Service 1998, 7–8, 23–25).

3. This result has been confirmed by several researchers. For example, one study using a different data set found that over 50 percent of AFDC recipients held a job over a thirty-six-month period in the mid-1980s (Harris 1993).

4. This is a heroic assumption because only 60 percent of women who earn under $25,000 per year work fifty or more weeks per year; the percentage is even smaller for women with young children and for those who earn the lowest wages (U.S. Bureau of the Census 1998a).

5. Calculated by the authors based on the union wage premium of 20 percent (Mishel and Bernstein 1994) and women's 1995 union representation rate of 14 percent (U.S. Bureau of Labor Statistics 1996).

6. Number of uninsured from Physicians for a National Health Program (1998). Other information in this paragraph is from Rassell (1994).

7. For example, despite lower average income levels, many industrialized countries have lower infant mortality and longer life expectancy than the United States (U.S. Council of Economic Advisors 1998).

References

Albelda, Randy. 1999. "Welfare to What? A Look at the Department of Transitional Assistance's Report on Families Leaving Welfare." Working paper, University of Massachusetts, Boston.

Bane, Mary Jo, and David Ellwood. 1994. *Welfare Realities: From Rhetoric to Reform.* Cambridge, MA: Harvard University Press.

Blank, Rebecca, David Card, and Philip Robins. 1999. *Financial Incentives for Increasing Work and Income among Low-Income Families.* Chicago: Joint Center for Poverty Research.

Burt, Martha. 1992. *Over the Edge: The Growth of Homelessness in the 1980s.* New York: Russell Sage Foundation.

Center for Law and Social Policy. 1999. *CLASP Update,* April. Washington, DC: Center for Law and Social Policy.

Congressional Research Service. 1998. *Welfare Reform: Financial Eligibility Rules and Benefit Amounts under TANF.* Washington, DC: U.S. Congress.

Daskal, Jennifer. 1998. *In Search of Shelter: The Growing Shortage of Affordable Rental Housing.* Washington, DC: Center for Budget and Policy Priorities.

Dreier, Peter, and John Atlas. 1996. "U.S. Housing Policy at the Crossroads: A Progressive Agenda to Rebuild the Housing Constituency." Working paper, International and Public Affairs Center, Occidental College, Los Angeles.

Ettlinger, Michael et al. 1996. *Who Pays? A Distributional Analysis of the Tax system in All Fifty States.* Washington, DC: Citizens for Tax Justice and Institute on Taxation and Economic Policy.

Families USA. 1999. *Losing Health Insurance: Unintended Consequences of Welfare Reform.* Washington, DC: Families USA. <http://www.famliesusa.org/uninten.htm>.

Figart, Deborah M., and June Lapidus. 1995. "A Gender Analysis of U.S. Labor Market Policies for the Working Poor." *Feminist Economics* 1, no. 3.

Friedlander, Daniel, and Gary Burtless. 1995. *Five Years After: The Long-Term Effects of Welfare-to-Work Programs.* New York: Russell Sage Foundation.

Gallagher, L. Jerome, Megan Gallagher, Kevin Perese, Susan Schreiber, and Keith Watson. 1998. *One Year after Federal Welfare Reform: A Description of State Temporary Assistance for Needy Families (TANF) Decisions as of October 1997.* Washington, DC: Urban Institute.

Gibson, Karen, and Peter Hall. 1993. *American Poverty and Social Policy: What Can Be Learned from the European Experience.* New York: Social Science Research Council. (Distributed by the National Center for Children in Poverty, Columbia University, New York.)

Greenberg, Mark. 1993. *Beyond Stereotypes: What State AFDC Studies on Length of Stay Tell Us about Welfare as a "Way of Life."* Washington, DC: Center for Law and Social Policy.

Harris, Kathleen Mullan. 1993. "Work and Welfare among Single Mothers in Poverty." *American Journal of Sociology* 99, no. 2 (September).

Institute for Women's Policy Research (IWPR). 1995a. "Unemployment Insurance: Barriers to Access for Women and Part-Time Workers." Research-in-Brief. Washington, DC: Institute for Women's Policy Research.

———. 1995b. "Using Temporary Disability Insurance to Provide Paid Family Leave: A comparison with the Family and Medical Leave Act." Research-in-Brief. Washington, DC: Institute for Women's Policy Research.

Kaplan, April. 1998. "Transportation: The Essential Need to Address the 'to' in Welfare-to-Work." *Welfare Information Network Issue Notes* 2, no. 10 (June). <http://www.welfareinfo.org/transitneed.htm>.

Karier, Thomas. 2000. "Welfare College Students: Measuring the Impact of Welfare Reform." Policy Notes 2000/3. Annadale-on-Hudson, NY: Jerome Levy Economics Institute.

Kramer, Fredrica D. 1998. "The Hard-to-Place: Understanding the Population and Strategies to Serve Them." *Welfare Information Network Issue Notes* 2, no. 5 (March). <http://www.welfareinfo.org/hardto.htm>.

Long, Sharon K., and Sandra J. Clark. 1997. *The New Child Care Block Grant: State Funding Choices and Their Implications.* Washington, DC: Urban Institute.

McFate, Katherine. 1991. *Poverty, Inequality, and the Crisis of Social Policy: Summary of Findings.* Washington, DC: Joint Center for Political and Economic Studies.

Mishel, Lawrence, and Jared Bernstein. 1994. *The State of Working America 1994–95.* Armonk, NY: M. E. Sharpe.

Mishel, Lawrence, Jared Bernstein, and John Schmitt. 1999. *The State of Working America, 1998–99.* Ithaca, NY: Cornell University Press.

Pauly, Edward (with Cristina DiMeo). 1996. *Adult Education for People on AFDC: A Synthesis of Research.* Washington, DC: U.S. Department of Health and Human Services and U.S. Department of Education.

Physicians for a National Health Program. 1998. "Number of Americans without Health Insurance Jumps to 43.2 Million." News release, September 25. <http://www.pnhp.org/press998.html> .

Raphael, Jody. 1996. "Domestic Violence and Welfare Receipt: Toward a New Feminist Theory of Welfare Dependency." *Harvard Women's Law Journal* 19 (spring).

Rassell, Edith. 1994. "Health Care: Expenditures Exceed Results." In *The State of Working America 1994–95,* by Lawrence Mishel and Jared Bernstein. Armonk, NY: M. E. Sharpe.

Savner, Steve, and Mark Greenberg. 1996. "Reforming the Unemployment Insurance System to Better Meet the Needs of Low-Income Families." Manuscript, Washington, DC.

Shellenbarger, Sue. 1996. "Family-Friendly Jobs Are the First Step to Efficient Workplace." *Wall Street Journal,* May 15, p. B1.

Spalter-Roth, Roberta, Heidi Hartmann, and Beverly Burr. 1994. "Income Insecurity: The Failure of Unemployment Insurance to Reach out to Working AFDC Mothers." Institute for Women's Policy Research, paper presented at the Second Annual Employment Task Force Conference, March 20–22.

Spalter-Roth, Roberta, Beverly Burr, Heidi Hartmann, and Lois Shaw. 1995. *Welfare That Works: The Working Lives of AFDC Recipients.* Washington, DC: Institute for Women's Policy Research.

U.S. Bureau of the Census. 1998a. *Money Income in the United States: 1997.* Current Population Reports P60–200. Washington, DC: Government Printing Office.

———. 1998b. *Poverty in the United States: 1997.* Prepared by Joseph Dalaker and Mary Naifeh. Current Population Reports P60–201. Washington, DC: Government Printing Office.

U.S. Bureau of Labor Statistics. 1996. *Employment and Earnings.* Washington, DC: Government Printing Office.

U.S. Council of Economic Advisors. 1998. *Economic Report of the President.* Washington, DC: Government Printing Office.

U.S. Department of Health and Human Services. Administration for Children and Families, Office of Planning, Research, and Evaluation. 1994. *Characteristics and Financial Circumstances of AFDC Recipients.* Washington, DC: Government Printing Office.

————. Administration for Children and Families, Office of Planning, Research, and Evaluation. 1998a. *Characteristics and Financial Circumstances of TANF Recipients.* Washington, DC: Government Printing Office.

————. 1998b. *Characteristics of State Plans for Aid to Families with Dependent Children,* 373. Washington, DC: Government Printing Office.

————. Administration for Children and Families. 1999. "Changes in Welfare Caseloads since Enactment of New Welfare Law." Accessed at <http://www.acf.dhhs.gov/news/stats/aug-sep.htm>, June 7.

U.S. General Accounting Office. 1998. *Welfare Reform: States' Efforts to Expand Child Care Programs.* HEHS-98-27. Washington, DC: Government Printing Office.

————. 1999. *Welfare Reform: Information on Former Recipients' Status.* HEHS-99-48. Washington, DC: Government Printing Office.

Wolfe, Barbara, and Steven Hill. 1993. "The Health, Earnings Capacity, and Poverty of Single-Mother Families." In *Poverty and Prosperity in the USA in the Later Twentieth Century,* edited by Dimitri B. Papadimitriou and Edward N. Wolff. New York: Macmillan Press.

What Would We Gain by Subsidizing Child Care?

Barbara R. Bergmann

Women's large-scale entry into the labor market is the major cause of the changes in women's position in the economy and in society that have taken place in the last third of the twentieth century. Greater participation in the workforce has increased the range of women's choices about the life they might lead, has enabled women to aspire to interesting careers, has increased the respect in which women are held, and has reduced their dependence on male support. These changes have, of necessity, altered the way our society finances and arranges for the care and rearing of young children. We have not yet faced up to the implications and requirements of that change. Mothers' paychecks are now an important source of support for millions of families and in a growing proportion of cases are indispensable. Yet the high cost of child care makes severe inroads on those paychecks and therefore on the standard of living of families. Child-care costs take away on average 20 percent of the incomes of the low-wage families who have to pay them.[1] And millions of children are not getting the quality of care that would do justice to their needs for nurturance and development.[2]

Almost two-thirds of mothers with children under six are now in the paid workforce;[3] the kind of care their children get and the effect of the cost of that care on their families' standard of living are problems that deserve national attention. The high cost of child care is one of the major causes of low living standards, lack of self-support, and social pathology in families with children. That is particularly true in the case of single-mother families, to which more than a quarter of American children now belong. Allied with the cost problem is the quality problem, since the cost of good-quality care is beyond the means of many families. The low quality of care that many young children are receiving is or should be of concern to their parents. It should also be of public concern, since it affects the kind of adult population we will have in the future—how psychologically secure, how socially mature, how economically productive the future citizens of this country will be. The care children get affects parents' ability to get to work reliably and while there to feel secure that their children are in good hands. This in turn affects worker productivity and labor turnover and thus employers' costs of production.

If there is general agreement that the U.S. child-care problem is serious, there is little agreement on what to do about it. Some say mothers (with the exception of single mothers, perhaps) should stay home with their children, and they attribute many of today's societal ills to mothers' job holding. Others would rely totally on the free market to evolve a supply of care that would be appropriate to the country's needs in terms of quality and cost, given our resources, and would favor withdrawing what government subsidies and regulations are now in place. Many advocates look to community action—business, charities, and foundations—to mobilize the resources to improve the quality and availability of care in each locality. Others hope that state and local governments will provide free prekindergartens and that employers might provide lengthy paid parental leaves. Finally, there are those, like the present writer, who believe that only a large, active, and expensive federal program, providing both finance and a national framework for quality improvement, will serve the nation's purposes adequately.

Back to Mother Care?

Some people regard the movement of mothers out of the home and into jobs as a terrible mistake. They believe that the lack of full-time care by mothers has produced cohorts of unsupervised, unhappy children, many without morals, poorly socialized, prone to crime. Highly publicized trials of foreign teenage baby-sitters, accused of killing the children they were taking care of, and allegations of child abuse against the personnel of child-care centers have provided ammunition to those opposed to the replacement of a mother's care by paid care.

Two groups adhere to this view. One consists of those who believe that a mother's undivided attention is a necessity for high-quality child rearing. Although there is now considerable evidence that children in nonmother care do as well as those in their mothers' care,[4] this is a belief that persists. The second group, not entirely distinct from the first, consists of those who regret the changes in behavior and attitudes that the movement for women's equality has caused and would like to see a return to the kind of lives most women and men led prior to the 1960s.

Those who would bring back full-time care by mothers (some, bowing to egalitarian trends, would now say, "parents") are, quite understandably, not inclined to join a campaign to fix the country's problems with paid-for child care. On the contrary, they oppose the infusions of government money that would make high-quality nonmaternal child care and early childhood education more affordable for parents. Nor are they in the forefront of those urging that the quality of out-of-home care be improved. A supply of out-of-the-home child care that was more affordable and of better quality would make it more convenient for mothers to leave off full-time mothering and get jobs, thus strengthening the very trends the proponents of mother-only care deplore.

Yet despite the realities of our present supply of child care—most of it high priced and much of it of mediocre-to-poor quality—a majority of the mothers of small children nevertheless do hold jobs and buy child care. Whether they "need to work," or want to work, or find that working is the best of all the alternatives open to them, they do work. A huge turn in public sentiment against working mothers or a major depression that raised the unemployment rate to depression-era levels might prompt the return of some of them to full-time care of their own children, but these are unlikely events. On the contrary, the outlook is for more mothers in jobs, not fewer. Currently, mothers who have participated in the job market of their own accord are being joined there by the millions of single mothers who would prefer to stay home supported by welfare but who are being forced into jobs.

Until recently, single mothers had a right to stay home with their children and be supported under the program of Aid to Families with Dependent Children that originated in the Social Security Act passed in 1935 as part of President Roosevelt's New Deal. In 1996 the Congress passed and President Clinton signed a "welfare reform" bill ending that right; it was designed to send as many single mothers as possible out of the home and into paid jobs. Ironically, the keenest advocates of ending the right of single mothers to care for their own children by refraining from paid work, and of pushing them into the workforce against their will, are the social conservatives—the very people who emphasize "family values" and who preach that mothers should not take paid work and should devote themselves exclusively to their children.

Whenever the question of government support for nonparental care arises, there are answering proposals for paid parental leave or for other types of subsidies for parents taking care of their own children. Child-care benefits for mothers at home create serious inequities, since they would go to families that are considerably better provided for than families with similar income but no adult at home, such as working single parents. Further, they are likely to seriously set back gender equality in employment, on which the improvement in women's status has rested. Quality and efficiency considerations may further argue against benefits for mothers at home. Children can receive good care with ratios of adults to children of 1:3 for infants; 1:7 for three year olds; and 1:8 for five year olds.[5] Most parents at home are caring for one or two children. Thus if public resources were used to subsidize parental care, the public would be paying for the labor time of far more adults than would be the case if subsidies were restricted to out-of-home care. Lengthy paid parental leave is particularly expensive.

In any case, the problems of child care in the United States are not likely in the foreseeable future to be resolved by a return to mothers' care, whether paid or unpaid. On the contrary, those problems will worsen as additional millions of poorly paid women will be needing to find care for their children.

"A Shortage of Affordable High-Quality Care"

When people say, "There is a shortage of high-quality affordable child care in this country," they are in effect complaining that there are large numbers of parents who cannot get their children into good-quality care at a price they feel comfortable paying—and that we, as a society, should do something about it. What the exact nature of the problem is and what, if anything, should be done about it are central issues in child-care policy. The problem of "affordability" arises because the prices parents have to pay to buy care are, for a large proportion of families, high relative to their incomes. Those prices keep some parents from buying any child care at all and so keep them from working. Other parents, because of those prices, put their children into care of a quality that they know or suspect is not of the best and might even bring harm. Still other parents feel themselves forced to use so much of their income for child care that their ability to buy the basics of family living is severely compromised.

There is an urgent problem with the affordability of child care that the country needs to remedy. Obviously, it is a problem that troubles low-income working people most acutely; however, as we shall see, it is also troubling to families whose incomes exceed the official poverty level by a large margin. Solving it would help millions of children to safer, better care; would help them and their parents to a higher standard of living; and would go far to relieve the country itself of some acute social problems that mar our general prosperity.

To say that the high price of care creates big problems for families is not to say that the price the market has set is abnormally high. Current prices are fully justified by costs that have to be met if minimally decent care is to be provided. If costs were cut, quality would go down. And costs would be higher than they are now if the child-care industry were to deliver a higher level of quality than it currently provides, as it should be encouraged and enabled to do. The question we face is not how to reduce or avoid those costs but who is to pay for them and how.

The commonly used phrase "shortage of affordable child care" conveys the suggestion that the problem is not just with price—that there is a problem of insufficient supply that should be remedied. Would increased funding—in the form of subsidies to the industry or vouchers to the parents—guarantee that an adequate quantity of care would be provided and that the services would be of high quality? On the matter of quantity, we can, based on past performance, put our confidence in the responsiveness of the U.S. economy. If sufficient funding were available, the child-care industry, like any other industry, could be expected to respond with a supply of its product that would meet the demand. While anxiety over quantity of care supplied would not be justified, anxiety would certainly be warranted concerning the quality of the child care that would result from an enlarged subsidy program. The quality provided would depend on the level of subsidies, the standards set, and the extent and efficacy of enforcement of those standards. If effective regulation of the providers were absent, a considerable portion of public subsidies would be likely to flow to care that is mediocre and to some that is outright poor, just as some parent fees do now. A subsidy level that did not cover the costs of high-quality care would not produce it, regardless of the nature of the regulations or the effort put into enforcing them. High quality depends on a combination of generous subsidies and effective regulation.

Subsidies for the Hardest-up Families

The simplest and most obvious case for subsidies is that of a single mother, working full-time at a minimum-wage job, who has one or more preschool children. Some families in this situation have recently moved off welfare; many others have never been on welfare. Some single mothers have had children out of wedlock; others have gone through marital breakups. The case of the low-wage single mother is not one that politicians find the most politically compelling. People like her do not vote in large numbers, and single mothers who need help are not popular with large segments of the U.S. public. Nevertheless, hers is a good case to start with because her need is so stark, obvious, and understandable. And whatever her history, she is now "playing by the rules."

Obviously, she needs someone to care for her children while she works. Some people assume that the typical single mother has a relative who will take good enough care of her children for free.[6] About half of currently working single mothers do get free care, mostly from relatives.[7] Some of those arrangements are far from ideal. But it is the half who must pay with whom we are concerned here.

What child-care fees would be "affordable" for such a family? One obvious way to think about the family's ability to pay for child care is to see how much money the family takes in during a year and how much it would cost to buy the goods and services (other than child care) that would provide a minimally decent standard of living. Out of her income the mother needs to pay taxes; buy adequate food; keep a roof over her head; get transportation to work; get clothes washed; and buy many other items, such as shoes, children's clothing, toothpaste, and, perhaps, diapers. We have left medical expenses out of the list because she is eligible for Medicaid. After accounting for the cost of buying a minimally necessary list of these things, we can see how much money is left over to cover the cost of providing care for the family's children. If the amount left over is insufficient to buy care of an acceptable quality, then keeping this family at a decent standard of living would require some form of government help to make child care "affordable."

The financial situation of the family of a working single mother with two preschool children is summarized in table 3.1. The first panel of the table gives information on the amount of money she will have to live on. Working at the minimum wage of $5.15 for 40 hours a week, 50 weeks a year, would bring in $10,300 per year. To see how much money she will have available—her "disposable income"—we need to subtract from her wage income the taxes the family owes, if any, and add in any benefits she will be entitled to. This family has income too low to owe any federal or state income taxes, but it does pay Social Security taxes of $788. Offsetting this subtraction are several benefits that families with earned income this low are entitled to receive: the Earned Income Tax Credit (EITC) and food stamps.[8] The EITC is a cash supplement sent by the federal government to low-wage workers with children.[9] It can be thought of as an income-tested child allowance for wage-earn-

TABLE 3.1. **Financial Situation of a Single Mother with Two Preschool Children and a Full-Time Job at the Minimum Wage, 1998**

1. Ability to spend	
Before-tax wages[a]	$10,300
Federal and state income taxes	0
Earned Income Tax Credit	3,556
Social Security taxes	−788
Food stamps	1,790
Disposable income	$14,858

2. Minimum budget, excluding child care (two versions)	
Official poverty line	$13,415
Required expenditure for food, clothing, shelter, transportation, services in the National Academy of Sciences budget (exclusive of child care and health insurance)	$15,000

3. Cost of child care	
Cost of licensed child care in a center of average quality for two preschool children	$16,000

[a]Assumes work of 40 hours per week, 50 weeks per year, at the September 1997 minimum wage of $5.15.

Source: Helburn (1995), Citro and Michael (1995), and Renwick and Bergmann (1993).

ing parents, disguised as a tax break.[10] The food stamp benefits for which the family is eligible are almost the same thing as cash, so they can be added in.[11] After these subtractions and additions, we arrive at a "disposable income" of $14,858.

The second panel of the table gives two alternative assessments of what a minimally decent standard of living would cost this family. The first is the official U.S. poverty-line figure of $13,415. The poverty line is specified as the cost of a thrifty food budget multiplied by three and is revalued yearly to take account of price changes.[12] The official poverty measure was set up in the early 1960s, when it was assumed that any family with children had a stay-at-home mother. So paying for child care was not considered an expense that needed to be taken account of.

The second assessment shown in the panel is based on the work of a committee of experts assembled by the National Academy of Sciences (NAS). They concluded that the poverty line ought to be based on a detailed family budget, rather than on the "food cost times three"calculation that produces the currently official poverty line.[13] The detailed budget provides a more realistic accounting for minimal needs for food, clothing, shelter, transportation, services, and taxes; and better consideration of health care needs and benefits and of the child-care needs of employed parents. According to the Academy's calculations, the minimal basic budget for a family of this composition, exclusive of taxes and health insurance, *and exclusive of child care costs,* would come to $15,000 for 1998.

The $14,858 disposable income of this family falls between these two assessments of what the family needs to spend in order to have a minimally decent package of goods and services, exclusive of child care and health care. Whichever of the two one adopts (and we believe the second assessment to be clearly superior) it is obvious that the family has little or nothing left over to pay for child care. Its disposable income will be exhausted in purchasing the goods and services needed for a minimally decent standard of living. If the family is required to divert any of its disposable income to pay for child care, it will be forced below a decent standard of living. It seems reasonable, then, to say that the only "affordable price" this family can pay for child care is zero.

The third panel in table 3.1, which deals with the cost of care, is not, as we have just seen, relevant to deciding what an affordable price would be for this family. But the kind of care we want to make affordable and its cost are relevant to the amounts of money the government would have to provide to achieve that. The panel shows the cost of one kind of care—"formal" care in a licensed child-care center that is about average in quality. It would cost about $8,000 per child, or $16,000 for two children.

There are lower-priced alternatives (that tend to be of still lower quality), Superficially, it might sound consistent to say that, since we are using a poverty-line minimally acceptable budget for food, clothing, and shelter, we should be talking of some minimally acceptable grade of child care. Cut-rate child-care arrangements of the informal, nonlicensed variety are certainly available and are used by many parents. Isn't using that kind of care the equivalent of using an eight-year-old, somewhat banged-up but still operable Chevrolet Caprice such as a family with a borderline income might own, which might serve well enough in function if not in style?[14]

Choosing care of a minimally acceptable quality might at first glance seem consistent with choosing a poverty-line basic budget. But it is not necessarily good public policy to relegate children who have low-level living standards to low-quality child care. Quite on the contrary, children from relatively poor families would benefit more than other children from high-quality child care and would be most severely hurt by the worst. Some informal unlicensed care can be high quality, but much of it is not. Unlicensed care that is performed without oversight is chancy.

Making care affordable certainly means relieving families at the poverty line or below of the need to dip into their incomes to buy care. The nation should be making available to such parents licensed care that is at least as good as the current average, at no cost to the parents. Present programs reach only a small fraction of those in that situation.

The Need for Child-Care Subsidies to Families above the Lowest-Earning Group

We proceed now to the question of extending subsidies for child care to families with more than minimum-wage earnings. We again use the example of families consisting of a single mother and two preschool children. For a wide range of earnings levels, table 3.2 shows the disposable income that would be left to this type of family after taxes have been subtracted from and income supplements added to its wage income.

TABLE 3.2. Wage Income and Disposable Income of a Single Mother and Two Preschool Children, 1997

Wage (+)	Federal Income Tax[a] (−)	Dependent Care Tax Credit (+)	State Income Tax[b] (−)	Social Security Tax (−)	Food Stamps (+)	EITC (+)	Disposable Income (=)
10,300	0	0	0	788	1,790	3,556	14,858
11,000	0	0	0	842	1,622	3,469	15,250
12,000	0	0	0	918	1,382	3,469	15,933
13,000	0	0	0	995	1,142	3,258	16,406
14,000	0	0	0	1,071	902	3,047	16,878
15,000	0	0	0	1,148	662	2,836	17,351
16,000	0	0	0	1,224	422	2,625	17,823
17,000	0	0	0	1,301	182	2,414	18,296
18,000	0	0	0	1,377	0	2,203	18,826
19,000	0	0	87	1,454	0	1,992	19,451
20,000	0	0	250	1,530	0	1,781	20,001
21,000	118	118	412	1,607	0	1,570	20,551
22,000	268	268	575	1,683	0	1,359	21,101
23,000	418	418	737	1,760	0	1,148	21,651
24,000	568	568	900	1,836	0	937	22,201
25,000	718	718	1,062	1,913	0	726	22,751
26,000	868	868	1,225	1,989	0	515	23,301
27,000	1,018	1,008	1,387	2,066	0	304	23,842
28,000	1,168	1,008	1,550	2,142	0	93	24,242
29,000	1,318	960	1,675	2,219	0	0	24,749
30,000	1,468	960	1,770	2,295	0	0	25,428
31,000	1,618	960	1,865	2,372	0	0	26,106
32,000	1,768	960	1,960	2,448	0	0	26,785
33,000	1,918	960	2,055	2,525	0	0	27,463
34,000	2,068	960	2,150	2,601	0	0	28,142
35,000	2,218	960	2,245	2,678	0	0	28,820
36,000	2,368	960	2,340	2,754	0	0	29,499
37,000	2,518	960	2,435	2,831	0	0	30,177
38,000	2,668	960	2,530	2,907	0	0	30,856
39,000	2,818	960	2,625	2,984	0	0	31,534
40,000	2,968	960	2,720	3,060	0	0	32,213
41,000	3,118	960	2,815	3,137	0	0	32,891
42,000	3,268	960	2,910	3,213	0	0	33,570
43,000	3,418	960	3,005	3,290	0	0	34,248
44,000	3,568	960	3,100	3,366	0	0	34,927
45,000	3,718	960	3,195	3,443	0	0	35,605

[a]Exclusive of dependent tax credit.
[b]Levels derived from Washington, DC, income tax.

Families who report child-care expenses are entitled to a federal tax credit for part of the expenditure. This credit can only be used to offset federal taxes that the family owes and is not "refundable" to those who owe no federal taxes. So the credit gives no help at all to lower-income families; the family we are using as an example—the single mother with two children under five—would not benefit from it unless the mother had a wage income of about $21,000. As can be seen from the table, the current tax-based child-care credits are modest and would pay for a small fraction of the $16,000 cost of child care of average quality for two preschool children.

A family with access to free health insurance would need a disposable income of at least $31,000 to be able to cover both the NAS minimal basic budget and the child-care fees out of its own resources. As the highlighted line of table 3.2 shows, to have this disposable income, the single-mother two-child family would need a wage income close to $38,000. Families with wage income of less than that amount (and this would include the vast majority of single-parent wage-earning families) would not have enough disposable income to cover the whole package. If a reasonable quality of child care were to be made affordable to them and a reasonable standard of living maintained, some assistance would have to be provided at least to those earning under $38,000.

Should Government Provide Child Care?

What is the rationale for government action to make child care "affordable"? Help with child-care expenses is clearly needed if the people of this country want to adhere to the principle that when people work and "play by the rules" in this richest of all countries, they and their children should have a standard of living that comes up to some basic minimum and their children should have care of a decent quality. Of course, not everyone is willing to subscribe to that principle. Some argue that people whose income does not allow them to support children decently and pay for their care out of their own resources simply should not have children, and they also feel that if such people do have children, it is best if they (and the children) suffer the consequences. Government help, in this view, merely encourages irresponsible behavior and dependency.

In thinking about which side of the argument to adopt, one should be mindful of the situation of single mothers who work full-time all year round at unskilled jobs, perhaps cleaning offices or hotel rooms; who have nobody to share family chores; and who are bringing up children who will be future citizens and hopefully future earners and taxpayers. Many of the nation's children live in families with characteristics like these or close to these. The question at issue is whether we as a nation want to insure that such children have a "nondistressful" standard of life.

Government help could take the form of allowing the children to enroll in specific child-care facilities at no charge or a reduced charge. Or it could take the form of giving the parent a voucher or certificate promising to a child-care provider that the government would pay a certain part of this family's fee. Either of these would amount to a government subsidy for child care.

Alternatively, it might be argued, the government could give enough cash to the family so it had enough to live at the minimum level and to be able to purchase care of the specified quality. However, a family so close to the poverty line would be unlikely to spend all or even most of a cash "child-care grant" on child care. Understandably, it would probably use a considerable proportion of the money to buy better food, housing, and so on. So quality care for the children could not be assured through such cash grants. For a similar reason, when we want to help a family to have medical insurance, we do not give cash that might be spent on other things.

In Sweden and France the government provides families from all income groups with free or highly subsidized child care.[15] A system of national health insurance benefits everybody. For single mothers, the wages they earn are supplemented by government-guaranteed child-support payments from absent parents. Family allowances supplement the incomes of families with children. The combination of wages and benefits enables low-paid parents in those countries to live in decency and better situated people to live well. The care the children of these countries receive is generally dependable, safe, and developmentally appropriate.

While the mothers in those countries are earning, their children spend their days in a safe and nonviolent environment in which their cognitive skills are developed; where they can be given nourishing meals and can learn the social requirements of mainstream culture; where any health and psychological problems can be diagnosed and attended to. In these countries, the preschool child is known to and regularly seen by nonfamily observers, both in the government baby clinics and in the day care centers. As a result, the likelihood that long-term child abuse would go undetected is very much diminished from what it is in this country. Federally provided child care in the United States could reduce abuse here and would also mean better nutrition for some children, more immunizations, and education for parents in health issues like asthma and nutrition. Parents might learn parenting techniques from professional child-care workers and would have someone to talk to about strategies concerning discipline and toilet training.

Should the U.S. government provide or subsidize child care even for families whose resources would allow more than a minimal budget and the purchase of decent care? Other countries do. There are a number of good reasons why we should also. Benefits only available to single mothers may promote single motherhood and discourage marriage. Benefits available only to low-income people reduce the incentive for low-income people to strive to raise their incomes. A system with an abrupt cutoff of benefits for those above a certain income creates serious inequities: those with incomes a few dollars above the cutoff income lose thousands of dollars worth of benefits and are far worse off than those with incomes a few dollars below the cutoff. A system that makes provision of care available to better-off, more politically adept people may give better services than a system catering only to the poor. Benefits available to broader groups have broader political support. With widely available publicly paid-for child care a greater share of the costs of rearing the next generation, now borne mostly by the parents, would be borne by the taxpayers in general.

The great bones of contention in the debate, of course, are the effect on children of nonparental care and the role of women in society. Government-provided child care that was broadly available would enable women who are mothers to choose the kind of life they wished to lead; it would enable women and men to share more equally in the satisfactions and frustrations of both the workplace and the home.

In France, where high-quality nursery schools are provided by the government and places are available for any toilet-trained child at zero fees, attendance is very high. Virtually 100 percent of preschool children aged three and above go to these nursery schools, and about 75 percent of toilet-trained two-year-old children attend.[16] The mothers of France have thus expressed their wishes about the life they wish to lead. They have also expressed their opinion about whether out-of-the-home child care is good for their children. Virtually all French mothers who do not hold a job send their children to nursery school as soon as they are eligible.

American mothers also appear to believe that their children gain from attendance at child-care centers. Both employed and nonemployed mothers of children make considerable use of them, despite substantial fees. If free nursery schools were provided in the United States as they are in France, it seems reasonable to suppose that considerably higher proportions of mothers would make use of them.

What Program Should We Try For?

A realistic approach to the problem of child care in the United States requires recognition of the need for a reliable flow of funds that would finance on a continuing basis, year after year, the provision of high-quality services to millions of children, while at the same time allowing hard-pressed parents to reduce what they currently pay for care out of their own pockets. The new funds that would be needed are in the tens of billions of dollars per year. The federal and state governments currently spend about $5 billion subsidizing care for a fraction of the low-income families eligible for such benefits and about $3 billion a year on tax credits for higher-income taxpayers with child-care expenses.[17] What is needed is a new national plan that would build on and go beyond our present system.

What might a reasonable program look like? Many child-care advocates argue that we should aim to set up a system that would provide free high-quality care to the children of all parents, regardless of their income. Only such a system, they believe, has any chance of receiving the political support of the middle class that would be needed for enactment. The problem, of course, is that the cost of such a program might be of the order of magnitude of $100 billion a year. An alternative system would cost annual sums on the order of $40 billion. It would offer full subsidies only to families at or close to the poverty line. From parents with higher incomes, it would require a co-payment, perhaps of 20 percent of their income above the poverty line.[18] Such a system might consist of full-day kindergarten in the public schools offered free to all five year olds, free full-day prekindergarten programs for four year olds, with a 20 percent co-payment scheme applied to children below four years old.

Of course, a case might be made that a program that confers on all families the ability to buy decent child care "pays for itself," at least in part. More child-care subsidies mean more women in jobs, paying taxes on their earnings. Besides, such a program might have beneficial results that could eventually save money that the government would otherwise have to spend. Better child care might be expected to promote improved performance in school, to reduce the need for special education instruction, and to reduce discipline problems. The better school performance would be expected to result in improved labor force productivity (resulting in higher tax payments) and reduced criminal behavior (reducing expenditures for the justice system and prisons, to say nothing of sparing trauma to those who would otherwise be victimized or undergo punishment).

The strongest case for programs of child-care subsidies such as those proposed here probably rests not on the calculation that they will save the government money (although they might) but on the fact that they are needed to keep many families, particularly single-parent families, out of a dire situation. Making quality child care affordable to all families would result in safer, more educational, and more enjoyable care for children and would give a financial boost to families pitifully short of resources, in a nonstigmatizing way. It would give parents a chance to participate in the world of work, and to achieve the gains in resources and status that such a participation would allow, while allowing them the knowledge that their children were getting reliable care of decent quality. Finally, subsidizing child care would raise women's status—by encouraging more of them to work without long interruptions, and by raising their career aspirations and thus changing the perceptions of women held by employers.

Notes

1. See Hofferth et al. (1991).
2. See Helburn (1995).
3. See U.S. Bureau of Labor Statistics (1999).
4. See NICHD Child Care Research Network (1999).
5. See National Association for the Education of Young Children (1998).
6. See Kaus (1992).
7. See U.S. Bureau of the Census (1995).
8. The EITC and food stamp allotments are "entitlements," which means that there is no cap to appropriations for them. Every eligible family receives the amount set out in the law. There are other benefits that are not entitlements and

where the appropriations are far lower than would be required to allow all families meeting the qualifications to receive them. These include housing benefits and presently available child-care subsidies.

9. This figure, which applied in the tax year 1997, is adjusted every year.

10. Formally speaking, the EITC is a refundable tax credit, which means that if the credit exceeds the amount of tax the family owes, the family gets the excess dollars.

11. Food stamps are used mostly for purchases of food that the family would buy even in the absence of the food stamp program. So they free up income that can be devoted to other uses equal to, or almost equal to, their retail value. Thus they add to the cash flow the family can use to cover its expenses. Some recipients of food stamps, particularly drug addicts and alcoholics, illegally sell their stamps, and the going rate is reported to be fifty cents on the dollar. However, these are the stamps least valued by the recipients most pressed for cash.

12. See Orshansky (1965, 1978).

13. The Academy's method of explicit budgeting also allows one to take account of regional differences in housing costs. See Citro and Michael (1995). See also Renwick and Bergmann (1993).

14. The National Academy experts did not tackle this problem by setting up a standard child-care cost, as for other family expenditures. In deciding whether to count a family as poor, they subtracted a family's actual child-care costs from its disposable income before comparing its resources to the basic budget.

15. For Sweden, see Mahon (1997). For France, see Bergmann (1996).

16. Bergmann (1996).

17. This does not include the $4 billion appropriation for Head Start, which, being mostly part-time, has not been organized to help working parents with their child-care needs. Nor does it include the Child and Adult Care Food program, which spends $2.5 billion for meals and snacks for children in care. State and local spending for preschools amounted to $0.7 billion in 1990 but probably has grown considerably since. The source of information on federal spending is U.S. Congress Committee on Ways and Means (1988, 679). Expenditure-based state outlays come from National Governors' Association/National Association of State Budget Officers (1998, 20). Other state spending estimates come from Stoney and Greenberg (1996).

18. For details of such a system, see Bergmann (1999).

References

Bergmann, Barbara R. 1996. *Saving Our Children from Poverty: What the United States Can Learn from France.* New York: Russell Sage Foundation.

———. 1999. "Making Child Care Affordable in the United States." *Annals of the American Academy of Political and Social Science,* Special issue, The Silent Crisis in Child Care, edited by Suzanne Helburn (May).

Citro, Constance F., and Robert T. Michael, eds. 1995. *Measuring Poverty: A New Approach.* Washington, DC: National Academy Press.

Devine, Theresa. 2000. "Women and Social Security Reform." Draft paper prepared for the American Economics Association meetings, Boston. Originally compiled from Congressional Budget Office calculations based on data from the March 1999 Current Population Survey.

Helburn, Suzanne, ed. 1995. *Cost, Quality, and Child Outcomes in Child Care Centers, Public Report.* Denver, CO: Department of Economics, Center for Research in Economic and Social Policy, University of Colorado at Denver.

Hofferth, Sandra et al. 1991. *1990 National Child Care Survey.* Washington, DC: Urban Institute.

Kaus, Mickey. 1992. *The End of Equality.* New York: Basic Books.

Mahon, Rianne. 1997. "Child Care in Canada and Sweden: Policy and Politics." *Social Politics* 4, no. 3:382–418.

National Association for the Education of Young Children. 1998. *Accreditation Criteria and Procedures.* Washington, DC: National Association for the Education of Young Children.

National Governors' Association/National Association of State Budget Officers. 1998. *The Fiscal Survey of States.* Washington, DC: National Governors' Association/National Association of State Budget Officers.

National Institute of Child Health and Human Development (NICHD) Child Care Research Network. 1999. "The NICHD Study of Early Child Care: Contexts of Development and Developmental Outcomes over the First Seven Years of Life." Working paper, NICHD.

Orshansky, Molly. 1965. "Counting the Poor: Another Look at the Poverty Profile." *Social Security Bulletin* 28:3–29.

———. 1978. "Measuring Poverty: A Debate." *Public Welfare* 36, no. 2:46–55.

Renwick, Trudi J., and Barbara R. Bergmann. 1993. "A Budget-Based Definition of Poverty, with an Application to Single-Parent Families." *Journal of Human Resources* 28, no. 1 (winter): 1–24.

Stoney, Louise, and Mark Greenberg. 1996. "The Financing of Child Care: Current and Emerging Trends." *Future of Children* 6, no. 2 (summer/fall): 83–102.

U.S. Bureau of the Census. 1995. *What Does It Cost to Mind Our Preschoolers?* Prepared by Lynne M. Casper. Current Population Reports P70–52. Washington, DC: Government Printing Office.

U.S. Bureau of Labor Statistics. 1999. "Labor Force Participation of Fathers and Mothers Varies with Children's Ages." *Monthly Labor Review,* the Editor's Desk, June 3.

U.S. Congress Committee on Ways and Means. 1998. *Green Book.* Washington, DC: Government Printing Office. Available at <http://www.access.gpo.gov/congress/wm001.html.>

Public Support for Parents

NANCY FOLBRE

Parents have joint primary responsibility for raising the child, and the nation shall support them in this. The nation shall provide appropriate assistance to parents in child-raising.
—United Nations Convention on the Rights of the Child
(ratified by all nations except Somalia and the United States)

Should we support and reward parents for the time, energy, and money they put into raising the next generation? Of course we should. Parenting is socially productive labor. It creates the productive capabilities that we call human capital, our most important economic resource. Parenting develops our culture and creates our future history. Parenting helps adults learn patience, humility, and love for others. Furthermore, without some kind of parenting, none of us would be here today.

As our hopes and expectations for developing children's capabilities have grown, so too has the cost of raising and educating them. Parenting is one of the primary activities that people perform for love rather than for money. But love (or at least loved ones) must eat. Raising children in the United States today is extremely costly, in terms of time as well as money. A recent report from the president's Council of Economic Advisors reports that the "rising number of single parents has increased the proportion of families that are 'cash-strapped' and 'time-poor' " (Council of Economic Advisors 1999). As result, families with children are disproportionately vulnerable to poverty.

The poor are not the only ones who suffer. When highly skilled labor is offered rich rewards in the marketplace, the costs of reallocating time from paid work to family work loom large, even for the affluent. As Sylvia Hewlett and Cornel West put it, "Contemporary moms and dads are trapped between the escalating requirements of their children, who need more resources (in terms of both time and money) for longer periods of time than ever before, and the signals of a culture that is increasingly scornful of effort expended on others" (1998, 36).

Proposing to provide more support for parents is not far fetched. We already funnel resources to families with children in a number of ways. We provide public education, allow families a dependent tax deduction and several tax credits, offer public assistance for parents with young children, and maintain a system of institutional and foster care for children whose parents cannot care for them. Economists Robert Haveman and Barbara Wolfe calculate that, in 1992, government spending covered about one-third of the total cost of children (1995, 1831). This probably represents an overestimate of public contributions, but, in any case, government programs and transfer payments have emerged in an ad hoc way without much analytical rationale. Perhaps because of discomfort with the nexus between love and money, the family and the economy (and more generally, between altruism and self-interest), economists have failed to systematically consider the optimal distribution of the costs of children (England and Folbre 199a). The lack of a coherent theoretical framework for analyzing the disjuncture between private costs and public benefits makes it difficult to argue for universal programs.

In this chapter, I outline some important issues to consider in making a stronger case for greater public support for parenting in the United States, asking three specific questions. (1) How much support should be offered parents? (2) What form should support for parenting take? (3) Who should pay for such support?

How Much?

Before trying to answer this first question it is helpful to review what we know (and do not know) about the current costs of children in the United States. Haveman and Wolfe estimate that average annual total costs per child in 1992 amounted to about $13,500, summing to about 15 percent of gross domestic product (1995, 1829). These costs include direct parental expenditures such as money spent on food and clothing, public education and other government transfers, and the opportunity cost of time devoted to children's care outside the market economy. These estimates are low for at least two reasons. They do not place any value on time devoted to child care beyond that which would have been devoted to wage work—that is, they ignore the time that parents could have devoted to other household chores or to their own leisure activities. Sometimes child rearing can be combined with these activities, but sometimes it cannot. A second problem is that children are defined as those eighteen or under, although many parents devote resources to children well beyond that age.

The costs of children vary enormously, depending on what kinds of families they live in. The average income of the top one-fifth of families with children in the United States is more than ten times that of the bottom quintile. Thus, if families spend about the same percentage of their income on children, expenditures on children vary by a factor of ten. Estimates of the actual percentages spent vary (Bainbridge and Garfinkel 1999; Betson 1991), but there is considerable evidence of economic stress. In the United States today slightly less than one-fifth of children live in families with income under the poverty line. The recent reduction in unemployment rates is having an ameliorative effect, as is the expansion of the Earned Income Tax Credit, which provides a significant tax refund for families with young children in which one or both parents are working for pay. Yet our rates of child poverty remain well above those of the social democracies of northwestern Europe.

Some social programs, such as Temporary Assistance to Needy Families (TANF), are targeted to families with incomes below the poverty line. Others provide in-kind or cash transfers to parents regardless of their income. Among the latter are the dependent tax exemption, the child-care tax credit, and public expenditures on education. These programs reflect some level of social agreement that children are public goods that benefit society as a whole and therefore merit public support (Folbre 1994a). Overall levels of support for parenting, however, are low compared to those in the countries of northwestern Europe. Barbara Bergmann calculates that the U.S. government would need to increase expenditures on children by about 60 percent to match what the French government spends per child (1996b, 18).

Despite much talk about economic restructuring and the dismantling of the welfare state, most of the countries of northwestern Europe remain strongly committed to pro-family policies (Kamerman and Kahn 1991, 1994, 1999). A number of historical factors—including the devastating demographic effects of World War II—help explain why these countries devote more collective resources to children (Folbre 1994b). Obviously, the United States has followed a different political trajectory. Nonetheless it is worth asking what level of public resources should be devoted to support for parenting.

"Quality" versus Quantity of Children

Would greater public support for parents encourage them to have more children than they otherwise would? Not necessarily. It could simply improve the lives—and the productive capabilities—of family members. Among economists, there is some disagreement about the best level of population growth, and concerns have been expressed, particularly in Europe, about birthrates dropping below replacement level. In this country, however, the historical role of immigration in adding to our population, combined with environmentalist concerns about the negative effects of population growth, has discouraged policies that might have the effect of increasing the birthrate.

The European experience is reassuring in this respect. In France, pronatalist policies that were explicitly designed to encourage families to rear more than two children have had only a small effect on fertility, which remains below replacement levels (Thélot and Villac 1998, 114). Even in Sweden, the most generous country in Europe, fertility rates are only slightly above replacement, and they remain lower than in the United States. It is also important to note that the average fertility of welfare recipients in this country is no higher than among the population as a whole.

Concern about the quantity/quality trade-off helps explain why many public programs for children involve in-kind transfers, such as subsidies for child care and education. The issue of the form of support will be discussed later, but one could argue that public support should be set at a level that best promotes the overall development of people's capabilities. We do not yet know how to achieve this goal. We do know, however, that poverty probably has negative effects on young children, measured in terms of psychological well-being and educational attainment (Duncan and Brooks-Gunn 1997).

A more modest goal would be to give parents sufficient assistance to keep their children out of poverty. The example of northwestern European countries suggests that this is not an unrealistic goal. If child rearing is considered part of the larger economy (as it should be!), the overall result would be an increase in the efficiency of the economy as a whole (Haveman and Wolfe 1993). The value of the output—children's productive capabilities—would increase by more than the cost of the additional inputs.

Equality of Opportunity

Efficiency, however important, is not the only goal of social policy. Another objective is equality of opportunity, a political principle embedded, though perhaps rather superficially, in the American ethos. Some economists argue that there are always costly trade-offs between efficiency and equality. Others insist that two principles can be complementary. Equality of opportunity can foster healthy competition by leveling the playing field. Why try hard if one has no chance of winning? Individuals who know they have little chance of success have little incentive to compete.

We could provide enough support for parents to foster equality of opportunity for all the children in our country. Some European countries make this an explicit goal, especially where the cultural integration of immigrant populations is concerned. In France, for instance, the extensive system of public subsidies for nursery schools (available free for all children ages three to five) is more generous in the so-called economic priority zones where poverty rates are high. Children for whom French is not a native language get the benefit of smaller class sizes, as well as special social services.

What level of support would be necessary to approach ideals of equal opportunity in the United States? Beyond the elimination of child poverty, it would be necessary to increase funding for schools in poor neighborhoods and more generously subsidize higher education to make it accessible to low-income students. This would represent increased support for parents and children. Note, however, that both of these principles focus on outcomes for children, ignoring the welfare of parents themselves. This would not be problematic if we could assume that everyone was equally likely to devote resources to raising the next generation. In fact, parenting responsibilities are very unevenly distributed, and they impose significant costs on mothers in particular (Joshi, Paci, and Waldfogel 1999). If we consider parenting socially productive work, we should reward it.

Rewarding Parenting

Parents derive a great deal of satisfaction from parenting. One could argue that they are paid in joy. But not all aspects of child rearing are totally joyous, and we expect good parents to act out of a sense of responsibility to their children even when they are not having a good time. Most northwest European countries offer universal family allowances designed to protect the standard of living of all parents and children. The United States does not. However, embedded in our tax and welfare policies are several programs that represent implicit family allowances with very different rules depending on family income and composition.

The federal income tax exemption for dependents, set at $2,748 in 1999, had a value equal to the taxes that would have been paid if that amount had not been exempt from taxation. This exemption is phased out in the top tax bracket. However, for a family in the 31 percent tax bracket, with annual taxable income between $104,050 and $158,550 for a family filing jointly, the benefit amounts to $852. For a family in the lowest bracket (15 percent), with annual taxable income between 0 and $43,050, it amounts to $405. Between 1948 and 1960, the value of this exemption almost completely offset income tax liability for families with children. However, its real value was undermined by inflation between 1960 and 1985. Economist Eugene Steuerle estimates that the tax rate of families with two children increased 43 percent over this period, while the average tax rate for families without children remained essentially unchanged (CDF-MN 1999, 1; Whittington 1992). If the exemption had remained at the same percentage of median family income at which it was originally set in the 1940s, it would have amounted to $6,500 in 1996 (Hewlett and West 1998, 263).

To the dependent exemption must be added a relatively new provision of the tax code, the child tax credit implemented in 1998. As of 1999, it offered a credit of $500 for each child under age seventeen. The credit phases out as income exceeds $110,000 ($75,000 if single, head of household, or a qualifying widow or widower). Because it is a credit and not a deduction, its value remains the same across different tax brackets. However, it can only be deducted from taxes that are due; at lower incomes it interacts with the Earned Income Tax Credit. As a result, families with incomes below about $15,000 do not benefit from it.

Even if the child tax credit is combined with the dependent tax exemption, the tax benefits for families raising children still fall below the original inflation-adjusted value of the original dependent exemption. For a family with an income of $110,000 (the 31 percent tax bracket), the implicit family allowance paid per child in 1999 amounted to $852 in tax savings and a $500 tax credit, for a grand total of $1,337.

Families receiving Temporary Assistance to Needy Families

(TANF) must have income below the poverty line, and since they seldom pay income taxes, they do not often benefit from these tax provisions. However, they do receive assistance based on their number of dependent children. In 1996, the average monthly amount per recipient amounted to $1,630 per year. That is, TANF recipients in that year enjoyed about $300 more per child than a family with an income of $100,000 in 1998. Unlike tax benefits, TANF benefits are subject to strict income and wealth eligibility, time limits, and work requirements.

Poor families who do not receive TANF are eligible for the Earned Income Tax Credit, which, unlike the tax credits discussed previously, is refundable. That is, if the amount of the credit exceeds the taxpayer's federal income tax liability, the excess is payable to the taxpayer as a direct transfer payment. Since 1993, low-income taxpayers with no children have been eligible for this credit, but the maximum amount they can receive is small, just $332. By contrast, taxpayers with one child could claim a credit in 1997 of 34 percent of earnings up to $6,500, or a maximum credit of $2,210. Taxpayers with two or more children could gain a maximum credit of $3,656 (U.S. Congress Committee on Ways and Means 1998, Sec. 13).

Among families receiving the maximum Earned Income Tax Credit benefit, the additional benefits that accrue from the first child amount to $2,110 minus $332, or $1,778, and for the second child, $3,656 minus $2,210, or $1,446. No extra benefits accrue from additional children. In other words, Earned Income Tax Credit recipients can receive a higher level of cash support for first and second children than either poor families on TANF or affluent families in the 31 percent tax bracket. Restrictions are less binding than those for recipients of TANF, but eligibility is strictly limited to low-income families in which a parent is working for pay. In the United States, expenditures on Earned Income Tax Credit now exceed those on TANF. The amounts provided are not sufficient to guarantee that working families with children will have incomes over the poverty line, though they certainly provide a boost for low-wage earners.

Another family allowance–type provision embedded in the Social Security system provides generous insurance against the economic ill effects of the death of a spouse—if that spouse worked in covered employment. In 1996, the average benefit to a widowed mother or father and two children was $1,475.29 per month (Social Security Bulletin 1998, table 3.C4). Taking a third of this as an estimate of the amount per child comes to $491.76, or an annual amount of $5,901. No work requirement or income eligibility concerns come into play. The benefits are universal, with no strings attached. If economic desertion of a co-parent were similarly insured through the Social Security system many low-income mothers would receive far more generous transfers than they do through TANF.

Finally, the U.S. offers an implicit family allowance for foster parents who take in children who have become wards of the state. These payments vary widely across states but are based on calculations of the cost of specific items such as room and board, supervision, and clothing. A survey by the American Public Welfare Association estimates that the national average for basic monthly foster care in 1996 was $356 for two year olds, $373 for nine year olds, and $431 for sixteen year olds. The annual amounts would be $4,272, $4,476, and $5,172, respectively. The estimated costs of institutional care in a group home are much higher—over $35,000 per child (U.S. Congress Committee on Ways and Means 1998, Sec. 11).

In-kind transfers such as food stamps and Medicaid complicate this picture. However, these benefits, limited to poor families, are largely counterbalanced by tax expenditures that primarily benefit the nonpoor. Tax expenditures are defined as deviations from normal tax policy that are functionally equivalent to spending programs. In fiscal 1996, the total federal tax expenditures budget came to about $455 billion, about two and a half times more than was spent on all means-tested direct spending programs (Citizens for Tax Justice 1999, 3). For example, the cost of the tax exemption offered to employer-paid health insurance amounted to $57 billion in that year, while the cost of the mortgage interest tax deduction, available only to homeowners, was $43 billion. Medicaid expenditures limited to poor families, but disproportionately spent on the aged elderly, amounted to about $92 billion in the same year (Citizens for Tax Justice 1999, 2; U.S. Congress Committee on Ways and Means 1998).

In sum, our implicit family allowance system provides between $1,352 and $1,900 in cash transfers a year per child for families in which children are living with their own parents. Families that are in the 31 percent tax bracket enjoy an exemption worth $852 and a credit worth $500. Low-income families receiving the Earned Income Tax Credit are not eligible for either tax benefit but can receive almost $1,900 in support for their first child, contingent on their participation in paid employment. TANF recipients receive an in-between amount.

We know that these implicit family allowances are low relative to the costs of children, not only because we have persistently high child poverty rates but also because more generous public assistance is provided to children who lose a parent through death or become wards of the state. Moreover, these implicit allowances have disparate impacts depending on family structure. The no-strings-attached tax benefits help the affluent, while the conditional transfers benefit the poor. Many income tax and Social Security provisions, as well as welfare policy, seem designed to punish single mothers who fail to work for pay but to reward married mothers who stay home. A high-income earner with a wife who stays home to take care of the children enjoys an additional dependent exemption from his taxes. However a single-parent low-income family is not eligible for assistance unless the parent works for pay or is specifically exempted from the work requirement by state TANF rules.

What Form?

Whatever the level of support for parents, the form this support takes matters a great deal. The loudest concerns usually center on cash versus in-kind transfers such as publicly subsidized child care or parental leaves from work. Feminist economists have been particularly concerned about the possibility that family allowances would reinforce traditional gender roles by encouraging mothers to stay home. Another issue that has recently surfaced concerns "pay for performance," in which support would be linked to child outcomes. And virtually all advocates of pro-family policies wrestle with the question of universal benefits versus more modest, but perhaps more practical, programs to assist the poor.

Family Leaves and Child-Care Subsidies
Apart from the direct expenditures, which are considerable, time that parents take out of the labor market reduces job experience and lowers their lifetime earnings. Indeed, research suggests that motherhood tends to lower women's earnings even if they continue to work full-time, full-year (Waldfogel 1997; England and Budig 1999). The growing incidence of out-of-wedlock births and increased probability of divorce mean that mothers face a substantial risk of poverty unless they marry and remain married to a steady wage earner. Their fear of the economic consequences of relationship dissolution puts them in a

weak bargaining position within the family. It is hard to argue with someone who controls one's only source of market income. Fathers who specialize in child rearing face similar risks.

Certain stages of child rearing are particularly demanding, especially those that involve the care of infants. This helps explain why about four-fifths of industrialized countries provide paid maternity leave. The United States offers only twelve weeks of unpaid leave, and that is only for employees of large firms (Grimsley 1998). Canada, by contrast, offers seventeen weeks of paid leave. Some countries offer at least one year of paid leave (Ruhm and Teague 1997). The level of pay is normally some percentage of the pay that the parent would have earned, representing the amount foregone when time is taken out of paid employment. High-wage earners, therefore, receive more for their parenting effort during this period than low-wage earners.

Federal support for child care, like our implicit family allowance system, takes two very different forms. Tax benefits are of primary relevance to nonpoor families. The child-care tax credit amounts to 20 percent to 30 percent of child-care expenses (depending on family income level), up to $2,400 for one child under thirteen and up to $4,800 for two or more children if these expenses are incurred as a result of parental work for pay. Thus, it can offer as much as $720 per child, though the average amount paid is considerably lower and most families are reimbursed at only 20 percent (it is worth noting that many other business- and work-related expenses are 100 percent deductible). Since this credit is not refundable, it offers no tax benefit for most families unless they have at least $15,000 in income. No upper income limit is imposed on this credit, and as high-income families are more likely to spend money on child care, they are the most likely to benefit.

A less well-known but more generous subsidy takes the form of dependent care pretax accounts, which allow working parents with child-care expenses to set aside up to $5,000 per year in an employer-sponsored account that is exempt from income and payroll taxes. Employers have an incentive to set up such accounts because their payroll taxes are reduced. Here again, the value depends on the tax rate, but a family in the top federal income tax bracket enjoys a subsidy amounting to $1,980, not counting the effect of payroll taxes. In sum, the range of tax subsidies generates reimbursements ranging from $480 a year (20 percent of $2,400 for those least eligible for the child-care credit) to a high of almost $2,000 (the benefit to a family in the highest tax bracket of a fully utilized dependent care tax account).

In the early 1990s, the cost of these tax expenditures far exceeded federal expenditures on programs aimed to serve low-income families. In 1993, the cost of the Child and Dependent Care Tax Credit alone was $2.5 billion, compared to $1.7 billion spent on child care for AFDC recipients, Transitional Child Care, At-Risk Child Care, and the Child Care and Development Block Grant (NAS 1996). Since that year, child-care funding targeted to low-income families has been significantly increased, and program delivery has been reorganized as part of the changes to the larger welfare system legislated in 1996. Still, the amount of total entitlement expenditures authorized for 1999, $2.2 billion, remained slightly below the overall cost of the Child and Dependent Care Tax Credit (U.S. Congress Committee on Ways and Means 1998, 684).

Furthermore, most of the administrative effort has gone into providing child care for recipients of TANF or parents making a transition off TANF, as a way of reducing the public assistance rolls. As a result, many of the working poor have found it difficult to find subsidized slots; this remains the group least likely to receive assistance with child-care costs (Hofferth 1995). As Sharon Long puts it, "Concerns about the potential costs of that increased level of demand, along with concerns about the implications of future economic downturns, have made some states hesitant to expand their child-care programs much beyond the welfare population" (Long 1999, 3). Even states that allocated additional state funds, such as Massachusetts and New York, have long waiting lists for low-income families.

The state of Wisconsin has successfully established a program that assists all eligible families. But there, as elsewhere, changes in reimbursement formulas, lags in adjusting for inflation, and waiting lists have created problems with continuity and quality of care. Concerns have been expressed about the effect of child-care vouchers used as a form of subsidy. Often, their value is set so low that only low-quality providers are willing to accept them. Private expenditures on child care consume an inordinate share of the total income of poor families. In short, the two-tiered system of public subsidy of child care currently in effect does not meet the needs of working poor and low-income families, despite increased pressure on parents to participate in paid employment. On the other hand, it is important to remember that the subsidies offered to middle-income and affluent families also represent only a small fraction—between 20 percent and 30 percent of the costs they pay.

Changing Gender Roles

Mothers have traditionally devoted more time and effort to child care than men, and women earn less than men, on average, in the labor market. As a result, financial support for parents in the United States today may well have the effect of reinforcing traditional gender roles. A boost in family allowances might make it "too easy" for mothers to stay home with their children and let fathers specialize in earning income, a choice that reinforces gender inequality (Bergmann 2000). While some mothers prefer this form of specialization, they may be unaware of the long-run disadvantages to them in a world with a high probability of separation and divorce. Furthermore, there are also disadvantages for their children. Fathers who do not participate actively in child rearing are less likely to maintain their relationships with children in the event of separation from their mother.

The traditional ideal of extreme specialization in child rearing is weakening. Sometimes economic stresses lead to rearrangement of the division of labor, as when parents adopt shift work in order to minimize the cost of purchasing child care (Presser 1994). Husbands who take on child care while their wives are at work end up spending far more time with their children than most fathers. Their numbers are small but significant. In 1993, about 19 percent of the 14.8 million U.S. husbands with preschool age children and wives working outside the home were the primary care providers for their children; an additional 25 percent of these husbands provided some care (U.S. Bureau of the Census 1994).

Many fathers are taking on more direct child-care responsibilities even in the absence of such external pressures. A spate of recent books emphasizes the benefits of shared parenting (Deutsch 1999; Coltrane 1996; Mahoney 1995; Peters 1998). Many voices in the emergent men's movement encourage fathers to play a more active role in child rearing (Hewlett and West 1998; Popenoe 1996). Many current economic policies, such as significantly lower hourly pay and benefits for part-time than for full-time work, reinforce undue specialization between breadwinner and homemaker. A recent *Business Week* article included the headline "Men face greater expectations at home. But work isn't giving them the slack they need" (Hammonds 1998, 56). Active efforts to lower such penalties and to promote shared parenting could counterbalance the temptation to use a family allowance to increase mothers' specialization.

We could design tax incentives that encourage both mothers and fathers to work between twenty and thirty hours in paid work, with each devoting substantial time to family care. Other policy measures could also help equalize gender roles. Direct pay for parenting can be time limited, as is the case with parental leaves from work. In countries such as Finland where parental leaves are relatively generously paid, mothers tend to leave the labor force for a period of more than a year when their children are young. However, the availability of subsidized child care for toddlers encourages them to resume paid employment relatively quickly (Bittman 1999). In other words, an increase in maternal specialization for the care of very young children is counterbalanced by a decrease in maternal specialization for the care of older children.

In some countries, such as Belgium and the Netherlands, family allowances are designed to discourage female labor force participation because they are conditioned on mothers staying home. But in other countries this is neither an explicit goal nor an actual side effect. In France, for instance, single mothers receive an extra stipend until their children reach age three but then are expected to utilize nursery schools and return to paid employment. Female labor force participation rates in France are similar to those in the United States (Thélot and Villac 1998, 21).

Small incentives, such as allowing fathers paid leave for work that cannot be traded for maternity leave, encourage paternal participation. In Sweden, for instance, parental leave can be shared or used by one parent, but one nontransferable month is reserved for the father and one for the mother, to encourage sharing (Haas 1992). During their child's first year, more than one half of fathers use some leave. Fathers use nearly one-third of all paid temporary leave to stay home and care for sick children (Kamerman and Kahn 1999). A stronger policy measure—not (yet) in effect anywhere in the world—would make provision of direct pay for parenting contingent on equal sharing of time devoted to child care. In the U.S. context, Sylvia Hewlett and Cornel West call for a paid *and* compulsory leave for new fathers, as well as for enforcement of the visitation rights and responsibilities of noncustodial parents (1998, 244).

In the absence of such stringent regulation, it seems likely that a boost in parental allowances would reduce mothers' labor market participation more than that of fathers. The size of the effect, however, is unknown. It is worth noting that child-care subsidies, as well as direct financial support for parenting, reinforce traditional gender roles because they increase the demand for paid child-care workers, an occupational category that is more than 95 percent female. The effect of increased family allowances on encouraging mothers to stay home more than fathers would be small compared to the effect of the current gender wage differential in paid employment, which means that families lose more earnings when fathers take time off than when mothers do. Implementing the policies discussed elsewhere in this book to raise women's market earnings would do a great deal to equalize the distribution of parenting responsibilities.

Pay for Performance

Most proposals to provide more direct support for parents are based either on a per child allowance or on earnings replacement. This is, obviously, a different principle than those applied to other forms of work, which presumably are based on performance or productivity. If we think that parents would be driven by extrinsic rather than intrinsic rewards, we should worry that parents will not be motivated to do a good job. It is not just that bad parents might spend the money on themselves. It is that some parents may work harder or more intelligently at parenting than others, in which case it seems unfair to reward all parents the same.

James Coleman has argued that parents should be paid for their "value added"—some calculation of how much better children turn out (in terms of measures such as educational attainment and staying out of prison) than might have been expected (1988). Even if one agreed with this approach, the measurement problems are rather formidable. A simpler solution, proposed by Paul Demeny in 1987 and developed in greater detail by economist Shirley Burggraf (1993, 1997), would give parents a legal claim on their children's earnings as a replacement for Social Security. In this way, parents would capture part of the economic benefits that children create and would have obvious incentives to maximize their children's earnings.

The disadvantages of this approach are twofold. First, actuarially speaking, no old age insurance system based on child rearing can provide the level of insurance that a larger pooling of income and risks provides. How would we provide for individuals whose children die or who simply, through no fault of their parents, are unable to earn enough income to pay this "private tax" to their parents? Second, extrinsic incentives that "pay for performance" could undermine or weaken parental altruism. If we believe that parents should take the best interests of their children to heart, why make their future economic welfare dependent on their children's economic performance? Among other problems that might emerge would be a distinct preference for sons, since men generally earn more than women.

Extrinsic incentives do not always undermine intrinsic ones. Sometimes the two are complementary, as when pecuniary rewards signal the value that society places on the activity. Bruno Frey, a scholar exploring the interface between economics and psychology, argues that "External interventions *crowd-out* intrinsic motivation if they are perceived to be *controlling* and they *crowd-in* intrinsic motivation if they are perceived to be *acknowledging*" (1998, 444, emphasis in original). It is difficult to think of a more "controlling" intervention than one that rewards parents for a narrow subset of child outcomes that are very difficult for them to control. Instead, public policies should acknowledge and honor the value of parental effort.

Universal versus Targeted Payments

If the primary reason to transfer resources to families is to reduce child poverty and to blunt unequal opportunity, then it makes sense to target low-income families with additional assistance. Barbara Bergmann makes a persuasive case for providing fully subsidized child care to the poor and phasing out the subsidy for higher-income families (1996a). The primary reason for this phaseout is strategic: it lowers costs. Arguably, some increase in support for parents is better than none. On the other hand, targeted transfers do not address the fact that parenting is socially productive work that should be rewarded and recognized no matter who is doing it. Furthermore, any benefit that is phased out as family incomes increase acts as an implicit tax on married women's labor force participation, thus indirectly reinforcing traditional gender roles (McCaffery 1997).

Few people realize that current transfers to parents and children in the United States benefit the rich as well as the poor or that low- and middle-income families may be slighted. Irv Garfinkel calculates that in 1992 families in the top one-fifth in terms of income received far higher benefits than lower-middle and middle-income families (1996, 63). Even with the expansion of the Earned Income Tax Credit in recent years, the dollar value of the tax credits offered affluent families approximates the dollar value of cash assistance and the EITC to the poor.

In other words, we already have a universal support system within place within the United States. It just happens to be complicated, inadequate, and inconsistent. We could simplify and expand this system by providing a more generous direct payment to parents and fully subsidizing child care as an extension of our public education system.

Who Pays?

Regardless of the level or the form that support for parenting takes, someone has to actually fork over the money. If the payment is indirect, as it almost always is, we need to consider who will actually bear the brunt of the higher taxes and/or higher prices that result. This issue has received remarkably little consideration in the literature on public finance, although some macroeconomists argue that national economic policies transfer too much money from the young to the old (Kotlikoff 1992) and I have argued that nonparents free ride on parental labor (Folbre 1994a). In the most abstract terms, one can ask how the costs of children should be distributed between employers and workers, parents and children, parents and nonparents, and men and women (England and Folbre 1999b). This question is not easy to answer.

Employers

Employers benefit from the labor power that parents create but pay a wage that is presumably determined by the forces of supply and demand in the labor market. The Marxist analysis of the wage relation led, at an early date, to the argument that employers should be forced to pay a "family wage" that would be sufficient for a male worker to reproduce himself, supporting a wife and children at home. This concept was often used as a bludgeon against women's competition with men in the labor market, with the male trade union movement arguing that women were undercutting men's wages because they had no (or fewer) dependents to support (Kessler-Harris 1990).

Similar arguments surface today in a less antifeminist context, with arguments that employers should pay all workers at least a "living wage," sufficient to support three dependents (Pollin and Luce 1998). Municipal living wage ordinances that require businesses with local government contracts to pay a living wage have been passed in a number of cities. This demand has also explicitly entered the national family policy debate: Sylvia Hewlett and Cornel West call for a minimum wage of $7 an hour, a level that would allow a full-time worker to keep a family of three above the poverty line (1998, 236).

Pressuring employers to pay higher minimum wages may have other merits, but it does not solve the problem. In the first place, the very way that Hewlett and West formulate the demand seems to suggest that one parent should specialize in full-time work and the other should stay at home taking care of the children, which would certainly tend to reinforce traditional gender roles. In the second place, by demanding a family wage for workers whether or not they are actually devoting resources to raising a family, this approach does nothing to diminish the parenting penalty. One could argue, of course, that individuals are unlikely to form a family unless they earn an adequate wage. This problem could be more directly addressed by offering them a family allowance (or tax credit) if and only if they are devoting time and resources to the care of children or other truly dependent family members.

Nonparents

The case for imposing greater taxes on nonparents derives from the observation that children grow up to provide services and pay taxes that help support nonparents as well as parents in their old age. All citizens currently make a claim on the earnings of the younger generation, whether they have helped to raise them or not. Our Social Security system provides benefits based on paid work history or marital status by taxing the current working-age population. The time, energy, and effort devoted to actually producing these workers go unrewarded. To take a more specific example, elderly people without children are much more likely to require nursing home care financed through Medicaid. Yet they pay very little more in taxes, on average, than elderly people who raised children whose informal assistance makes it possible for them to continue living on their own rather than entering a nursing home (Wolf 1999).

In framing the argument that nonparents should assume a share of the costs of children that reflects the benefits they derive from those children, it is important to specify that we want to reward the effort of parenting, not the fact of biological parenthood. Provision of the genetic material required is the least costly aspect of the child rearing process. We think of parenthood as a dichotomy—either someone has produced biological offspring or not. But parenting is not confined to biological kin, and it reflects a continuum in which some parents contribute far more than others. Therefore, if we want to make nonparenting a criterion for taxation we need to define a threshold, some minimum level of responsibility that must be met in order to qualify as a parent. Defining parenting in these terms would acknowledge the efforts of gay and lesbian parents, who are often currently excluded from eligibility for legal adoption of children. It also points to the significance of differences in effort provided by mothers and fathers and by custodial and noncustodial parents.

Mothers and Fathers

Currently, mothers pay a disproportionate share of the costs of raising children (Folbre 1994a, 1994b; England and Folbre, 1999b). Some would argue that they also derive a disproportionate share of the psychological benefits and that mothering must, by definition, be its own reward (Fuchs 1988). There is no meaningful way to ascertain whether or not this is the case; one could argue that mothers are, in a sense, prisoners of love. In any case, whatever the distribution of emotional benefits, it is clear that mothers are unable to claim a fair share of the economic benefits of their child rearing efforts. Specialization in family work lowers their personal income. Unless they have been married for at least ten years to a covered worker, it can leave them ineligible for Social Security benefits.

Assume that women in stable marriages are fully compensated for their child rearing efforts by transfers within the family from fathers to mothers (an assumption inconsistent with data showing that mothers have far less leisure time and suffer greater loss of earning power in the market). Even if this were the case, about 40 percent of all children in this country are living in single-parent households, over 90 percent of which are headed by women. Less than half of these households receive adequate and reliable child-support payments. Recent efforts to improve child-support enforcement have focused on the low-income population as a way of reducing public expenditures. Little increase is evident in transfers to separated or divorced mothers (Sorensen and Halpern 1999).

Two specific policy measures could help increase paternal contributions to parenting. First and most obvious, the state could more closely stipulate and more vigorously enforce parental responsibilities. Today the legal responsibility of a parent is simply to provide for the child's "subsistence." Nothing is stipulated beyond that. It is difficult to argue that a noncustodial parent should pay a specific percentage of his or her income to the children when similar rules do not apply to resident parents. Second, the state could regulate work hours and pay practices to reduce the competitive pressures that make active parenting costly and risky for both fathers and mothers.

Most of the changes that we are currently witnessing in paternal involvement reflect a more indirect set of pressures—the increased bargaining power of women whose participation in paid employment has given them economic independence. Women probably will continue to use this bargaining power to pressure coresident fathers to take on more responsibilities for care. In this context, however, virtually the only threat that they can make to increase contributions from noncustodial fathers is to cut off access or visitation rights, hardly a healthy or desirable outcome. A more explicit set of "rules of the game" could push parental bargaining in more constructive directions.

Increasing public support for parenting could also reduce gender inequality. Since men earn more and pay slightly more in taxes than women do, redistribution to parents through taxation has an equalizing effect. Furthermore, there is evidence that the provision of in-kind services such as subsidized child care makes it easier for men and women to equally share child-care responsibilities (Juster and Stafford 1991).

Children

Last, but not least, children could help pay for their own costs. In effect, they already do, since the Social Security taxes that they pay as working-age adults go to help support their parents' generation. But in public discussion these taxes have been conceptualized as a way that youth are providing for their own old age, a kind of intergenerational transfer that performs the same function as a private pension. Taxes in general are often described as money that is taken away from individuals and spent on others, as in the publicity regarding "Tax Freedom Day," the date on which a person would meet all his or her tax obligations if all that individual's earnings had been transferred to the Internal Revenue Service. This creates the impression that taxpayers have received no benefits from the government.

Why don't we ever hear about "Tax Pay Back Year," the point in time at which children have repaid in taxes what was spent to pay for their education, their health, their infrastructure, and the public support given their parents? Instead of describing expenditures aimed at young children as a transfer, we could describe them as a loan that they are required to pay back, a literal investment in their future capabilities that offers an excellent rate of return. Our current government accounting structure makes it very difficult to see the intergenerational flows that are actually taking place. Some conceptual reorganization could help taxpayers understand the economic advantages of public support for the development of children's capabilities.

Conclusion

I have outlined several ways we could provide more public support for parenting, without specifying exactly how much or what form this support should take. In my opinion, the failure to directly address some of the difficult issues raised earlier in the chapter helps explain the relative lack of political support for pro-family policies in this country. Advocates tend to make their case in simplistic moral terms without explaining their underlying economic logic. Still, many of the questions raised previously are difficult to answer, and I do not think that the formulation of a progressive family policy should wait until we can devise precise answers.

Here are some guidelines. We already provide some public support for parenting but not enough to keep parents and children out of poverty or to make it clear that we collectively value the work that parents do. Greater expenditures could increase economic efficiency by improving the development of children's capabilities and enhancing equality of opportunity. In principle, universal programs make sense, supplemented by some extra targeted provisions for the poor. We could pay for these expenditures both by taxing nonparents more heavily and by making "loans" to children that will be later repaid.

Among family policy advocates, there is considerable debate over the merits of cash versus in-kind transfers, child-care subsidies versus family allowances, and state-based versus employer-based approaches. In closing, I will hazard my own opinion and argue for a lot of everything. We should create a more generous universal family allowance. We should provide universal publicly subsidized, high-quality child care, especially for children ages three and above. We should legally specify and strenuously enforce parental responsibilities. Finally, we should require employers to adopt policies that encourage both men and women to devote a healthy portion of their day to the care of those they love.

Note

This chapter was written with the financial and intellectual support of the MacArthur Foundation Research Network on the Family and the Economy. I gratefully acknowledge the comments and criticisms of Lee Badgett, Irving Garfinkel, Sheila Kamerman, Mary King, Julie Nelson, Robert Pollak, and Timothy Smeeding.

References

Bainbridge, Jay, and Irving Garfinkel. 1999. "The Cost of Children in the U.S." Manuscript, Department of Social Work, Columbia University.

Bergmann, Barbara R. 1996a."Child Care: The Key to Ending Child Poverty." In *Social Policies for Children,* edited by Irwin Garfinkel, Sara S. McLanahan, and Jennifer L. Hochschild, 112–35. Washington, DC: Brookings Institution.

———. 1996b. *Saving Our Children from Poverty: What the United States Can Learn from France.* New York: Russell Sage Foundation.

———. 2000. "Subsidizing Child Care by Mothers at Home." *Feminist Economics* 6, no. 1.

Betson, David. 1991. "Alternative Estimates of the Cost of Children from the 1980–86 Consumer Expenditure Survey." Special Report 51, Institute for Research on Poverty, University of Wisconsin,

Bittman, Michael. 1999. "Parenthood with Penalty: Time Use and Public Policy in Australia and Finland." *Feminist Economics* 5, no. 3:1–16.

Burggraf, Shirley. 1993. "How Should the Cost of Child Rearing Be Distributed?" *Challenge* 37, no. 5:48–55.

———. 1997. *The Feminine Economy and Economic Man.* New York: Addison-Wesley.

Children's Defense Fund–Minnesota (CDF-MN). 1999. "Family Tax Policies." Available at <http://www.cdf-mn.org/family.htm>. Accessed on November 19.

Citizens for Tax Justice. 1999. *The Hidden Entitlements.* Available at <http://www.ctj.org/hig_ent/part-1.htm>. Accessed on November 18.

Coleman, James. 1998. "Social Capital in the Creation of Human Capital." *American Journal of Sociology* 94 (supplement): S95–S120.

———. 1998. "Fathers' Role at Home Is under Negotiation." *Chronicle of Higher Education,* October 2.

Demeny, Paul. 1987. "Re-Linking Fertility Behavior and Economic Security in Old Age: A Pronatalist Reform." *Population and Development Review* 13, no. 1:128–32.

Deutsch, Francine M. 1999. *Halving It All: How Equally Shared Parenting Works.* Cambridge, MA: Harvard University Press.

Duncan, Greg, and Jeanne Brooks-Gunn, eds. 1997. *Consequences of Growing up Poor.* New York: Russell Sage Foundation.

England, Paula, and Michele Budig. 1999. "The Effects of Motherhood on Wages in Recent Cohorts: Findings from the National Longitudinal Survey of Youth." Paper presented at the annual meetings of the American Economic Association, January 4.

England, Paula, and Nancy Folbre. 1999a. "The Cost of Caring," *Annals of the American Academy of Political and Social Science* 561:39–51.

———. 1999b. "Who Should Pay for the Kids?" 1999. *Annals of the American Academy of Political and Social Science* 562:194–207.

Folbre, Nancy. 1994a. "Children as Public Goods." *American Economic Review* 84, no. 2:86–90.

———. 1994b. *Who Pays for the Kids? Gender and the Structures of Constraint.* New York: Routledge.

———. 1998. "Institutions and Morale: The Crowding-out Effect." In *Economics, Values, and Organization,* edited by Avner Ben-Ner and Louis Putterman, 437–60. New York: Cambridge University Press.

Fuchs, Victor. 1988. *Women's Quest for Economic Equality.* Cambridge, MA: Harvard University Press.

Garfinkel, Irwin. 1996. "Economic Security for Children: From Means Testing and Bifurcation to Universality." In *Social Policies for Children,* edited by Irwin Garfinkel, Sara S. McLanahan, and Jennifer L. Hochschild, 33–82. Washington, DC: Brookings Institution.

Grimsley, Kirsten. 1998. "U.S. Mothers Face Stingy Maternity Benefits." *Washington Post,* February 16.

Haas, Linda. 1992. *Equal Parenthood and Social Policy: A Study of Parental Leave in Sweden.* Albany, NY: State University of New York Press.

Hammonds, Keith. 1998. "The Daddy Trap." *Business Week,* September 21, 56–64.

Haveman, Robert, and Barbara Wolfe. 1993. "Children's Prospects and Children's Policy." *Journal of Economic Perspectives* 7, no. 4:153–74.

———. 1995. "The Determinants of Children's Attainments: A Review of Methods and Findings." *Journal of Economic Literature* 33:1829–78.

Hewlett, Sylvia Ann, and Cornel West. 1998. *The War against Parents.* New York: Houghton Mifflin.

Hofferth, Sandra. 1995. "Caring for Children at the Poverty Line." *Children and Youth Services Review* 12, no. 1/2:1–31.

Joshi, Heather, Pierella Paci, and Jane Waldfogel. 1999. "The Wages of Motherhood: Better or Worse." *Cambridge Journal of Economics* 23, no. 5:543–64.

Juster, F. Thomas, and Frank Stafford. 1991. "The Allocation of Time: Empirical Findings, Behavioral Models, and Problems of Measurement." *Journal of Economic Literature* 29:471–522.

Kamerman, Sheila B., and Alfred J. Kahn. 1991. *Child Care, Parental Leave, and the Under Three's: Policy Innovation in Europe.* New York: Auburn House.

———. 1994. *A Welcome for Every Child: Care, Education, and Family Support for Infants and Toddlers in Europe, Zero to Three.* New York: National Center for Clinical Infant Programs.

———. 1999. "Child and Family Policies in an Era of Social Policy Retrenchment and Restructuring." Paper presented at the Luxembourg Income Study Conference on Child Well-Being in Rich and Transition Countries, September 30–October 2.

Kessler-Harris, Alice. 1990. *A Woman's Wage.* Lexington: University of Kentucky Press.

Kotlikoff, Laurence J. 1992. *Generational Accounting: Knowing Who Pays, and When, for What We Spend.* New York: Free Press.

Long, Sharon. 1999. "Child Care Assistance under Welfare Reform: Early Responses by the States." Testimony before the U.S. House Committee on Ways and Means, Subcommittee on Human Resources, March 16. Available at <http://www.urban.org/TESTIMON/long3-16-99.html>.

Mahoney, Rhona. 1995. *Kidding Ourselves: Breadwinning, Babies, and Bargaining Power.* New York: Basic Books.

McCaffery, Edward J. 1997. *Taxing Women.* Chicago: University of Chicago Press.

National Academy of Sciences (NAS). 1996. *Child Care for Low Income Families.* Washington, DC: National Academy of Sciences. Available at <http://www.nap.edu/readingroom/books/childcare>.

Peters, Joan K. 1998. *The Parent Trap: Loving Our Children without Sacrificing Our Selves.* Reading, MA: Addison-Wesley.

Pollin, Robert, and Stephanie Luce. 1998. *The Living Wage: Building a Fair Economy.* New York: New Press.

Popenoe, David. 1996. *Life without Father.* New York: Free Press.

Presser, Harriet B. 1994. "Employment Schedules among Dual-Earner Spouses and the Division of Labor by Gender." *American Sociological Review* 59:348–69.

Ruhm, Christopher J., and Jacqueline L. Teague. 1997. "Parental Leave Policies in Europe and North America." In *Gender and Family Issues in the Workplace,* edited by Francine D. Blau and Ronald G. Ehrenberg, 133–56. New York: Russell Sage Foundation.

Social Security Administration. 1998. *Annual Statistical Supplement to the Social Security Bulletin.* Washington, DC: Government Printing Office.

Sorensen, Elaine, and Ariel Halpern. 1999. "Child Support Is Working Better than We Think." Urban Institute Report Series A, A-31, Washington, DC: Urban Institute. Available at <http://www.urban.org>.

Thélot, Claude, and Michel Villac. 1998. Politique familiale, bilan et perspectives. Paris: Rapport à la ministere de l'emploi et de la solidarité et au ministre de l'economie, des finances, et de l'industrie.

U.S. Bureau of the Census. 1994. *My Daddy Takes Care of Me! Fathers as Care Providers.* Prepared by Lynne M. Casper. Current Population Reports P70–59. Washington, DC: Government Printing Office.

U.S. Congress Committee on Ways and Means. 1998. *Green Book.* Washington, DC: Government Printing Office. Available at <http://www.access.gpo.gov/congress/wm001.html>.

U.S. Council of Economic Advisors. 1999. *Families and the Labor Market, 1969–1999: Analyzing the "Time Crunch."* Washington, DC: Government Printing Office.

Waldfogel, Jane. 1997. "The Effect of Children on Women's Wages." *American Sociological Review* 62, no. 2 :209–17.

Whittington, Leslie A. 1992. "Taxes and the Family: The Impact of the Tax Exemption for Dependents on Marital Fertility." *Demography* 29, no. 2:215–26.

Wolf, Douglas A. 1999. "The Family as Provider of Long-Term Case: Efficiency, Equity, and Externalities." *Journal of Aging and Health* 111, no. 3 (August): 360–82.

Are Older Women Economically Secure? Reforming Social Security

Lois B. Shaw and Catherine Hill

Social Security reform is a women's issue. On average, women earn less and live longer than men. Because of these characteristics, older women are more dependent than men on Social Security. Without Social Security, more than half of women aged 65 or older would be poor. For 25 percent of unmarried elderly women (widowed, divorced, separated, or never married), Social Security is their only source of income.

Social Security "reform" is under serious consideration in Washington. While the program is fully solvent for the next three decades, the Social Security trustees predict that a shortfall will occur in the year 2037 if no measures are taken. While many commentators believe the possibility of a future shortfall warrants action, even dramatic action, now, others believe continued economic growth together with modest changes will generate sufficient revenues to keep the system solvent. How this issue is resolved will have enormous implications for women and their families.

Politicians and policy analysts involved in the debates on Social Security reform often ignore implications of their proposals for women. In part, this omission stems from the perception that women's situation will improve over time as more women work in the paid workforce for longer periods of time. Certainly, the past three decades have seen a dramatic increase in the number of women working in the paid labor force. However, most women still have very different working lives than men. Women who work full-time year-round earn only 75 percent as much as men. Moreover, women are much more likely than men to work part-time. For example, in 1996, only half of women aged 25–44 worked full-time year-round (compared with three-quarters of men). If part-time workers are included, women earn only 60 percent as much as men. Women also remain much more likely to take time out of the labor force to care for children and elderly relatives. Shorter and less lucrative careers result in lower incomes in retirement for women.

Despite women's increased participation in the labor market, researchers predict that poverty rates among elderly women will be as high in the 2020s as those today (Smeeding, Estes, and Glasse 1999). This is partly due to the fact that more retired women in the future will be divorced, separated, or single and therefore much more vulnerable to poverty. In other words, while future generations of women will be economically disadvantaged for different reasons, they are not likely to fare much better than their mothers and grandmothers. For the foreseeable future, women face a high likelihood of poverty and near poverty in old age and have special reasons for wanting to protect and enhance Social Security.

This chapter addresses the implications of Social Security reform for women. We begin with a discussion of poverty in old age, highlighting differences in women's risk of poverty based on age, race, and marital status. Next, we discuss the issue of Social Security's long-term solvency and some of the major proposals being considered for changing the system. We also consider ways of improving the adequacy and equity of Social Security for women, discussing proposals to achieve these goals while keeping costs affordable. We conclude by discussing options for raising revenue both to ensure the solvency of the system in the future and to fund a "women's agenda" for Social Security reform.

Poverty among the Elderly

Women are more likely than men to be poor in old age. In 1998, about 13 percent of women age 65 and over had incomes below the poverty level compared with 7 percent of men of the same age. Women of color are particularly at risk for poverty in their old age. Older African American and Hispanic women are much more likely than white women to be poor. Almost 30 percent of black women aged 65 and over were poor in 1996, compared with 28 percent of Hispanic women and 12 percent of aged white women. Poverty at older ages also varies markedly by marital status and living arrangement. Married women are much less likely to be poor than nonmarried women, especially those who are living alone or with unrelated persons (see table 5.1).

The risk of poverty increases with age. Of women aged 75 and older, 15 percent had incomes below the poverty line, while 11 percent of all women aged 65 and 74 are poor (see table 5.1). In large part, poverty among women aged 75 and older can be explained by the increase in the number of women living alone. Widows lose part of the couple's Social Security benefits and, in many cases, part or all of their husbands' private pension benefits. Income tends to decline for other reasons as well. Sometimes income falls when assets are spent down for health care or other expenses. Sometimes income falls when work is no longer possible. Women who supplement their Social Security benefits by part-time employment when they first retire may become poor as they age into their seventies or eighties and can no longer work (Shaw, Zuckerman, and Hartmann 1998).

Poverty among the elderly, though still high for some groups of women (and men), has decreased markedly over the last forty years. In 1959 the overall poverty rate for the elderly was 35 percent, considerably higher than the 22 percent rate for the whole population. Today the poverty rate among the elderly is 10.5 percent compared with an overall poverty rate of 13.3 percent. Most of the improvement in elderly poverty came in the first fifteen years of this period. By 1979 poverty among the older population had fallen to about 15 percent (17 percent for women). Since then, the decline has been much slower.

Much of the improvement in living standards of the elderly can be attributed to the increase in coverage and benefits made available through improvements in Social Security. Today, Social Security benefits account for slightly over half of the income of unmarried elderly women (compared with about 40 percent for unmarried men) and 36 percent of couples' incomes.

Women depend more on Social Security because they enter retirement with fewer resources than men. The greatest disparity lies in accumulated pension wealth and savings, with Social Security credits partially compensating for this gap (Mitchell, Levine, and Phillips 1999). For example, of women age 65 and older in 1995, only 26 percent received income from an employer-based pension compared with 46 percent of the men age 65 and older. At the same time, women's pensions were worth 58 percent of the value of men's pensions (Employee Benefit Research Institute 1997). These figures reflect not only women's lower earnings and fewer years of work but also that the survivor benefits widows receive from their husbands' pensions typically pay 50–60 percent of the amount their husbands received.

The percentage of women receiving income from employer-based pensions is likely to increase in the future, but, because of men's and women's different work patterns, the gap between their pension coverage is likely to remain large. While coverage rates for men and women who currently work full-time are nearly the same (about 50 percent), only 15 percent of women working part-time were covered by pension plans (National Economic Council Interagency Working Group on Social Security 1998). Because of the continuing pay gap, women's pensions will also continue to be smaller than men's pensions.

The Social Security system provides protections that are likely to remain particularly important to women. First, Social Security replaces a higher proportion of the earnings of lower earners. As women tend to earn less than men, this provision benefits women. Second, Social Security provides benefits for wives (or husbands) and wid-

TABLE 5.1. Poverty Rates of Women Age 65 and Older, by Marital Status and Living Arrangement, 1998

Marital Status	Percentage in Poverty
Married	4.7
Widowed	16.8
Divorced	22.7
Married with spouse absent/separated	30.6
Never married	24.2

Living Arrangements	Percentage in Poverty
Alone	21.4
Spouse	4.6
Spouse and other family members	5.4
Other family members only	10.4
Nonfamily	28.2
All women aged 65–74	10.8
All women aged 75 and older	15.1

Source: Theresa Devine, "Women and Social Security Reform," Draft paper, prepared for the American Economics Association meetings, Boston (2000). Originally compiled from Congressional Budget Office calculations based on data from the March 1999 Current Population Survey.

ows (or widowers) who earned significantly less than their spouses. Women (or men) divorced after ten years of marriage can claim these benefits, even if their former partner remarries. Third, because women tend to live longer than men, the fact that Social Security provides an inflation-adjusted lifetime income is particularly important to them.

The life and disability insurance provided by Social Security are also particularly important to women. While Social Security is usually thought of as a retirement program, it also provides valuable life and disability insurance to U.S. workers. For example, for a married worker of average earnings history with two children, Social Security provisions are equivalent to about $374,000 in life insurance and $223,000 in disability insurance coverage (Orio Nicholas, personal communication, 2000). This coverage is provided to all workers regardless of age, occupation, or preexisting health conditions. Of particular importance to women is the provision of benefits to spouses caring for children under 16 if the worker retires, becomes disabled, or dies. Women represent 98 percent of the beneficiaries of this provision. (For major benefit provisions and how benefit amounts are determined, see table 5.2.)

Current Debates: The Long-Term Solvency Problem—Why Privatization Is Not the Answer

In spite of its success in reducing poverty among the elderly, Social Security's future has become uncertain. According to current projections by the Social Security trustees, the system will be unable to continue to pay the present level of benefits in about thirty-four years. The system is not about to be "bankrupt" in the usual sense of the word since benefits could always be reduced or the payroll tax or other taxes increased. However, due to the increased longevity of the population as well as a forecast for slower economic growth in the future, the Social Security trustees project that, if no changes are made, the program will not be able to pay full benefits after the year 2037.

In order to understand what we refer to as the long-term solvency problem, it is necessary to understand how the system is financed. Social Security is funded largely by the payroll tax on workers and employers. It is mainly a pay-as-you-go system, which means that about 90 percent of the payroll tax paid by current workers goes to pay benefits for current retirees and other beneficiaries; the other 10 percent is deposited in the Social Security trust fund, which is invested in government bonds. Interest on these bonds as well as income taxes paid on current benefits also go into the trust fund. It is estimated that as the baby boom generation retires, payroll taxes will no longer cover all benefits and the trust fund will gradually be drawn down. When the trust fund is exhausted, the payroll taxes coming into the system will be sufficient to pay only 70 percent of promised benefits unless changes are made.

It is important to remember that these are estimates based on assumptions about the future. By law the Social Security trustees are required to make forecasts over a seventy-five-year period. Uncertainties in these forecasts are unavoidable, since they must depend on estimating future economic growth as well as changes in the birthrate,

TABLE 5.2.   An Overview of the Current Social Security System's Benefits

The benefit formula is a progressive calculation that replaces a higher percentage of earnings for low-income workers than for high earners.

Benefits are adjusted annually to account for inflation and are paid as long as the recipient lives.

Currently, the normal retirement age (for receiving full benefits) is 65; the earliest age for eligibility for retirement benefits is 62. The age for full Social Security benefits has been revised from 65 to 67 years of age, to be phased in by the year 2022.

Early retirement (before the normal retirement age) results in reduced benefits.

A married person is eligible for the larger of either 100 percent of his or her own retired worker benefit or 50 percent of his or her spouses's retired worker benefit. Benefits are reduced if taken before the normal age.

Widow(ers) are entitled to the larger of 100 percent of the deceased spouse's benefit or her (his) own retired worker benefit. Benefits are reduced if taken early.

A divorced person who was married for at least 10 years and is not married at retirement is entitled to the same benefits as a wife (husband) or widow(er): spousal benefits of 50 percent of the former spouse's retired worker benefit during his or her lifetime and 100 percent of the benefit after the death of the former spouse unless one's own retired worker benefit is larger. Divorced spouse benefits are paid even if the former spouse remarries and has other dependents receiving benefits.

Disabled worker benefits based on covered earnings are available at any age before normal retirement age.

Children of disabled or deceased workers are eligible for benefits until age 18. Parents of these children are also eligible to receive benefits until the children are age 16, if the parents' earnings do not exceed specified levels.

immigration, and longevity. Some researchers believe that the trustees overestimate the seriousness of the system's problems because the assumptions they make about economic growth are too pessimistic (Baker and Weisbrot 1999). Others believe the forecasts understate the "crisis" because the assumptions about increases in longevity are too low (Social Security Advisory Board 1999). It is probably prudent to assume that there is a potential solvency problem that should be addressed by making modest changes, as we discuss subsequently.

All proposals to achieve long-term solvency recommend either ways to reduce benefits or to raise the amount of revenue available to the system. As discussed later in the chapter, these approaches for reducing benefits and/or raising revenue have different implications for different groups of women and men.

Proposals to partially privatize the Social Security system have been put forward by some analysts as a way to improve the financial health of Social Security. Privatization plans would establish private retirement accounts for individual workers, who would have some degree of control over how their funds were invested. Some plans would divert part of the payroll tax to pay for private accounts, and others would increase the payroll tax or add funds from some other source. Payroll taxes diverted into private accounts would not be available to cover current benefits and would therefore make the system's solvency problem worse. If private accounts were added through tax increases, this would make it harder to raise taxes to pay promised benefits. Therefore, nearly all privatization plans call for cuts in Social Security benefits.

Proposals of the Cato Institute and those put forward by Senators Archer and Shaw are exceptional in claiming that there would be no benefit cuts, at least initially. The Archer/Shaw plan proposed using general revenues to fund private accounts but did not specify whether these funds would come from tax increases or cuts in other government spending. The Cato Institute calls for borrowing and cuts in government spending. Women should be especially wary of unfunded programs that directly or indirectly call for cuts in other important domestic programs, which essentially "rob Jill to pay Jane." Privatization proponents claim that retirement income from the private accounts would make up for lower Social Security benefits because the rate of return from stocks is higher than returns on government bonds. However, women and other low earners would be at risk of doing much worse for reasons we detail later.

The basic reason that establishing private accounts does not, in itself, achieve solvency for Social Security is that there will be a long and costly transition period when funds must be found to pay for private accounts at the same time that Social Security benefits must continue to be paid to current recipients and workers who will become eligible for benefits before the private system matures. In essence, the generations living through the transition must pay for two systems at once, one for their grandparents' and parents' generations and another for their own retirement.

If these plans would not help Social Security achieve solvency, why are they so often suggested? Several influences are at work. One is a concern that our country does not save enough; private savings are an important source of funds for business and government investment. Many believe that more savings would be available if individuals saved more for their retirement and depended less on social insurance. Sometimes the fear is expressed that support of such a large retired population will crowd out other needed social spending on education, health, and other programs. The investment industry, including brokers and investment companies, backs privatization because it stands to make large profits from administering a large number of new accounts. Some high earners believe they would be better off under a private system than in the present social insurance system where some of their dollars help support lower earners. The recent strength in the stock market also tends to make many people believe that high returns are possible with little risk; the risk of a serious downturn is not considered.

Adequacy and Equity for Women

While ensuring long-term solvency is necessary, improving the adequacy and equity of Social Security for women should be part of any reform package. Women are a diverse group, and their different work and marital histories greatly influence their prospects for economic security in retirement. Divorce, widowhood, disability, a history of low-wage employment (and/or marriage to a low earner), and taking time out of the paid workforce to care for children or elderly increase a woman's risk of poverty in retirement. While improving adequacy (raising benefits for low-income women) should be at the core of a feminist agenda for Social Security, improving equity in benefits between traditional one-earner families and two-earner families is also important. The needs of today's two-earner families are often not well served by Social Security rules, which were designed for a society made up mainly of single-earner couples with homemaker wives.

In this section of the chapter, we present an overview of proposals to improve Social Security for women. First, one of the oldest proposals, earnings sharing, is described, along with its impacts on women with different work and marital histories. Next, we discuss proposals to strengthen the existing system by increasing benefits for widows, divorced women, and low earners. We suggest ways for limiting the cost of these proposals and targeting them to those in need.

The Spousal Benefit and Earnings Sharing

Unpaid caregiving work is at the heart of women's issues in Social Security. Presently, Social Security recognizes the value of unpaid family work by giving women (and men) the option of receiving a benefit based on their own work history or a benefit based on half that of their spouse's earning record. Because women earn less than men and tend to work for fewer years for pay, it often makes sense for women to claim a spousal benefit, rather than a benefit based on their own work record. These women are said to be "dually entitled" because they can claim benefits either as a worker or as a wife (whichever is higher).

An unintended consequence of the spousal benefit is an equity problem. As table 5.3 shows, couples with different work histories receive different "returns" on their payroll tax contributions. In spite of her considerable work experience, the wife of couple 2 receives only slightly higher benefits than the wife of couple 1, who did not work in the paid labor force at all. Couple 3, in which the spouses had equal earnings, received considerably less than the traditional one-earner couple, even though the couples had the same total earnings and paid the same amount of payroll taxes. This difference is even more pronounced when the wives become widows.

Spousal benefits reward caregiving imperfectly. While the wife of a high-wage earner can receive a spousal benefit, regardless of whether she actually had children or performed other unpaid caregiving activities, single parents and divorced spouses from marriages that lasted fewer than ten years are not eligible for the spousal benefit. Of course, gay couples can not use the spousal benefit, even though one partner might take time out of the paid workforce to care for children or elderly parents. As Steuerle, Spiro, and Carasso (1999) point out, the principles behind the spousal benefit are contradictory. On the one hand, the spousal benefit recognizes that households with two people need more money. On the other hand, it provides benefits to high-income one-earner households, while low-income dual-earner couples do not benefit from it. Thus, while an important provision for many women, the spousal benefit remains an imperfect tool for recognizing unpaid caregiving.

"Sharing" a couple's Social Security credits equally between partners in a marriage has been put forward as fairer way of recognizing unpaid family work. The principle behind earnings sharing is that the husband and wife are equal partners in a marriage. A Social Security system that used earnings sharing would combine the annual earnings total of the couple and credit each of them with one-half of this total for his or her Social Security earnings record. Each individual's benefit, therefore, would be based on the individual's own earnings for the years he or she was single, plus half of the combined couple earnings for the years of marriage. The advantage of earnings sharing is that inequities between one-earner and two-earner couples are eliminated. Since no one would receive a spousal benefit, one-earner families and two-

TABLE 5.3. A Comparison of Social Security Benefits for Families with Different Work Histories

	Single-Earner Family (1)	Dual-Earner Family (where the wife earns half of her husband's earnings) (2)	Equal Earners (3)
Husband earns	$36,000	$36,000	$18,000
Wife earns	$0	$18,000	$18,000
Benefits paid on retirement at age 65	Husband $1,215 Spouse $607 Family $1,822	Husband $1,215 Spouse $756 Family $1,971	Husband $756 Spouse $756 Family $1,512
Benefits to widow (or widower) under curent system	$1,215	$1,215	$756
Benefits to widow if formula is changed to 3/4 of combined benefits	$1,366 (12% raise)	$1,478 (21% raise)	$1,134 (50% raise)
Benefits to widow if formula is changed to 2/3 of combined benefits	$1,215 (no change)	$1,314 (8% raise)	$1,008 (33 1/3% raise)

Source: Author's calculations based on Social Security Administration, *Annual Statistical Supplement to the Social Security Bulletin* (Washington, DC: Government Printing Office, 1998), table 2. A11, 48.

earner families would get the same "return" on their payroll taxes. In the event of divorce, Social Security credits could be divided like other commonly held property.

Earnings sharing is not a new idea. Women's organizations have been interested in earnings sharing as a way of solving the "dual entitlement" problem since the early 1970s. However, while earnings sharing would indeed eliminate the dual entitlement problem, this does not automatically mean higher benefits for the majority of women. A study by the U.S. General Accounting Office (1996) found that earnings sharing would result in lower benefits for many women. While homemakers would gain half of their husbands' earnings in their own accounts, they would lose access to the spousal benefit (50 percent of their husbands' benefits) that currently exists. The retirement income for traditional families, where the wife stayed at home, would decline relative to that of the dual-earner couples. Second and third wives, and their children, would be particularly hard hit by earning sharing because they would have no access to the credits earned by their husbands prior to or after their marriage. Overall, while the goal of improving equity among different kinds of households is admirable, earnings sharing is not the best vehicle because it could leave many women worse off than under the current system.

Survivor Benefits

Widows make up a majority of the poorest elderly, with the oldest widows facing the greatest economic hardships. Because widows are much less likely to remarry than widowers, they are generally unable to benefit economically from sharing expenses with another person. The average household income of married women falls sharply when their husbands die, even when income measures are adjusted to account for the smaller household size (Holden and Zick 1999). Older widows are particularly vulnerable economically because they are less likely to be able to supplement their income with earnings and more likely to incur high medical expenses.

Under current law, a widow is entitled to the larger of the benefit based on her husband's account or the benefit based on her own work record. If only one member of a couple has been in the workforce, the widow's benefit is equal to her husband's benefit, which is two-thirds of the couple's combined benefit (see table 5.3). As shown in table 5.3, the second widow, who earned half as much as her husband, will receive the same amount as the widow who never worked. Worst off will be the widow who earned as much as her husband. She will receive much less than the first widow in spite of the couples' equal payroll tax contributions; furthermore, her Social Security income will be only half the couple's combined income, a much larger decline in benefits than the first widow will experience. Since the period of widowhood is the time of greatest economic vulnerability for women, this distribution of benefits is undesirable.

One approach to helping all widows, but especially those with their own work records, is to raise the benefits payable to the survivors of married couples to 75 percent of the couple's combined benefits. Such a policy would result in a 50 percent raise for the widow of an equal earner couple, with more modest increases for other widows. This provision would partially offset the inequity between traditional one-earner households and dual-earner households, without the problems associated with full-scale earnings sharing.

If the program were set up in this way the largest benefits would often go to upper-income widows who do not need them. To limit costs, the widow's benefit could be capped at the maximum benefit Social Security pays to individual workers. Alternative ways to limit costs call for somewhat less generous provisions. For example, the survivor benefit could be calculated as two-thirds rather than three-quarters of the combined benefit. In this formula, the benefits for survivors of one-earner couples would not increase. Some proposals have also called for reduction of the spouse benefit to one-third of the husband's benefit to help pay for increased survivor benefits.

Divorced Women

Benefits for divorced women were not added to Social Security until 1965, when women divorced after a twenty-year marriage became eligible for the same spouse and widow benefits they would have received if their marriages had not ended. In 1977, in recognition that divorce was becoming much more prevalent, the number of years of marriage required for eligibility was reduced to ten. Treating divorced spouse benefits like spouse or widow benefits has the odd effect that a divorced women may see a substantial increase in her benefit when her former spouse dies. While their ex-spouses are alive, however, divorced women have a high rate of poverty because the spouse benefit was designed as supplemental income rather than intended for a person living alone.

In spite of their high rates of poverty, little attention has been given to improving benefits for divorced women. In fact, proposals to increase benefits for widows while reducing the spouse benefit would make the situation worse for divorced women who depend on the spouse benefit. At a recent conference of women's organizations convened to discuss Social Security reform for women, it was suggested that divorced spouse benefits should be increased to 75 percent of the former spouse's benefits during his lifetime (Hill and Hartmann 2000). Another suggestion was to extend benefits to women married at least seven years, the average length of marriage before divorce.

Some researchers have suggested instituting earnings sharing in cases of divorce only (Smeeding, Estes, and Glasse 1999). Social Security assets would be divided like other marital property. Costly administrative expenses would be avoided because accounts would be divided only once, at the time of divorce. Earnings would be shared and divided for the years of marriage only, thus giving credit for marriages of less than ten years that now receive no benefits, while giving larger credits for longer marriages. When added to their own accounts, this would help many divorced women achieve adequate benefits. One downside of earnings sharing at divorce is that investments in human capital are no longer shared. For example, in the current system, if a wife (or husband) puts her husband (or his wife) through college or graduate school, and if the marriage lasted ten years or more, the divorced spouse can benefit from her (or his) ex-spouse's future earnings. In earnings sharing, only the working spouse's current credits are divided, and ex-spouses have no claim on future earnings.

Family Service Credit

Another possible avenue for helping divorced women, as well as other women and men who performed unpaid caretaking work, is a "family service credit." The idea of giving women and men "credit" for unpaid caretaking work has been raised by a number of prominent women leaders as a way to improve women's benefits in an equitable fashion (Hill and Hartmann 2000). The advantage of a child-care or family service credit is that it recognizes unpaid caretaking work, regardless of marital status. For example, a divorced woman whose marriage lasted fewer than ten years does not have access to a spousal benefit, but she could benefit from a family service credit. Likewise, a single mother (or father) does not benefit from a spousal benefit but could benefit from a family service credit. Theoretically, family service credits could also be available to those who care for elderly or disabled relatives as compensation for time these individuals took out of the paid workforce. A family service credit explicitly recognizes the value of caretaking and provides a monetary reward to the women and men who do this work.

The idea of crediting unpaid caretaking work within the Social Security system is not new. While the United States recognizes women's work indirectly through the spousal benefit, many other industrialized nations provide direct compensation for women's unpaid family responsibilities. For example, Canada has a "child rearing dropout" provision that allows women (or men) who care for children under the age of 7 to "drop" these years when their pensions are calculated. A parent does not need to have left the labor force entirely for the child rearing dropout credit to apply; if the earnings in years she was caring for a child under 7 are lower than her average of her other pensionable years, the government will drop these years when calculating the average earnings. Because retirement benefits are based on average earnings over forty years, dropping low-earning years raises her (or his) retirement benefits. While men can use this provision as well, it is less likely that their wages will drop significantly when they have children because they tend to remain working in the labor force full-time even when their children are young. It is still too early to judge how this provision will affect Canadian women's retirement income, because the first generation that could use the child-care provision has not yet reached retirement. However, it is expected to increase benefits most for women who do not work when their children are young but who have high incomes and a strong attachment to the workforce at other times. Iams and Sandell (1994) simulated the effects of instituting dropout years in the United States and found that the greatest benefits went to high-income women, with only small increases for other women.

In order to better target benefits to low- and moderate-income earners, the Social Security Administration could structure the family service credit as a credit toward the alternative "special minimum" formula provided for workers with long careers with low earnings. Adding a family service credit to the special minimum could especially help women (and men) who combine low-wage, part-time work with family responsibilities. While the increase in benefits is likely to be modest, such a credit would be a step toward acknowledging the unpaid, but societally important, work of caregiving in the calculation of Social

Security benefits. This credit, of course, does not reflect a true valuation of caregiving, but it is a step in the direction of compensating caregiving financially.

The most serious obstacle to establishing a family service credit is the cost. In addition to the cost of additional benefits to retired caregivers, administrative costs may be prohibitive, particularly if care for elderly or disabled relatives is included. Child-care credits can be administered relatively simply; the parent who earns less during the first years of a child's life receives the credit if he or she has custody of the child during that time period. Birth certificates, divorce agreements, and Social Security work records are the only paperwork needed to establish who has earned the family service credit. However, if care for elderly and disabled adults is included, additional administrative procedures will be needed to determine who has earned the family service credit. Tax records that report adult economic dependency may be one avenue for establishing credit for adult caregiving.

At present, little research has been done on family service credits. We do not have reliable estimates of overall costs or the probable distribution of benefits by income. Recommending the introduction of family service credits is premature until this kind of information is available.

Increasing Benefits for Low-Wage Workers

Raising the income of the poorest elderly can be tackled by raising Social Security benefits for the lowest earners and improving Supplemental Security Income (SSI). One approach would change the formula used by the Social Security Administration to calculate benefits in order to raise benefits for the lowest earners. A second approach would be to make the special minimum benefit, offered by Social Security for low earners with long work records, more generous. An advantage of these approaches is that they are targeted to a needy population. An alternative suggested by Smeeding, Estes, and Glasse (1999) is a minimum benefit, similar to Canada's Guaranteed Income Supplement, which would be available for all recipients with low benefits and little or no other income.

Supplemental Security Income is a means-tested program designed to provide income support for the poorest aged or disabled Americans. Approximately 62 percent of SSI beneficiaries are women. Those eligible for SSI are also entitled to Medicaid, the means-tested medical assistance program for low-income people. Increasing SSI benefits is perhaps the most efficient approach to ensuring adequate income to very poor elderly and disabled households. It also has the advantage of using an independent program in which benefit increases do not affect Social Security's solvency.

However, if SSI remains the main supplement for low Social Security benefits, better coordination between the two programs would be essential. For example, increasing a widow's Social Security benefit to 75 percent of the couple's combined benefits could have negative consequences if some poor elderly women are lifted over the SSI eligibility limit and lose Medicaid coverage as a result. For some low-income widows, an increase in Social Security benefits will simply result in a transfer of funds between programs and no additional benefits for the widow herself. Raising the "income disregard"—the amount of money SSI recipients are allowed to keep that is not deducted from their SSI benefits—would allow low-income widows to receive additional money from Social Security without losing their eligibility for Medicaid.

Although increasing benefits under SSI is an efficient way to improve living standards for the poorest elderly and disabled Americans, it is means tested and carries the stigma of a "welfare" program. For this and other reasons, many poor people do not apply for SSI. Moreover, SSI is less popular politically than Social Security because its benefits are based on need and are not tied to contributions. While increasing SSI benefits is the most appealing approach in theory, it is important to recognize the practical difficulty of properly funding a welfare program. Historically, universal programs have enjoyed far more political support than means-tested programs. As noted earlier, there are ways to increase benefits for low earners within the Social Security system.

Social Security Policy: Achieving Long-Run Solvency while Providing Adequate Benefits

The challenge facing policymakers is to improve benefits for the most economically vulnerable elderly within the context of ensuring Social Security's solvency for future generations. As some increases in revenues or reductions in benefits will almost certainly be needed, it is important to find the least harmful solutions. One place to start is to increase the amount of earnings subject to the payroll tax. At present only the first $72,400 of earnings is subject to the payroll tax. This represents a lower percentage of total earnings than has been subject to the tax in the past. Increasing the amount of wages subject to the Social Security taxes is appealing because it places the financial burden on those most able to pay. If all earnings were subject to the payroll tax (and credited toward benefit calculation) 74 percent of the solvency problem forecasted by the Social Security actuaries would disappear (Fontenot 1999).

Another way to generate revenue would be to tax all Social Security benefits like private pensions. This would, in effect, lower benefits for many people. However, losses would be modest and widely spread, and low-income households would be protected through the usual income tax deductions and exemptions.

Investing part of the Social Security trust funds in the stock market could also be considered. This would be likely to raise the rate of return on the trust fund, which is now entirely invested in government bonds. Collective investment leads to smaller shared risk, unlike individual accounts, which concentrate risk on individuals. Many state and local government pension funds have diversified investments that include stocks. Allowing the Social Security Administration to diversify a modest portion of its surplus could be a wise decision. If 40 percent of the trust fund is invested in stocks, assuming the market continues to do well, 48 percent of the solvency problem can be solved (Smeeding, Estes, and Glasse 1999). However, if the stock market does poorly, much less would be achieved; negative earnings in the stock market could even make the solvency problem worse.

If these changes do not raise sufficient revenue to achieve long-term solvency and improve benefits, less desirable changes may be necessary. Proposals to raise the payroll tax rate are less desirable because this is a regressive tax: low earners pay a larger percentage of their total earnings than high earners. However, a small gradual increase in the payroll tax might be more desirable than some of the proposed benefit cuts. An increase of the payroll tax by 2.2 percentage points (from 6.2 to 8.4 percent not including Medicare) would achieve solvency by itself, but a much smaller increase could be implemented if other changes were also undertaken.

Especially undesirable are proposals to reduce cost of living adjustments. These plans exact the largest cuts from the oldest elderly, who are more likely to be women and already poorer than their younger counterparts. Increasing the number of years of earnings used in calculating benefits from 35 to 38 or 40 also hurts women more than men and those with irregular work patterns the most. Of workers retiring in 1996, the median woman had worked 27 years over her lifetime (Mannella 1998). The Social Security Administration has estimated that only 30 percent of women and 60 percent of men retiring in 2021 will have 38 years of work experience (Mannella 1998). If cutting benefits becomes necessary, a 3 percent across-the-board cut would be fairer and less harmful for most women than either of these other proposed cuts.

Reducing Social Security benefits and hoping to replace the losses with private accounts is another path that should be avoided. Lifetime benefits adjusted for inflation are particularly important for women, and annuities that might be bought from the proceeds of private accounts rarely offer inflation protection. Private accounts, especially small ones, are costly to administer (and annuities costly to buy), so that much of the individual account is lost to administrative expenses. Most plans do not require the kind of survivor benefits now offered by Social Security, let alone enhanced benefits. Provision for divorce is rarely mentioned. Plans often call for decreases in disability benefits in line with decreases in guaranteed retirement benefits, undermining the protection of disabled workers and their dependents. Stock market investments are the central feature of individual accounts, and those that offer large gains are inherently risky. Persons unlucky enough to retire during stock market downturns, which have often been prolonged, would see the value of their pensions plummet. For example, a worker who retired between 1975 and 1980 would have achieved less than half of the benefits of a worker who retired between 1965 and 1970 (Aaron and Reischauer 1998, 35).

In the long run, if the economy does not continue to grow rapidly, some unpopular changes may be necessary. Unless workers become willing to postpone retirement, the increasing number of years benefits must be paid will continue to put pressure on the system. In fact, the expected increase in the length of retirement, and hence the total benefits each person will receive, rather than just the size of the baby boom generation is a major cause of the long-term solvency problem. If life expectancy continues to increase, it may be appropriate to increase the ages of eligibility for reduced and/or full benefits.

At present, the earliest age of eligibility for retirement benefits is 62, and the normal retirement age when full benefits are available is 65; benefits taken before age 65 are reduced by 20 percent of full benefits if taken as early as 62 (to take into account the extra years that the retiree will collect benefits). The normal retirement age is currently scheduled to increase gradually from 65 to 67 years between 2000 and 2022, at which time benefits taken at age 62 will be reduced by 30 percent of the full benefit. Proposals have been made to increase the earliest age of eligibility to 65 or higher along with further increases in the normal age.

Any further changes in retirement age should be made carefully with attention to the needs of the most vulnerable workers. People in physically demanding jobs are less likely than white-collar workers to be capable of working at older ages. Nurses, waitresses, and maids are examples of women holding physically demanding jobs. Many people now take early retirement when they have difficulty finding or keeping jobs because of health or other problems that do not qualify them for disability benefits.

One change could be broadening qualifications for receiving disability benefits to protect more of those who no longer meet the physical qualifications of their occupations. Increasing the length of time that older unemployed workers could collect unemployment insurance might also be a way to help workers who have difficulty finding employment suitable for their age and abilities. Another concern is that as the age of eligibility for benefits increases, more women near retirement age would lose benefits when they quit work to care for their elderly relatives or husbands. If unemployment insurance is extended for maternity leave, as currently proposed, it might be extended for elderly caregiving as well.

If the retirement age is to be increased, it will be essential to monitor developments in the labor market for older workers. Employers have often cut payrolls during times of retrenchment by laying off older workers or offering incentives for early retirement. When they are laid off, older workers typically stay unemployed longer than younger workers and are likely to find jobs, if at all, that provide much lower wages and benefits. If labor shortages develop when the large baby boom generation retires, problems of obtaining employment at older ages might lessen. This outcome is not assured, however; employers might prefer other solutions, such as automation and moving jobs abroad, rather than employing older workers.

Changes in some employment and private pension practices may be needed. Because employers offering private pension plans benefit from tax breaks, it is appropriate that they should be required to offer fair annuities that pay larger monthly benefits to workers who want to retire at older ages (to make up for fewer years of benefits that must be paid). Employers may need to be encouraged, through legislation, union action, or other strategies, to provide working conditions that make a longer working life possible for their employees. Perhaps some system of reduced work schedules and partial retirement benefits could be devised for employees unable to work full-time. To insure that older workers are not forced out of the labor market, stronger enforcement of age discrimination laws will be crucial.

Conclusion

Achieving long-term solvency for Social Security is necessary if we are to protect more older women from poverty in the future. Politicians and researchers have put forward numerous proposals for assuring the future of Social Security (see Aaron and Reischauer 1999 for a summary and evaluation of some of these proposals). Many proposals involve changes that are likely to be especially harmful for women with modest incomes. Privatization schemes usually involve large reductions in regular Social Security benefits in the hope that private accounts will make up the difference; this is risky, especially for small accounts with high administrative costs. Plans that maintain the current benefit structure, while making smaller cuts, sometimes favor policies such as scaling back cost of living increases, which would be most harmful for the oldest elderly, predominantly women. We believe that other policies that are less harmful for women and other low earners should be adopted. These include increasing the amount of earnings subject to the payroll tax, taxing Social Security benefits like other pensions, including new state and local government employees in Social Security, and investing part of the trust fund in the stock market. According to recent estimates, the projected shortfall in funds could be eliminated or nearly eliminated by these changes alone (calculated by authors from Fontenot 1999).

Raising benefits for the poorest elderly with particular attention to those living alone should be at the heart of Social Security reform. At a minimum, we recommend increasing benefits for surviving widows, divorced wives, and the lowest earners. It is possible that a family service credit should be part of the improvement package. This would have the advantage of providing recognition for unpaid caregiving directly, rather than indirectly through spouse and widow benefits, which leave out single and gay couple caregivers and those from short-term marriages. As noted previously, however, further research is needed to determine the cost and distribution of benefits before this policy can be recommended.

To pay for these benefit improvements requires extra funds beyond the measures to address long-term solvency addressed earlier. Several widely discussed plans have included increased survivor benefits for widows, usually paid for in part by reducing the spouse benefit (Aaron and Reischauer 1999; Smeeding, Estes, and Glasse 1999). The proposal by Smeeding, Estes and Glasse includes all three of our recommendations for improving benefits for women. This plan would achieve solvency in much the way we suggested previously and in order to pay for additional benefits would also raise the ages for Social Security eligibility and receiving full benefits. If raising retirement ages seems likely to cause too much hardship, a .5 percentage point increase in the payroll tax and a 3 percent across-the-board benefit cut could also pay for achieving the goal of improvements for the most vulnerable women. In summary, we believe that achieving solvency and better economic security for women is attainable with modest changes to the system.

There is no silver bullet for Social Security reform. Instead, reforming Social Security will be a balancing act requiring careful attention to the diversity of Americans' working lives and family arrangements. The recent campaign to privatize Social Security has raised the stakes, putting the economic security of millions of Americans in jeopardy. Young women should not sit back and assume that working in the paid labor force alone will take care of their retirement. The persistence of the wage gap, differences in women's and men's family responsibilities, and the rise in divorce and single motherhood are expected to leave many elderly women economically insecure in the future. Thus, strengthening Social Security should be at the top of young women's agendas, not only for their mothers and grandmothers but for their future selves as well.

References

Aaron, Henry J., and Robert D. Reischauer. 1998. *Countdown to Reform: The Great Social Security Debate.* New York: Century Foundation Press.

Baker, Dean, and Mark Weisbrot. 1999. *Social Security: The Phony Crisis.* Chicago: University of Chicago Press.

Devine, Theresa. 2000. "Women and Social Security Reform." Draft paper prepared for the American Economics Association meetings, Boston. Originally compiled from Congressional Budget Office calculations based on data from the March 1999 current Population Survey.

Employee Benefit Research Institute (EBRI). 1997. *EBRI Databook on Employee Benefits.* Prepared by Paul Fronstin et al. Washington, DC: Employee Benefit Research Institute.

Fontenot, Keith. 1999. "Memorandum to Jane Ross on Information on the Distributional Effects of Various Security Solvency Options by Gender and Income," May 18. Washington, DC: Social Security Administration.

Hill, Catherine, and Heidi Hartmann. 1999. *Strengthening Social Security for Women—A Report from the Working Conference on Women and Social Security.* Washington, DC: Institute for Women's Policy Research.

Hill, Catherine, Lois B. Shaw, and Heidi Hartmann. 2000. "Why Privatizing Social Security Would Hurt Women: A Response to the Cato Institute's Proposal for Individual Accounts." Washington, DC: Institute for Women's Policy Research.

Holden, Karen, and Cathleen Zick. 1999. "Widowhood in a Reformed Social Security System." In *LaFollette Policy Report* 9, no. 2 (Madison, WI: Robert M. La Follette Institute of Public Affairs).

Iams, Howard, and Steven Sandell. 1994. "Changing Social Security Benefits to Reflect Child-Care Years: A Policy Proposal Whose Time Has Passed." *Social Security Bulletin* 57, no. 4 (winter).

Mannella, Kenneth. 1998. "Analysis of Cato Papers Advocating Social Security Privatization for Women." Washington, DC: Social Security Administration.

Mitchell, Olivia, Phillip Levine, and John Phillips. 1999. "The Impact of Pay Inequality, Occupational Segregation, and Lifetime Work Experience on the Retirement Income of Women and Minorities." Washington, DC: Public Policy Institute, American Association of Retired Persons.

National Economic Council Interagency Working Group on Social Security, Women, and Retirement Security. 1998. "Women and Retirement Security," October 27.

Shaw, Lois B., Diana Zuckerman, and Heidi Hartmann. 1998. *The Impact of Social Security Reform on Women.* Washington, DC: Institute for Women's Policy Research.

Smeeding, Timothy, Carroll Estes, and Lou Glasse. 1999. *Social Security Reform and Older Women: Improving the System.* Washington, DC: Gerontological Society of America.

Social Security Administration. 1998. *Annual Statistical Supplement to the Social Security Bulletin,* table 2.A11, 48. Washington, DC: Government Printing Office.

Social Security Advisory Board. 1999. Report of the Social Security Technical Panel. Washington, DC: Social Security Advisory Board.

Steuerle, Eugene, Christopher Spiro, and Adam Carasso. 1999. "Does Social Security Treat Spouses Fairly?" In *Straight Talk on Social Security and Retirement Policy,* no. 12 Washington, DC: Urban Institute.

U.S. General Accounting Office. 1996. *Social Security: Issues Involving Benefit Equity for Working Women.* Washington, DC: Government Printing Office.

PART 2

Raising the Pay for "Women's Jobs"

6

Raising the Minimum Wage and Living Wage Campaigns

Deborah M. Figart

What women need, no matter what their jobs, is a living wage, a salary that can make ends meet, help balancing work and family, and respect on the job.
—Karen Nussbaum, director of the Working Women's Department, AFL-CIO, in *New York Times,* March 5, 1996

Growing numbers of young adult women, including former public assistance recipients, are struggling to earn money in the service economy—for rent, for tuition, and for food. They are employed in restaurants, fast food chains, and retail stores. These women often work for the minimum wage or subminimum wages, relying on tips and commissions to make ends meet. But the current federal minimum wage is inadequate. At $5.15 per hour ($10,712 a year), it is not sufficient for a single person and would leave a woman with only one child in poverty. A *Ms.* magazine article noted that "More and more young people are struggling to turn their McJob—the name given to these minimum-wage, low-security jobs—into work that provides benefits and a living wage" (Klein 1996, 32). This chapter will evaluate two public policies under the broad umbrella of "living wages" that can aid their efforts: raising the national minimum wage and launching living wage campaigns.

The federal minimum wage is the lowest wage that may be legally paid to nonsalaried workers in the United States. Advocates propose regular increases in the minimum wage, even indexing it to keep pace with inflation or productivity growth. However, the federal minimum wage leaves many people in poverty, forcing workers to rely on public sector support in the form of food stamps, housing assistance, and the Earned Income Tax Credit.

A *living wage* is a more general term used to express the idea that wages should adhere to an accepted social norm. The call for a living wage goes further than providing minimal subsistence to incorporate notions of economic independence and economic justice. As a response to growing income and earnings equality in the past few decades, community, religious, and labor union leaders have initiated campaigns to raise low wages, arguing that tax dollars should not be used to subsidize employers who pay poverty wages. During the 1990s, the living wage movement focused on ordinances that require private sector employers who receive public funds (through contracts, tax breaks, or subsidies) to pay their workforce a "living wage." The living wage typically advocated is defined as the hourly rate needed to keep a family of four above the federal poverty line.

Although not explicitly targeted to women or people of color, both strategies would help both groups, who are overrepresented in the low-wage labor market. The U.S. Department of Labor (1997a) classified one in five poor Americans as "working poor," poor people who spend at least twenty-seven weeks per year in the labor force, with the majority working full-time. Most of the working poor are women, many employed in poorly paid female-dominated occupations. In fact, 53 percent of the working poor were employed in just two occupational groups: service occupations or the category of technical, sales, and administrative support occupations (U.S. Department of Labor 1997a, table B). Further, women, African Americans, and Latinos are more likely to be poor than men or whites in all occupational groups.[1] Therefore, the families of all women and men of color are the primary beneficiaries of increases in the minimum wage and passage of living wage ordinances.

The policies would have the added benefit of decreasing income inequality. According to the 1999 edition of the biennial report *The State of Working America 1998–99* (Mishel, Bernstein, and Schmitt 1999) the most important developments regarding U.S. incomes since 1979 have been slow growth and increasing inequality. The percentage of poor adults who work year-round, full-time has increased steadily since 1975. Over 17 percent of poor families are headed by women (Albelda and Tilly 1997, 10, 37). Women's earnings, though, are crucial to the economic survival of all family types. Increased work hours and income of wives is the safeguard for America's families, enabling them to keep pace with or barely ahead of inflation. Finally, both raising the minimum wage and living wage ordinances could help reverse a growing gap between the earnings of white and African American or Latino workers.

Historical Background

Living wage movements at the turn of the last century were promoted by organized labor. Workers sought to increase their standard of living, which they defined qualitatively rather than quantitatively. According to historian Lawrence Glickman, author of *A Living Wage: American Workers and the Making of Consumer Society* (1997), the fight for better living standards was an attempt to link economics to morality and politics. Yet women wage earners, like immigrants and unskilled workers, were accused of threatening (devaluing?) the so-called American standard: "It is the standard of living which determines wages, . . . that is why women get less wages than men, and children less than either" (Edwin Chamberlain, labor advocate, quoted in Glickman 1993, 234). It was widely believed that women had fewer needs than men, justifying a "woman's wage," as discussed in Alice Kessler-Harris's book *A Woman's Wage* (1990). The quest for living wages turned into a fight for a legislated minimum wage, from early state legislation to the national Fair Labor Standards Act (FLSA) (for historical accounts, see Grossman 1978; Nordlund 1997).

In the United States, the first national minimum wage, established in 1938, was 25¢ per hour. The original bill in 1938 and an earlier bill in 1937 called for 40¢ per hour. The minimum was reduced to 25¢ per hour for the first year of the act to secure votes from southern members of Congress. Many categories of workers were initially exempted from the legislation mandating payment of a minimum wage. The 1938 act was applicable to employees "engaged in interstate commerce" or "in the production of goods for interstate commerce." Most individual states have their own minimum wage laws. Several states link their state minimum wage to the federal rate. A few states set their minimum wages higher than the federal standard. Only Arizona and Louisiana lack state minimum wage laws. In 1997, Louisiana enacted a law prohibiting any parish or municipality from establishing a minimum wage rate.

Arizona prohibits any political subdivision from adopting a minimum wage that exceeds the federal rate (Nelson 1998).[2] In the November 1998 general election, the state of Washington became the first state to index the minimum wage to the rate of inflation, a measure that easily passed a statewide ballot initiative.

The changing level of the federal minimum wage is summarized in table 6.1. The minimum hourly wage reached $1.00 by 1956, $2.00 by 1974, and $3.10 by 1980. Prior to the 1980s, maintaining the value of the minimum wage had steady support in the U.S. Congress across party lines. The minimum wage was raised regularly, especially in periods of high inflation. For example, it was increased in all but three years during the 1970s. After years of not keeping pace with price changes during the 1980s, the minimum wage received two stepwise increases in 1996 and 1997, to $4.75 and $5.15 per hour.

From 1938 through the 1960s, the minimum wage hovered at or above 50 percent of the average hourly wage of production and non-supervisory workers in the private sector. Fifty percent was seen as a target for fairness by policymakers. Since the 1970s, wages in general, and the federal minimum wage in particular, have lost more and more of their buying power. Table 6.1 shows the value of the minimum wage in constant dollars as well as the ratio of the minimum wage to the average hourly wage. Using the Consumer Price Index for Urban Consumers (CPI-U) to adjust for inflation, we can see that the real value of the minimum wage rose steadily in its first thirty years, peaking in 1968. (In 1997 dollars, adjusting for inflation using the CPI-U-X1 deflator, the minimum wage in 1968 was $6.81 per hour.) Whatever deflator or base year is chosen, the value of the minimum wage has eroded since 1968.[3] Not only has the real value of the minimum wage fallen, it has fallen relative to average wages since 1968. In 1997, the minimum wage was equivalent to only 41.9 percent of the average hourly wage. Wages have also lagged behind profits (Levin-Waldman 1998a).

Data from the U.S. Bureau of Labor Statistics reveal that workers' hourly wages have not kept pace with productivity gains, defined as output per person per hour. According to Robert Pollin and Stephanie Luce, coauthors of a new book titled *The Living Wage,* if the minimum wage had grown at the same rate as productivity since 1968, the minimum wage in 1997 would have been $11.20 (1998, 40). The decline in the real value of the minimum wage from 1979 to 1988 accounts for 30 percent of the rise in wage inequality among women during this period (DiNardo, Fortin, and Lemieux 1996). In the 1980s and early 1990s, professional and managerial women fared much better, compared to inflation, than their working-class sisters.

Amendments to the minimum wage law in 1961 extended coverage to employees in local transit, construction, and large retail and service enterprises and to gasoline service station workers. The 1966 and later amendments extended coverage to state and local government employees, to workers in retail and service trades previously exempted, and to domestic workers employed in private households (Elder and Miller 1979). Although amendments have broadened coverage, many employees are still excluded from the legislation. Executive, administrative, and salaried professional employees and some retail sales employees are excluded on the basis of their responsibilities (the duties test). Generally, workers on salary are not covered (the salary test). The exceptions now amount to one-third of the labor force, and the scope of coverage is continually shrinking as the economy adds relatively more jobs classified as exempt (see Golden 1998).[4]

TABLE 6.1. The Federal Minimum Wage in Current Dollars, in Constant Dollars, and as a Percentage of Average Wages, 1938–97

Date Effective	Hourly ($)	Constant 1982–84 $/Hour	Share of Average Wage (%)
October 24, 1938	0.25	1.79	N.A.
October 24, 1939	0.30	2.14	N.A.
October 24, 1945	0.40	2.21	N.A.
January 25, 1950	0.75	3.19	56.4
March 1, 1956	1.00	3.73	55.6
September 3, 1961	1.15	3.83	53.7
September 3, 1963	1.25	4.07	54.8
February 1, 1967	1.40	4.26	52.2
February 1, 1968	1.60	4.68	56.1
May 1, 1974	2.00	4.18	47.2
January 1, 1975	2.10	4.03	46.4
January 1, 1976	2.30	4.14	47.3
January 1, 1978	2.65	4.24	46.6
January 1, 1979	2.90	4.25	47.1
January 1, 1980	3.10	3.98	46.5
January 1, 1981	3.35	3.85	46.2
April 1, 1990	3.80	2.95	38.0
April 1, 1991	4.25	3.14	41.2
October 1, 1996	4.75	3.00	40.2
September 1, 1997	5.15	3.19	41.9

Note: To calculate the real value in constant dollars, the CPI-U was chosen for the month of the minimum wage increase. The last column is based on payroll records in surveys of establishments, from U.S. Department of Labor, 1998b and U.S. Department of Labor 1991.

Source: U.S. Department of Labor 1997c, 1998a, 1998b.

For example, a store manager is an exempt employee because of the job title of "manager." Yet store managers in a variety of workplaces have routine duties that include checking inventory, stocking shelves, and helping customers, in addition to their supervisory responsibilities. While an entry-level management position at a fast food franchise or convenience store may have a salary higher than the minimum wage, it is important to point out that employees exempted from the minimum wage are also excluded from receiving the time-and-one-half (150 percent) premium for hours worked above the forty-hour threshold. Any hours worked above forty are not paid at all, thereby reducing the average take-home wage of these workers, calculated when wages or salaries are divided by hours worked.

How Are Women Helped by the Minimum Wage?

Increases in the minimum wage do effectively reach those who need them most—poor working adults in low-income families, especially women with children. This is what prompted President Bill Clinton to lobby vigorously for an increase in the minimum wage in 1996 on behalf of working women. A press release from the White House Office for Women's Initiatives and Outreach quotes the president.

> [Minimum wage earners] are among our hardest working people. Six out of ten of them are working women, many trying to raise children and hold their families together. Others are just getting started in the work force, trying to get a hold on the first rung in the ladder; all of them are trying hard to do the right thing—to work. Raising the minimum wage would honor both work and family. We should not leave anyone behind who is willing to work hard as our country moves forward. (White House Update for Women, July 10, 1996)

Minimum Wage Workers: A Profile

Historically, about one in ten workers at any given time is earning the minimum wage; one estimate suggests that more than 60 percent of workers have earned the minimum wage at some point in their lives (Spriggs and Schmitt 1996, 163). In the past two decades, the proportion of minimum wage workers in the total labor force has declined as the minimum wage fell increasingly behind entry-level wages in the marketplace. Only 5 percent of workers earned the minimum wage by

1995. The 1996 and 1997 increases in the minimum wage reached almost 10 million workers, raising the proportion again to over 7 percent of the labor force.

Looking more closely at the demographics, it can be seen that minimum wage workers average thirty hours of paid work per week; 47 percent work full-time year-round. Nearly 40 percent are the sole breadwinners in their families. The average minimum wage worker brings home half of his or her family's earnings. Only 12 percent of minimum wage workers are teenagers in families with above average incomes (Mishel, Bernstein, and Rasell 1995, tables 1, 7). In 1997, 62 percent of workers earning the minimum wage were women. Compared with their representation in the U.S. labor force as a whole, minimum wage earners are disproportionately African American (15 percent) and Hispanic (20 percent). Sixty-six percent were adults over the age of twenty (U.S. Department of Labor 1997b).

The Economics of a Wage Hike:
Theory versus Reality

Many economists and employers oppose the minimum wage, reasoning that the minimum wage would generate job losses. It is argued that any wage "above equilibrium" would result in the quantity of laborers supplied exceeding the quantity of laborers demanded, that is, unemployment. If massive layoffs were not the consequence, surely the growth rate of jobs in firms would slow (see, e.g., Welch 1995; Taylor 1995). Opponents also add that an increased wage bill would drive up business costs, thereby leading to inflation. Up through the 1980s, traditional economists generally regarded the issue of whether the minimum wage had adverse effects on employment as settled.

However, recent empirical evidence of unemployment associated with minimum wage increases is weak (for a summary, see Rix 1996; Levin-Waldman 1996; or Rodgers 1995). Economic studies over the past few years have shown that there is little or no negative effect on employment (Card and Krueger 1994, 1995). Even some longtime opponents of minimum wage increases have found a negligible effect on employment (e.g., Neumark and Wascher 1995). The work of economists David Card and Alan Krueger, summarized in their book *Myth and Measurement* (1995), was instrumental in helping to pass the phased minimum wage increases of 1996 and 1997. Their research, based upon prior federal increases and increases in state minimum wages, demonstrated that "modest" wage increases may even create jobs rather than destroy them. The reason is that wage earners have more money to spend, increasing demand for many products and therefore employment. The key word, though, is *modest*. What is a modest wage increase? It depends. An increase in prosperous times is more affordable than during recessionary times. Large and irregular hikes in the minimum wage are likely to have a more negative effect than smaller, regular increases. As with many empirical questions in the social sciences, especially the economics discipline, there is contention about these newer conclusions, however: "Effects on employment of minimum-wage increases have not been easy to find in noisy data" (Kosters 1996, 105).[5]

Debate over statistical studies is one thing. Looking at the actual aggregate U.S. economy and employers' hiring decisions is another. Concrete evidence is beginning to mount from the two-part federal minimum wage increases of 1996 and 1997 to $5.15 per hour.[6] These increases appear not to have resulted in an increase in unemployment or inflation, according to careful research by the Economic Policy Institute in Washington, DC. After controlling for seasonal factors and economic growth, the data suggest that even the most vulnerable employees, minority teenagers, were not significantly harmed by the minimum wage hike. Instead, the minimum wage increases went primarily to low-income families, boosting their income substantially and helping to maintain economic growth (Bernstein and Schmitt 1997, 1998). Inflation has remained moderate. A new, nationally representative survey of small businesses by the Jerome Levy Economics Institute found that hiring and employment practices were hardly affected in response to the minimum wage hike. Moreover, over 75 percent of the businesses in the survey responded that a minimum wage hike to $6.00 per hour would not alter hiring or employment (Levin-Waldman and McCarthy 1998).

The Minimum Wage and Poverty

Today's minimum wage workers are concentrated in poor families because their earnings are not high enough to keep them above poverty. Furthermore, minimum wage jobs typically do not provide benefits such as health insurance, causing families even more economic stress. Figure 6.1 compares annual minimum wage earnings with the federal poverty thresholds for a family of three and a family of four.[7] In the 1960s, the minimum wage was slightly above or near the federal poverty threshold for a family of four. Its value shrank to the poverty level for a family of

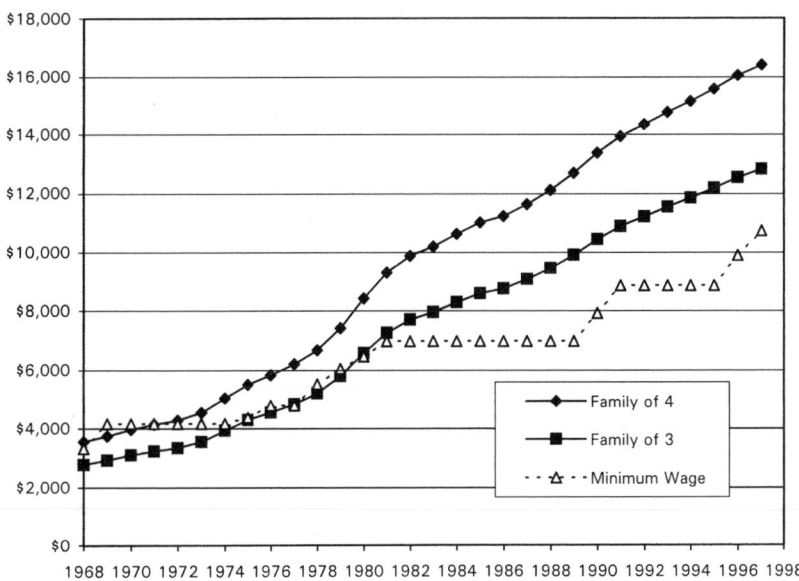

FIG. 6.1. Annual minimum wage earnings versus poverty thresholds. (From U.S. Bureau of the Census and U.S. Bureau of Labor Statistics.)

three in the 1970s. Beginning in 1980, workers earning the minimum wage for a forty-hour week, fifty-two weeks per year, saw the value of their pay fall further and further from these two poverty lines. The gap between a minimum wage and the poverty line for a family of four—often defined as a living wage—has widened appreciably. The difference did narrow with each of two rounds of minimum wage increases in the late 1980s and mid 1990s. Nevertheless, it would take regular boosts in the minimum wage for earnings to reach the poverty line for a family of three; and substantial increases to reach its 1968 value, the earnings necessary to exceed the poverty line for a family of four.

A minimum wage increase does narrow the gap between rich families and poor families. One of the first economists to study the distributional impact of the minimum wage was Edward Gramlich (1976), who later became director of the Congressional Budget Office. He found a slightly beneficial effect on poor workers and the distribution of income. The gains from the 1996–97 minimum wage increases went disproportionately to the neediest families. Specifically, the bottom 20 percent of families received 35 percent of the benefits, and the bottom 40 percent received 58 percent of the gain (Bernstein and Schmitt 1998).

Many skeptics in the 1980s argued that the minimum wage was at best a blunt instrument for battling income inequality and poverty. In a country the size of the United States, with an economy of approximately $9 trillion in 1999 (nominal gross domestic product [GDP] figures), it takes an immense amount of income transfer to affect overall poverty rates. Therefore, modest increases in the minimum wage did not significantly reduce the percentages of families below the poverty line (Card and Krueger 1995). Similarly, the effect of transfer programs such as welfare or temporary assistance payments alone has been relatively small (Sawhill 1988; Northrup 1991).[8]

Yet, labor economists David Card and Alan Krueger found that the 1990 and 1991 increases in the federal minimum wage helped reverse a part of the wage inequality that grew in the 1980s. Their conclusions are echoed by DiNardo, Fortin, and Lemieux (1996), whose work was published in a highly regarded statistics journal called *Econometrica*. In newer research focusing on the period from 1983 to 1996, two economists have found that increases in minimum wages in the 1990s have indeed served to reduce poverty (Addison and Blackburn 1999). Linda Martin and Demetrios Giannaros (1990) estimate that if the minimum wage had remained at its 1968 level for the next twenty years, poverty rates among families headed by women would have declined appreciably.

Fighting poverty requires an amalgamation of policies. The minimum wage alone is insufficient. A combination of policies to help the poor, including labor market income and the Earned Income Tax Credit (EITC), is most effective (Blank and Blinder 1986; Spalter-Roth, Hartmann, and Andrews 1992).

A Ripple Effect

One reason the minimum wage does help low-income families, especially families headed by women, is a "ripple effect." When the minimum wage is raised, millions of other workers also receive pay increases. The minimum wage serves as a reference point for hourly employees in retail and service industries. Employers like to maintain their internal wage structures when the minimum wage rises. For example, if an employee earns $1.00 more than the current minimum wage and the minimum is then raised by $1.00, an employer gives a raise to that employee to preserve the existing rank of jobs at the workplace. Workers like this one whose wages are linked to the minimum wage are said to be on a *minimum wage contour*.[9] People who earn up to $1.00 more than the minimum wage have similar demographic, industrial, and occupational characteristics to those of minimum wage workers. Therefore, raising the minimum wage helps still more women support their families. Approximately 65 percent of all workers on the minimum wage contour are women (Figart and Lapidus 1995). In the latest (1996–97) round of minimum wage increases, there were 12 million workers earning between $4.25 and $5.15 per hour who directly benefited and still another 9 million who likely received raises from the ripple or contour effect (Bluestone and Ghilarducci 1996).

The Debate Today

Naturally, politics plays its part each time an increase in the minimum wage is considered. The debate swings from speeches about helping the working poor, fairness, and economic justice on the one hand to projections for economic doom on the other. Proponents call the minimum wage a women's issue, a children's issue, a civil rights issue, and a labor issue. Support in the Congress depends in part upon the health of the economy, the strength of organized labor, and leadership from the president. (For an excellent discussion of the politics of the minimum wage and congressional voting patterns, see Levin-Waldman 1998b, 1998c.)

Several bills were introduced in the 105th U.S. Congress to raise the minimum wage to $6.15, $6.50, $6.65 per hour by 2000 or sooner and to $7.25 by 2002. The bills had titles such as the Fair Wage Act (H.R. 685), the American Family Fair Minimum Wage Act (H.R. 2211, S. 1009, H.R. 3100), the Liveable Wage Act (H.R. 2278), and the Fair Minimum Wage Act (S. 1573, S. 1805, H.R. 3510). One feature of several bills is a provision allowing the minimum wage to be automatically increased for inflation (utilizing the Consumer Price Index).

Other efforts to raise wages are local. An example is the work of one grassroots organization, United for a Fair Economy, in Boston, Massachusetts, which conducts research, provides education, and supports legislation focused on reducing income and wealth inequality. Part of their "Wage Gap" campaign includes the push for wages that enable workers to support families. The minimum wage, however, is only one avenue for raising women's pay.

The Contemporary Living Wage Movement

The goal of living wage campaigns is to enable workers to support themselves and their families, regardless of their particular family type and number of family members employed. A headline from the *Duluth News-Tribune* succinctly describes the origins of the contemporary living wage movement: "Safety Net Wearing Thin: Social Service Agencies and Churches Are Seeing More Wage-Earners in Line for Free Food, Clothes and Shelter" (Levey 1997). The first campaign is believed to have started in Baltimore, Maryland. Volunteers in many of the city's shelters and soup kitchens began to notice that more and more families were hungry although at least one member of the family was employed. One soup kitchen in Duluth, Minnesota, estimates that between a quarter and a third of the people they serve do paid work, arguing, "We're seeing a whole new group of people coming in here. It's massive. [The working poor] are like serfs. No one cares about them" (quoted in Levey 1997, 1A).

The living wage movement is also a general response to inequality in today's economy (see Bernstein 1998). Specifically mentioned are those economic policies that have led to the decline of cities, the outsourcing of public sector jobs through privatization, and welfare reform. Executive compensation has skyrocketed while low- and middle-income earners suffer. An implicit (or explicit) ethical argument in many living wage campaigns is that corporate America should be concerned about its workers and has a responsibility to treat its employees decently, in addition to piling up quarterly dividends for owners and shareholders.

As a result, religious groups working with the hungry and poor joined with labor unions and community organizations to push for local living wage ordinances. Religious leaders have been at the forefront of the living wage movement, saying, "It's our mission to take part in this debate" and "[The living wage] is a moral precedent" (quoted in Levey 1997, 1A). Social services providers are ardent supporters of living wages because they are serving more and more clients given the shrinking social safety net. The AFL-CIO and its affiliates, especially public sector unions such as the American Federation of State, County, and Municipal Employees (AFSCME), are active in living wage movements. They are battling privatization efforts, the outsourcing of public sector union-paying jobs to cost-cutting private contractors. The living wage was also part of AFL-CIO president John Sweeney's "America Needs a Raise" campaign, a national call to reverse stagnant living standards by lifting the wage floor for millions of low-paid and minimum wage workers (see Sweeney 1996; Kusnet

1998). Through its state affiliates, a national clearinghouse of community groups, the Association of Community Organizations for Reform Now (ACORN), has been active in nearly every living wage campaign.

In living wage campaigns, the monetary target is often a wage where annual earnings for a full-time, year-round worker exceed the federal poverty level for a family of four, $16,333 in 1997. Calculated on a hourly basis (2,080 hours), the living wage would be roughly $7.85. The share of workers in jobs paying less than this in real terms—adjusted for inflation—remained virtually the same between 1989 and 1997, at 28 percent (Mishel, Bernstein, and Schmitt 1999, table 3.10). In the second quarter of 1998, after the 1996 and 1997 minimum wage increases took effect, 45 percent of women earned below $8.00 per hour, as shown in table 6.2. The median wage of women is color is less than a living wage, making it virtually impossible for most to support families. Forty-three percent of African Americans (50.4 percent of black women; 34.0 percent of black men) and 49 percent of persons of Hispanic origin (59.1 percent of Latina women; 41.5 percent of Latino men) earn less than $8.00 per hour.

Earlier efforts to seek more livable wages resulted in the federal Davis-Bacon Act and comparable "little Davis-Bacon" laws at the state level. The Davis-Bacon Act, first passed in 1931, requires that construction contractors pay the "prevailing wage" in the area, usually the local union wage, to counter low bidding and/or the substitution of nonunion for union labor. Later amendments extended coverage to most nonconstruction firms (1936); service contractors (1965); and all categories of workers except professionals, managers, and administra-

TABLE 6.2.   A Profile of Low-Wage Workers, 1998

Group	Below Living Wage (%)	Median Wage ($)
Women	45.0	8.17
White	44.1	8.25
Black	50.4	7.79
Latina	59.1	7.09
Men	29.5	10.04
White	29.0	10.10
Black	34.0	9.24
Latino	41.5	8.22

Note: The living wage used is $8.00 per hour.
Source: U.S. Department of Labor, 1998c.

tors (1976). New York City and San Jose, California, have used prevailing wage ordinances in an attempt to raise the pay of private sector service workers. According to AFSCME's spring 1996 *Collective Bargaining Reporter,* a key difference between recent living wage laws and earlier prevailing wage laws is the method by which wages are set. Prevailing wage laws rely upon an administrative finding to set wages for a specific job in a geographical area, whereas living wage laws set wages by statute. Living wage laws have generally set a specific dollar amount or tie the wage to a percentage of the poverty level.

The nation's first living wage ordinance was passed in Baltimore in December 1994. A living wage was defined as an hourly wage rate of $6.10 in 1995, increasing to $7.70 by 1999. The Baltimore ordinance was followed a year later by ordinances in the city of Milwaukee, Wisconsin; and Santa Clara County, California. Thirty-three ordinances were passed between December 1994 and July 1999, as summarized in table 6.3. As of this writing, twenty-four cities have adopted living wage ordinances, including, among others, Boston, Massachusetts; San Antonio, California; Durham, North Carolina; Chicago, Illinois; Jersey City, New Jersey; and Pasadena, California. Eight counties have passed living wage ordinances: Santa Clara County, California; Milwaukee County, Wisconsin; Cook County, Illinois; Multnomah County, Oregon; Hudson County, New Jersey; Dane County, Wisconsin; Miami-Dade County, Florida; and Los Angeles County, California. One local board, the Milwaukee School Board, passed a living wage ordinance in January 1996. Many ordinances call for wages between $6.50 and $8.50 an hour, with a range of $6.25 to $10.75 an hour.

Living wage campaigns have suffered initial defeats in Denver and Houston. But there are many second efforts and ongoing campaigns across the country, including efforts in Philadelphia, Pennsylvania; New Orleans, Louisiana; Albuquerque, New Mexico; St. Louis, Missouri; Pittsburgh, Pennsylvania; Buffalo, New York; and Sacramento, California; and in counties such as Marin County, California; and Albany County, New York. There are dozens of campaigns in cities both large and small, some very established and some just beginning.

Because they are local and do not cover the entire low-wage labor market, living wage ordinances do not reach as many workers as minimum wage laws. They apply only to businesses with contracts with or receiving public tax subsidies or abatements from the municipality. The Baltimore ordinance, for instance, requires service and professional contractors to pay employees enough to keep a family of four above poverty. This ordinance affects employees of engineering and construction firms who have contracts with the city; concession workers at the professional baseball stadium and the airport; and people in several female-dominated occupations such as cleaners, stenographers, and food service employees. In a statewide effort, the state of Maryland announced a pilot living wage program in July 1996. One beneficiary

TABLE 6.3. Living Wage Ordinances

Year	Localities (in order of passage)
1994	Baltimore, Maryland
1995	Santa Clara County, California Milwaukee, Wisconsin
1996	Milwaukee School Board Portland Oregon (amended 1998) Jersey City, New Jersey New York City, New York (prevailing wage rate)
1997	St. Paul, Minnesota Minneapolis, Minnesota Los Angeles, California New Haven, Connecticut Milwaukee County, Wisconsin Boston, Massachusetts (amended 1998) Duluth, Minnesota West Hollywood, California
1998	Durham, North Carolina Oakland, California San Antonio, Texas (prevailing wage rate) Chicago, Illinois Cook County, Illinois Pasadena, California Multnomah County, Oregon Detroit, Michigan San Jose, California
1999	Hudson County, New Jersey Dane County, Wisconsin Madison, Wisconsin Hayward, California Cambridge, Massachusetts Miami-Dade County, Florida Somerville, Massachusetts Ypsilanti, Michigan Los Angeles, California

Note: The year 1999 is January through July only.
Source: Association for Community Organizations for Reform Now (ACORN), http://www.livingwagecampaign.org

group was private sector cleaners in the state-owned World Trade Center, who were to receive stepwise raises to $7.70 per hour by 1998.

Other jurisdictions have incorporated some variation of the Baltimore model. Some specify covered job categories; some contain a minimum dollar threshold to define contract eligibility. Sixteen ordinances require or encourage some form of health benefits for covered workers, and five require vacation benefits. The strongest ordinances are those that provide for an automatic cost of living adjustment or wage increase linked to the U.S. poverty level, providing some protection from inflation. In January 1997, a bill was introduced into the U.S. House of Representatives (H.R. 182) calling for a nationwide livable wage for employees under federal contracts and subcontracts exceeding $10,000. However, this Federal Living Wage Responsibility Act is unlikely to pass in a Republican-led Congress.

Another even more comprehensive alternative to living wage ordinances is to raise state minimum wages above the federal threshold, perhaps even to index them to rise with inflation (Weisbrot and Sforza-Roderick 1996). Hawaii, the state with the most expensive cost of living in the nation, raised its state minimum wage to $5.25 per hour, effective January 1, 1993 (Nelson 1994). As of August 1, 2000, ten states and the District of Columbia have minimum wage rates higher than the federal standard. In addition to Hawaii, they include Alaska ($5.65 as of 1997), California ($5.75 as of 1998), Connecticut ($6.15 as of 2000), Delaware ($6.15 as of 2000), District of Columbia ($6.15 as of 1997), Massachusetts ($6.75 to become effective in 2001), Oregon ($6.50 as of 1999), Rhode Island ($5.65 as of 1999), and Vermont ($5.75 as of 1999). The State of Washington is the first state to index their minimum wage to inflation. Voters first approved an increase in the minimum wage to $5.70 per hour, effective January 1, 1999. A statewide ballot initiative (I-688) also provided for a raise to $6.50 per hour in 2000. Beginning in 2001, it will automatically be increased to keep pace with the cost of living (Nelson 1997, 1998, 1999, 2000).

The Economic Debate Today

The living wage movement and supporters of a minimum wage increase share the same opponents. A primary concern is potential job loss. We can look to states that have raised their minimum wages well above the federal minimum, including New Jersey and California, and infer that a living wage would have a negligible effect on employment. Studies of implemented living wage ordinances reveal that job loss and other hypothesized negative economic and fiscal consequences have not occurred. In Baltimore, the increase in the cost of city-awarded contracts from 1995 to 1996 was less than one-quarter of 1 percent in current dollars; after adjusting for inflation, the average contract price was less than the year before (Weisbrot and Sforza-Roderick 1996). Contractors reported in telephone interviews that the higher living wage resulted in less job turnover, a positive outcome, and none of the companies interviewed reported any reduction in staff due to the living wage requirement. The president of Able Temporaries, who has contracted services to Baltimore for twenty-five years, stressed the positive effects of the ordinance: "We found that by paying people a little more, they did a better job more efficiently" (quoted in Wood 1996, 3). These findings were confirmed by the Economic Policy Institute in Washington, DC, for living wage–covered contracts established up through August 1997 (Niedt et al. 1999).

Several economic analyses were conducted during the Los Angeles living wage campaign in advance of its passage (Pollin et al. 1996; Luce 1996; Zabin 1997; Pollin and Luce 1998). All estimated net benefits for the city. In their statistical analysis, Robert Pollin and Stephanie Luce (1998) painstakingly demonstrate that the impact of living wages on both firms' and city budgets is negligible, even when considering the ripple effects of a new living wage on other wages. In addition, subsidies and transfer payments that branches of government disburse to working families should decline. Workers' higher earnings would be reinvested in their communities. In sum, policies that reduce income inequality are not incompatible with policies for economic growth (Zabin 1997, 14).

Who Benefits?

Compared with the minimum wage, there is very little empirical evidence about the impact of living wage ordinances. The campaigns are relatively new. Once again, drawing upon research about the minimum wage, we would expect that women and people of color would disproportionately benefit from the living wage pay adjustments.[10] From prior research on the minimum wage, we know that increasing wages of low-paid workers has the potential to lift some women workers out of poverty. In one study of a hypothetical minimum wage increase including the ripple effect, the percentage of women among the working poor was estimated to fall by 17 percent under one scenario, to 54 percent with other assumptions (Figart and Lapidus 1995).

A few simple statistics and calculations from the March 1998 Current Population Survey demonstrate the harsh reality of low wages. For women aged 18 to 64 from poor families, the mean hourly wage is $6.71 for an average of 32 weekly hours and 36 weeks per year in the labor force. One out of five women from poor families earns the federal minimum wage, $5.15 per hour. More than two-thirds of women from poor families, 68 percent, earn between the current minimum wage and a living wage of $8.00 per hour. For poor women earning between $5.15 and $8.00 per hour, the typical work week (the mode) is 40 hours, and year-round work, 52 weeks, is the norm. However, assuming the mean 32-hour work week and 36 weeks per year, if poor women earned $8.00 instead of $5.15 per hour, their annual family income would rise by $3,283. Even without increasing her weekly hours in the labor force, a woman earning $8.00 per hour year-round would have an annual income of $13,312, or $510 above the 1997 poverty line for a family of three.

Putting aside the statistics, we can listen to women themselves. Many working women assert that they cannot feed their families in low-wage jobs. Testifying at a community hearing in Sacramento, California, home-health-care worker Gina Brown asserted, "I deserve a fair, livable wage. I want to show my [9-year-old] daughter that hard work pays off." Her cries were echoed by Paula Reynosa, a janitor who has also worked in canneries and the fields. "My job keeps me in poverty," said health-care employee Christina Lane, who has two children. "This is simply unfair" (quoted in Teichert 1997, B1).

Advocates for a living wage argue that low wages are tearing families apart and robbing workers of their dignity. Workers in Duluth, Minnesota, could not understand why there was such controversy surrounding their living wage proposal. Politicians and business leaders paid lip service to family values and reforming welfare and yet opposed a living wage that would help workers sustain their families through work and not public assistance. In the *Duluth News Tribune,* one women who supports herself and her two children responded, "I'd love for them to see what it's like for just one day" earning $5.20 an hour as a food production worker. Her child-care expenses are partly met by public funds, and she lives in a subsidized apartment. She has also tried making ends meet by serving hamburgers at McDonalds, delivering newspapers, and pouring concrete as a general laborer.

A married couple with two children, a small home, an old minivan, and no telephone does not find it any easier, the newspaper reports. Even with two incomes, "It's not enough" (quoted in Adams 1997). In the Chicago living wage campaign, a South Side Chicago woman employed as a maid echoes, "I've just about had it; I'm paid next to nothing" (quoted in Tyson 1996). Another mother is struggling to support her family and pay off debts on a fast food job and child-support payments (Levey 1997).

Concluding Thoughts: Policy in the Welfare Reform Era

One of the lessons of these legislative efforts is that women workers can benefit from policies that are not specifically written to address gender inequality. Because the working poor are disproportionately women struggling in low-wage jobs, gender-neutral efforts to make work pay can alleviate gender inequality. Therefore, minimum wage and living wage campaigns provide important opportunities for alliances between feminist activists and other organizations committed to economic justice.

Women's wages, and the need for women to support their families, are now an integral part of minimum and living wage campaigns. Changes to the U.S. social welfare system have brought the issue of a fair or living wage into the center of political discussions. The vast majority of adults affected by welfare program are women. Critics of welfare policy changes have turned their attention to the jobs that these women leaving welfare are likely to hold. Mary Jo Maynes, chair of the New Party affiliate in the Twin Cities area, states, "All levels of government should use the living wage standard as a guide for public spending. If we are going to kick more and more people off welfare, we need to guarantee that they'll be able to find jobs that pay enough to keep them out of poverty" (quoted in Macek 1997).

Neither the current minimum wage nor existing living wage ordinances are sufficient to reduce women's poverty. The minimum wage must be increased substantially and regularly to keep up with the costs of living. One way would be to link federal minimum wage increases to productivity or inflation. The Consumer Price Index is already used to calculate cost of living adjustments for Social Security recipients. Indexing would keep increases regular and modest.

However, we need to go beyond these two policies to raise women's incomes and reduce women's poverty rates. Many important strategies are discussed in other chapters of this book. The living wage movement has focused attention on employers' social responsibilities. In an era of smaller government, policies that require employers to pay fair wages and benefits are an important supplement to public programs.

Notes

1. Although almost 75 percent of the working poor were white workers, compared with their representation in the total labor force, black and Hispanic workers experienced poverty rates that were more than twice the rate of white workers.

2. The states with the highest proportion of workers earning the minimum wage or less are Louisiana, North Dakota, Mississippi, Alabama, Arkansas, Montana, Wyoming, and West Virginia.

3. The CPI-U is the most comprehensive price index and represents the expenditures of about 87 percent of the total U.S. population. The Bureau of Labor Statistics publishes several price indexes with a reference base more recent than 1982, such as the CPI-U-X1, but these are not dated back to the early twentieth century.

4. Card (1992) estimated that 15 percent of the workforce was exempt a decade ago, or 85 percent coverage.

5. Economists are now searching for ways to resurrect their textbook analysis. A recent reanalysis of time-series data for 1954–93 by two labor economists critical of the minimum wage estimates a negative impact on teenage males and females; employment falls between 2 and 4 percent over a two-year period (Williams and Mills 1998). Another study explores the possibility of "publication bias" in prior research (Neumark and Wascher 1998). Marvin Kosters, a resident scholar and labor economist at the conservative "think tank" the American Enterprise Institute, concludes: "In my judgment, the empirical evidence that is available now, taken together, should lead us to reject the view that adjustments by employers in response to increasing the minimum wage can be disregarded because they are likely to be small and insignificant" (Kosters 1996, 106).

6. Some fine print in the legislation creates the possibility for exceptions to the new minimum. First, employees aged twenty or less may be paid only $4.25 per hour for their first ninety days of consecutive employment. Second, employers could apply for special certificates from the Department of Labor that allow wages below the minimum for full-time students, student learners, apprentices, and workers with disabilities. Employers who hire workers who rely on tips must pay at least $2.13 per hour, as long as they make up the difference if the tips combined with the wage do not equal the minimum wage.

7. The dollar value is for weighted average poverty thresholds for families of specified size, from the U.S. Census Bureau's historical poverty tables. The methodology used to derive the federal poverty thresholds dates back to 1964 and is based upon a standard of minimal physical subsistence. These poverty lines have been extensively critiqued as unrealistically low, especially for the working poor and families headed by women (see Ruggles 1990; Renwick and Bergmann 1993).

8. Differences in transfer payments seem more important in evaluating relative poverty trends across countries (see, e.g., Hanratty and Blank 1992).

9. Through longitudinal analysis, Spriggs and Klein (1994) identified work-

ers with a high school education or less on a minimum wage contour, classifying them by major industry and occupation (see also Grossman 1983; Katz and Krueger 1992; Spriggs and Schmitt 1996).

10. In order to verify that living wage ordinances cover workers in female-dominated and minority-concentrated jobs, we need empirical studies of municipalities where they have been implemented.

References

Adams, Paul. 1997. "Living Wage Stirs Debate: Northland Workers Struggle to Get By." *Duluth (Minnesota) News Tribune,* May 11, p. 1A.

Addison, John T., and McKinley L. Blackburn. 1999. "Minimum Wages and Poverty." *Industrial and Labor Relations Review* 52, no. 3:393–409.

Albelda, Randy, and Chris Tilly. 1997. *Glass Ceilings and Bottomless Pits: Women's Work, Women's Poverty.* Boston: South End Press.

American Federation of State, County, and Municipal Employees. 1996. *Collective Bargaining Reporter* (spring).

Association of Community Organizations for Reform Now (ACORN). <http://www.livingwagecampaign.org>.

Bernstein, Jared. 1998. "Living Wage Campaigns: A Step in the Right Direction." Task Force working paper WP01, Economic Policy Institute, Washington, DC.

Bernstein, Jared, and John Schmitt. 1997. "The Sky Hasn't Fallen: An Evaluation of the Minimum-Wage Increase." *Working USA* 1, no. 3:81–91.

———. 1998. *Making Work Pay: The Impact of the 1996–97 Minimum Wage Increase.* Washington, DC: Economic Policy Institute.

Blank, Rebecca M., and Alan S. Blinder. 1986. "Macroeconomics, Income Distribution, and Poverty." In *Fighting Poverty: What Works and What Doesn't,* edited by Sheldon H. Danziger and Daniel Weinberg, 180–208. Cambridge, MA: Harvard University Press.

Bluestone, Barry, and Teresa Ghilarducci. 1996. "Making Work Pay: Wage Insurance for the Working Poor." Public Policy Brief 28. Annandale-on-Hudson, NY: Jerome Levy Economics Institute.

Card, David. 1992. "Do Minimum Wages Reduce Employment? A Case Study of California, 1987–89." *Industrial and Labor Relations Review* 46, no. 1:38–54.

Card, David, and Alan B. Krueger. 1994. "Minimum Wages and Employment: A Case Study of the Fast-Food Industry in New Jersey and Pennsylvania." *American Economic Review* 84 (September): 772–93.

———. 1995. *Myth and Measurement: The New Economics of the Minimum Wage.* Princeton: Princeton University Press.

DiNardo, John, Nicole Fortin, and Thomas Lemieux. 1996. "Labor Market Institutions and the Distribution of Wages, 1973–1992: A Semiparametric Approach." *Econometrica* 64, no. 5:1001–44.

Elder, Peyton K., and Heidi D. Miller. 1979. "The Fair Labor Standards Act: Changes of Four Decades." *Monthly Labor Review* 102, no. 7:10–16.

Figart, Deborah M., and June Lapidus. 1995. "A Gender Analysis of U.S. Labor Market Policies for the Working Poor." *Feminist Economics* 1, no. 3:60–82.

Glickman, Lawrence B. 1993. "Inventing the 'American Standard of Living': Gender, Race, and Working-Class Identity, 1880–1925." *Labor History* 34, no. 2/3:221–35.

———. 1997. *A Living Wage: American Workers and the Making of Consumer Society.* Ithaca, NY: Cornell University Press.

Golden, Lonnie. 1998. "Comp Time versus Overtime." *Dollars and Sense* 215 (January/February): 40–42.

Gramlich, Edward. 1976. "Impact of Minimum Wages on Other Wages, Employment, and Family Incomes." In *Brookings Papers on Economic Activity,* vol. 2, ed. Arthur M. Okun and George L. Perry, Washington, DC: The Brookings Institution.

Grossman, Jean Baldwin. 1983. "The Impact of the Minimum Wage on Other Wages." *Journal of Human Resources* 18, no. 3:359–78.

Grossman, Jonathan. 1978. "Fair Labor Standards Act of 1938: Maximum Struggle for a Minimum Wage." *Monthly Labor Review* 101, no. 6:22–30.

Hanratty, Maria J., and Rebecca M. Blank. 1992. "Down and Out in North America: Recent Trends in Poverty Rates in the United States and Canada." *Quarterly Journal of Economics* 107, no. 1:233–54.

Katz, Lawrence F., and Alan B. Krueger. 1992. "The Effect of the Minimum Wage on the Fast-food Industry." *Industrial and Labor Relations Review* 46, no. 1:6–21.

Kessler-Harris, Alice. 1990. *A Woman's Wage: Historical Meanings and Social Consequences.* Lexington: University Press of Kentucky.

Klein, Naomi. 1996. "Can a McJob Provide a Living Wage?" *Ms.* (May/June): 32–38.

Kosters, Marvin H., ed. 1996. *The Effects of the Minimum Wage on Employment.* Washington, DC: AEI Press.

Kusnet, David. 1998. "The New Labor Movement and the Politics of Living Standards." *Working USA* 2 (September/October): 26–35.

Levey, Noam. 1997. "Safety Net Wearing Thin: Social Service Agencies and Churches Are Seeing More Wage-Earners in Line for Free Food, Clothes, and Shelter." *Duluth (Minnesota) News Tribune,* May 13, p. 1A.

Levin-Waldman, Oren M. 1996. "The Minimum Wage and the Path towards a High Wage Economy." Working paper 166, Jerome Levy Economics Institute, Annandale-on-Hudson, NY.

———. 1998a. "Automatic Adjustment of the Minimum Wage: Linking the Minimum Wage to Productivity." Public Policy Brief 42. Annandale-on-Hudson, NY: Jerome Levy Economics Institute.

———. 1998b. "Exploring the Politics of the Minimum Wage." *Journal of Economic Issues* 32, no. 3:1–30.

———. 1998c. "State Type and Congressional Voting on the Minimum Wage." Working paper 243, Jerome Levy Economics Institute, Annandale-on-Hudson, NY.

Levin-Waldman, Oren M., and George W. McCarthy. 1998. "Small Business and the Minimum Wage." Policy Notes 1998/3. Annandale-on-Hudson, NY: Jerome Levy Economics Institute.

Luce, Stephanie. 1996. "Business Subsidies in Los Angeles: Getting a Return on Our Investment." Prepared for the Los Angeles Living Wage Coalition, December.

Macek, Steve. 1997. "New Party Report: Making Work Pay." *Z Magazine,* June.

Martin, Linda R., and Demetrios Giannaros. 1990. "Would a Higher Minimum Wage Help Poor Families Headed by Women?" *Monthly Labor Review* 113, no. 8:33–37.

Mishel, Lawrence, Jared Bernstein, and Edith Rasell. 1995. "Who Wins with a Higher Minimum Wage?" Briefing paper, Economic Policy Institute, Washington, DC.

Mishel, Lawrence, Jared Bernstein, and John Schmitt. 1999. *The State of Working America 1998–9.* Ithaca, NY: Cornell University Press.

Nelson, Richard R. 1994. "State Labor Legislation Enacted in 1993." *Monthly Labor Review* 117, no. 1:36–52.

———. 1997. "State Labor Legislation Enacted in 1996." *Monthly Labor Review* 120, no. 1:29–41.

———. 1998. "State Labor Legislation Enacted in 1997." *Monthly Labor Review* 121, no. 1:3–22.

———. 1999. "State Labor Legislation Enacted in 1998." *Monthly Labor Review* 122, no. 1:3–15.

———. 2000. "State Labor Legislation Enacted in 1999." *Monthly Labor Review* 123, no. 1:3–19.

Neumark, David, and William Wascher. 1995. "The Effects of New Jersey's Minimum Wage Increase on Fast Food Employment: A Re-evaluation Using Payroll Records." Working paper 5224, National Bureau of Economic Research, Cambridge, MA.

———. 1998. "Is the Time-Series Evidence on Minimum Wage Effects Contaminated by Publication Bias?" *Economic Inquiry* 36, no. 3:458–70.

Niedt, Christopher, Greg Ruiters, Dana Wise, and Erica Schoenberger. 1999. "The Effects of the Living Wage in Baltimore." Working paper 119, Economic Policy Institute, Washington, DC.

Nordlund, Willis J. 1997. *The Quest for a Living Wage: The History of the Federal Minimum Wage Program.* Westport, CT: Greenwood Press.

Northrup, Emily M. 1991. "Public Assistance and Antipoverty Programs or Why Haven't Means-Tested Programs Been More Successful at Reducing Poverty?" *Journal of Economic Issues* 25, no. 2:1017–27.

Pollin, Robert et al. 1996. *Economic Analysis of the Los Angeles Living Wage Ordinance.* Prepared for the Los Angeles Living Wage Campaign, October.

Pollin, Robert, and Stephanie Luce. 1998. *The Living Wage: Building a Fair Economy.* New York: New Press.

Renwick, Trudi J., and Barbara R. Bergmann. 1993. "A Budget-Based Definition of Poverty." *Journal of Human Resources* 28 (winter): 1–24.

Rix, Sara E. 1996. "Protecting Workers at the Bottom: The Minimum Wage and America's Minimum-Wage Workers." Public Policy Institute Issue Brief. Washington, DC: American Association of Retired Persons.

Rodgers, William M. III. 1995. "Prepared Statement of William Rodgers." *Evidence against a Higher Minimum Wage,* Part 1, Hearing before the Joint Economic Committee, 104th Congress, February 22. Washington, DC: Government Printing Office.

Ruggles, Patricia. 1990. *Drawing the Line: Alternative Poverty Measures and Their Implication for Public Policy.* Washington, DC: Urban Institute Press.

Sawhill, Isabel V. 1988. "Poverty in the U.S.: Why Is It So Persistent?" *Journal of Economic Literature* 26, no. 3:1073–119.

Spalter-Roth, Roberta M., Heidi I. Hartmann, and Linda Andrews. 1992. *Combining Work and Welfare: An Alternative Anti-Poverty Strategy.* Washington, DC: Institute for Women's Policy Research.

Spriggs, William E., and Bruce W. Klein. 1994. *Raising the Floor: The Effects of the Minimum Wage on Low-wage Workers.* Washington, DC: Economic Policy Institute.

Spriggs, William, and John Schmitt. 1996. "The Minimum Wage: Blocking the Low-Wage Path." In *Reclaiming Prosperity,* edited by Todd Schafer and Jeff Faux. Armonk, NY: M. E. Sharpe.

Sweeney, John J. 1996. *America Needs a Raise: Fighting for Economic Security and Social Justice.* New York: Houghton Mifflin.

Taylor, Lowell. 1995. "Prepared Statement of Lowell Taylor." *Evidence against a Higher Minimum Wage,* Part 1, Hearing before the Joint Economic Committee, 104th Congress, February 22. Washington, DC: Government Printing Office.

Teichert, Nancy Weaver. 1997. "Low Earners Appeal for Living Wage." *Sacramento Bee,* March 9, p. B1.

Tyson, James. 1996. " 'Living Wage' Drive Accelerates in Cities." *Christian Science Monitor,* April 10, p. 1.

U.S. Department of Labor. 1991. *Employment, Hours, and Earnings, United States, 1909–90,* vol. 1, 3. Washington, DC: Government Printing Office.

———. 1997a. *A Profile of the Working Poor, 1996.* Report 18. Washington, DC: Bureau of Labor Statistics.

———. 1997b. Unpublished tabulations from the Current Population Survey, Table A-7: "Hourly earnings of employed wage and salary workers paid hourly rates by age, sex, race, and Hispanic origin, 1997 annual averages."

———. 1997c. "History of Federal Minimum Wage Rates." <http://www.dol.gov/dol/esa/public/minwage/chart.htm> (November 18, 1997).

———. 1998a. "Consumer Price Index: All Urban Consumers—(CPI-U)." <ftp://ftp.bls.gov/pub/special.requests/cpi/cpiai.txt> (November 16, 1998).

———. 1998b. *Current Employment Statistics,* table B-2, "Average Hours and Earnings of Production and Nonsupervisory Workers on Private Nonfarm Payrolls by Major Industry, 1964 to Date." <ftp://ftp.bls.gov/pub/special.requests/ee/ceseeb2.txt> (November 16, 1998).

———. 1998c. Unpublished tabulations from the Current Population Survey, Table 7: "Hourly earnings of employed wage and salary workers paid hourly rates by age, sex, race, and Hispanic origin, second quarter 1998."

Weisbrot, Mark, and Michelle Sforza-Roderick. 1996. *Baltimore's Living Wage Law: An Analysis of the Fiscal and Economic Costs of Baltimore City Ordinance 442.* Washington, DC: Preamble Center for Public Policy.

Welch, Finis. 1995. "Prepared Statement of Finis Welch." *Evidence against a Higher Minimum Wage,* Part 1, Hearing before the Joint Economic Committee, 104th Congress, February 22. Washington, DC: Government Printing Office.

White House Office for Women's Initiatives and Outreach. Press release, "White House Update for Women," July 10, 1996.

Williams, Nicolas, and Jeffrey A. Mills. 1998. "Minimum Wage Effects by Gender." *Journal of Labor Research* 19, no. 2:397–414.

Wood, Daniel B. 1996. "Debate Escalates over 'Living Wage' as Antipoverty Tool." *Christian Science Monitor,* October 17, p. 3.

Zabin, Carol. 1997. "Assessing the Costs and Benefits of the 'Living Wage Ordinance': A Review of the Evidence." Policy Brief, University of California Los Angeles Center for Labor Research and Education, January 7.

7

Pay Equity: Did It Work?

Margaret Hallock

The year was 1986. Women workers were gathered at a hearing with Oregon legislators to discuss their jobs and wages. Women lined up with pay stubs in hand and described their work, from feeding hordes of students at the university to managing cases of welfare recipients. They listed in detail their responsibilities in coordinating and administering complex projects and holding together the systems that made the workplace hum. Most tellingly they inquired, "Why do we earn less because we take care of *people* rather than taking care of *things?*"

These women then asked the legislators to guess their monthly pay. To a person the legislators overestimated the women's pay by at least 15 percent, and they were shocked when the women revealed their actual pay, sometimes below the official poverty threshold. At that moment activists in Oregon turned the corner on the struggle of state workers to achieve pay equity—equal pay for work of equal value.

The Oregon pay equity struggle was one of dozens of such campaigns in the 1980s, mostly in the public sector, which attempted to upgrade wages for undervalued female-dominated jobs. A major reason for the gender wage gap is that men and women do not do the same jobs. Women remain concentrated in clerical and service jobs as well as female-dominated professions such as nursing and teaching. These jobs pay less than jobs that men hold that require similar or comparable education and experience. Economists and other students of the labor market have demonstrated again and again that wages are not set in a "free" market according to skill but that the very notion of skill has a gendered aspect, so that a clerical worker is commonly viewed to be less skilled than a "skilled" craftsperson. The higher the proportion of women in an occupation, the lower the wage. Women's wages are depressed due to decades of sex stereotyping of jobs and the fact that many women's jobs incorporate work that was once done in the home without pay rather than in the market.

The movement for pay equity—also known as comparable worth—set about to eliminate the portion of the wage gap that is due to occupational segregation and the undervaluation of women's jobs. Most pay equity projects evaluate and compare jobs according to the level of skill, effort, and responsibility required for the job and seek to equalize the pay for jobs that have equal value in terms of these factors.

The experience in Oregon illustrates the achievements and disappointments of pay equity. Most of the campaigns resulted in pay increases for women, but the upgrades often fell short of original expectations. The impact on the wage gap within an organization could be profound, but these gains were not translated to other jurisdictions. The reforms occasionally bogged down in the technical aspects of comparing jobs or stalled because of recalcitrant management or divisions among advocates.

Undoubtedly there were clear achievements. The pay equity movement transformed women's workplace consciousness, empowered a new generation of leaders, brought together union and gender issues, and invoked a widespread debate on the nature of the gender wage gap. But after a decade of activity, the disappointments seem to tip the scales. No lasting legislation or pay equity policy was enacted in the United States, and progress toward pay equity is not generally viewed as responsible for the recent decline in the gender wage gap.

Pay equity efforts have been more aggressive, coherent, and successful in Canada. Legislation in nine of twelve Canadian provinces and the federal sector explicitly calls for achieving equal pay for work of equal value, and pathbreaking legislation in Ontario covers the private sector as well as the public sector in a proactive, economy-wide regulatory approach. But here, too, disappointments prevail despite even greater achievements such as improving traditional wage setting mechanisms and launching a widespread dialogue about wages and gender. The Ontario legislation did not reach most women, particularly unorganized women in the lowest-wage jobs who need pay equity the most. It too fell prey to the myriad technical disputes and pitfalls experienced in the United States. The approach in other provinces and the federal sector has been even less effective in reducing the gender wage gap because it does not require all firms to achieve equity but instead relies on individual women to launch and win complaints.

The pay equity movement tapered off in the early 1990s as the women's movement was forced to defend gains in other areas and as unions turned to fight other battles, but equal pay remains the top issue among working women in the United States as shown in the AFL-CIO's *Ask a Working Woman* survey (AFL-CIO n.d.). In the late 1990s there was a resurgence of activity in state and local government legislative efforts as well as in union organizing and bargaining. But the struggle for pay equity now confronts a wholly different political economy than that of the 1980s. The public sector is under attack, and fundamental economic changes have wrought enormous shifts in the nature of work and the distribution of income. The rise of temporary and contingent work, the shift to services, smaller enterprises, and an astonishing increase in inequality all pose new challenges and threaten to eclipse the struggle for equal pay.

Given these fundamental shifts in the workplace and the political economic context, what is the best strategy for pursuing pay equity? Are there lessons to be learned from the campaigns and policies of the 1980s? How can women mobilize and organize for pay equity without succumbing to endless and expensive battles over technical issues such as how to evaluate and compare jobs? Should unions and other advocates approach pay equity from a more inclusive, solidaristic stance of confronting inequality and low pay generally?

This chapter attempts to address these issues by reviewing pay equity efforts in the United States and, to a lesser extent, in Canada. I examine the Oregon case in particular, noting that women did achieve significant wage gains with a long struggle that also energized and mobilized women union activists. However, ten years later, women remain concentrated at the bottom of the salary hierarchy in Oregon state government. Gender is still a significant factor in explaining wages, signifying in part that women's jobs were not fundamentally revalued through the pay equity process.

The main conclusion is that pay equity, as it has been practiced, has been disappointing. Wage gains were not widespread, and pay equity has not been credited with reducing the gender wage gap. The practice of pay equity has been centered too heavily on technical job evaluation that has been problematic both for women and unions. The dilemma, however, is that pay equity achieved its limited successes by focusing on revaluing what women do, and this was the key to mobilizing women, so future efforts should continue to speak to the value of the work women do. Therefore, the best course for the next decade may be to emphasize the broad issues of economic justice and equality such as in campaigns for "living wages" and upgrading low-wage service jobs while at the same time highlighting the gendered nature of specific jobs and wages. Such projects would speak to women as both women and workers, the key to the successful campaigns of the past.

Attacking the Wage Gap—from Affirmative Action to Pay Equity

The gender wage gap has been one of the more durable features of the wage structure in North America. In the late 1960s women began organizing around the theme of 59¢ on the dollar, the average earnings of working women compared to working men. Since then the wage gap between men and women has indeed shrunk, but the news is not all good.

The current wage gap is closer to 75¢ on the male dollar, though African American women earn only 63 percent of male wages. Researchers at the Institute for Women's Policy Research (IWPR) show that women did make progress during the 1980s, as their real income increased by 10 percent, but that this progress stalled in the 1990s. Meanwhile, men's real earnings have fallen steadily since the mid-1970s. Nearly 60 percent of the improvement in the weekly wage gap is due to falling men's wages (IWPR 1998). The rest of the improvement can be traced mainly to advances women have made in professional and technical fields (Blau and Kahn 1997).

Income inequality among women has grown; not all women shared in the gains (Gregory 1998). Mirroring the growing gap between the rich and the poor generally, highly educated women have enjoyed rising wages while pay remains stagnant for women in low-wage clerical and service jobs.

Activists and policymakers in the United States have pursued two basic approaches to reducing the wage gap. One approach, equal employment opportunity, focused on reducing discrimination against women in hiring, promotion, and pay as well as affirmative action to move women into higher paying and male-dominated jobs. Affirmative action helped establish a sense of how discrimination happens in the job market and the need for remedial efforts, and it gave a push to eliminating occupational segregation by race and gender (Blum 1991; Gunderson 1989). But these programs primarily affect women in professional or managerial jobs and those who can or will change jobs. Such programs have little effect on the millions of women who continue to work in predominantly female clerical and sales jobs. Worse, the underlying message of affirmative action to these women reinforces the message of the market—that their jobs are not valued and that they should change jobs if they want to earn a decent income.

The second approach was pay equity. While affirmative action was directed at individuals, pay equity was a collective reform targeted at the sex segregation of jobs as a whole and the undervaluation of women's jobs. It held the promise of upgrading wages in the jobs where women already worked and closing the wage gap between male- and female-dominated jobs. It attempted to expand the reach of the Equal Pay Act of 1963, which had been interpreted to require equal pay only for workers in the same job and therefore did not have a major impact on the pay gap between men's and women's jobs. Instead, pay equity sought equal wages for jobs that are dissimilar but of equal skill and value.

In the United States, pay equity was launched with litigation and carried through by countless localized initiatives led by unions and feminists. Attorneys waged a creative litigation campaign beginning in the 1970s in an attempt to have the courts recognize gender-based wage disparities as discrimination. Women sued companies and public jurisdictions under the 1964 Civil Rights Act, claiming discrimination because they earned less than men in comparable jobs. Several landmark cases in the early 1980s briefly opened a legal door for comparable worth, but the door was slammed shut by later, increasingly conservative court decisions that effectively allowed employers to say that it was the "free market" and not discrimination that led to depressed wages for female-dominated jobs (see McCann 1994).

The early victories, however, were a catalyst for widespread grassroots and legislative activity in states and localities, mostly in the public sector and mostly where women were represented by unions. By the end of the 1980s some twenty states had made pay equity wage adjustments along with hundreds of cities, counties, and municipalities.

In Canada, pay equity policies evolved in a similar vein, moving from demands for equal pay for equal work to equal pay for work of equal value. Canada's movement was ahead of that in the United States in that legislation called for comparisons across occupations as early as the 1950s. By the 1980s, most jurisdictions had adopted some form of pay equity legislation or formal initiative.

The context of pay equity efforts in the United States and Canada is that of a decentralized wage setting process with rather limited collective bargaining, particularly in the United States. Also in the United States there is no explicit recognition of male and female wage structures and the influence of historical and societal processes in creating a gender wage gap. Rather, the dominant discourse emphasizes market processes and individual choice, creating a major barrier for pay equity activists to conquer just to get the issue on the agenda.

So, pay equity policies in both the United States and Canada are focused on identifying and eliminating gender disparities for workers employed with a single firm or establishment at a time, an awesome task, and both tend to use job evaluation as the major tool. These dual characteristics—a decentralized approach and an emphasis on job evaluation—are also the major reasons for the disappointments of pay equity.

Doing Comparable Worth or Pay Equity

The dominant practice of pay equity involves a process of job analysis and job evaluation to identify and eliminate wage disparities. *Job evaluation* is a generic term that refers to a variety of methods used to compare jobs. Job evaluation systems attempt to objectively assess the complexity of jobs, not the performance of the jobholder, but it is an inherently subjective process that ranks jobs in order to establish a hierarchy of difficulty and basis for comparison.

Early advocates documented the pay gap using traditional management job evaluation tools that gave points to jobs according to their level of skill, effort, and responsibility. While unionists were wary of these job evaluation schemes because they emphasized managerial tasks, they were successfully used in the early court cases and were adopted by many advocates of comparable worth (McCann 1994; Steinberg 1991). Comparable worth or pay equity thus came to be seen as setting wages according to the skill, effort, and responsibility of the job, regardless of gender (Evans and Nelson 1989; Acker 1989).

The question of how to document the undervaluation of women's jobs is at the heart of the dilemma of comparable worth. Job evaluation is a double-edged sword; while it can yield concrete evidence of a pay gap and raise consciousness about discrimination, it is a cumbersome and expensive management tool that is often biased against women and can inhibit collective bargaining (Hallock 1993; Acker 1989; McCann 1994).

There are several problems with job evaluation. First, these systems were developed primarily as a management tool to evaluate management jobs, and they therefore miss some aspects of women's jobs such as the demands of dealing skillfully with patients, clients, and co-workers. Second, the value placed on skills that *are* measured, such as human relations skills, rewards these skills less in female than male jobs (see Acker 1989; Steinberg 1992, 1999). Thus job evaluation systems, although consistently applied, will still leave women's jobs undervalued to the extent that they ignore or continue to undervalue traditionally female duties and skills. Third, these systems are technical tools that are not easy for unions and workers to use to advantage. Finally, job evaluation reinforces hierarchy and meritocracy in an organization even while advocates critique these very concepts as a basis for setting wages (Blum 1991; Brenner 1987).

Job evaluation is only one of numerous steps in a pay equity initiative, all of which involve a myriad of technical details that have become the grist for disputes and battles. The main steps include the following.

- Dividing the workforce into job classes, obtaining current and reliable information about job duties (called job analysis), and determining the gender dominance of classes. In Ontario, a job is defined as male dominated if 70 percent of incumbents are men and female dominated if 60 percent are women.
- Selecting a job evaluation method and defining the specific factors that will be measured to determine the relative value of jobs.
- Evaluating jobs, usually by a committee that is representative of the workforce. This committee applies the job evaluation system to determine which jobs can be compared. The selection and training of the committee are crucial and often a point of struggle among workers and management.
- Analyzing and adjusting wages. The technical issues here are equally sobering, ranging from choosing which jobs to compare to each other to implementing wage adjustments.

Gender bias can enter at any of these steps. For example, in job analysis **it is common** to find women's jobs described in general terms with **stereotypes and** assumptions about duties. Job evaluation factors often do not capture key aspects of women's jobs. For example, child development specialists can be mistakenly described as "watching children" and secretaries evaluated for typing rather than coordinating office workflow. Men's jobs are often assumed to have poorer working conditions, such as working outdoors, ignoring the poor and hazardous conditions for women's jobs in places such as hospitals.

Although pay equity seeks to improve the fairness and justice of the wage structure, it typically evolves into a lengthy exercise in which basic questions of values masquerade as highly technical decisions. Further, these technical issues are hammered out on a case-by-case basis due to the decentralized nature of the wage setting process. This has two important results. First, the answers to the myriad technical questions will depend on the interests of the parties at the table. Pay equity is, after all, a highly political initiative, and labor, management, and pay equity advocates will make decisions based on their perceived interests in each case.

Second, these decisions are not easily transferred to other situations or adopted as standard policy. Only in Ontario is there a pay equity tribunal that wrestles with such issues and has the ability to set policy. Unfortunately, it has declined to issue standards or mandates on such questions as what constitutes a bias-free job evaluation system, claiming this would unduly influence the ability of employers to manage their enterprises (Fudge 1991).

Thus, pay equity in the United States and Canada emerges as a long stream of somewhat isolated initiatives, many of which are long-simmering disputes. An example is found in the situation of the Canadian federal employees of the Treasury Board who have been locked in a contentious pay equity battle for over fifteen years. The absence of a centralized wage setting scheme prohibits an efficient and economy-wide approach and ironically increases the need for technical job evaluation systems to rationalize the wage changes at each location. Broadbrush "rules of thumb" that could be widely applied would make the process smoother and more efficient (Gregory 1998).

The Promise and Practice of
Pay Equity—the Oregon Case

The contradictions of the comparable worth strategy are illustrated in the campaign for pay equity for Oregon state workers. I was the chair of the Oregon Task Force on State Compensation and Classification Equity, commonly known as the Comparable Worth Task Force, and director of research for the Oregon Public Employees Union (OPEU) during this campaign. Joan Acker, a member of the task force, eloquently described the dilemmas and contradictions of the campaign in *Doing Comparable Worth* (Acker 1989). We both think of the campaign in two separate phases, what I call the "expert's phase" from 1983 through 1985 and the "mobilizing phase" from 1985 until the implementation of a new classification system and final wage upgrades in 1990.[1]

From Technique to Dignity and Respect

The problems were visible from the start, as unions, management, and feminists began the effort with multiple and conflicting objectives. A feminist legislator introduced and successfully passed legislation calling on the state to identify and eliminate gender-based wage inequities. She garnered strong support for the bill, building on the judicial victories of the early 1980s as well as the momentum of the women's rights movement. Management signed on to this legislation on the condition that the effort would include an analysis of the entire classification system for state employees, in order to resolve some long-standing problems with the personnel system. The major union representing state employees also favored a full classification and compensation study because they had experienced years of difficulties negotiating wages for job classes that were too large and general—primarily women's classes—as well as some that were too small and detailed—mostly male-dominated classes. The union was attracted to the promise that a full study would treat all jobs more fairly, identify career ladders and opportunities, and revalue the skills of workers.

The initial legislation required that a "single, bias-free, sex-neutral point-factor job evaluation system shall be applied to all jobs in state service, across job families to rank order jobs, to set salaries, and to create career ladders for advancement according to the value of the work performed."

The stage was set for a full-blown technical study of the state's classification and compensation system, including job evaluation. The task force adopted the Hay system of job evaluation despite criticisms that the Hay system emphasized managerial tasks and undervalued traditionally female duties such as taking care of people. The task force attempted to deal with these criticisms by increasing the value given to human relations skill or dealing with people, but these enhancements were largely negated later in the actual process of job evaluation (see Acker 1989).

The first phase of the study was a painful exercise for all concerned. The scope of the study was massive, more than could be accomplished in two years. The project first surveyed over thirty-four thousand jobs, then reclassified positions, and finally evaluated the new job classifications. The task force reported finding significant gender bias in both the classification and pay systems and recommended a complete overhaul of both based on the point-factor system. But the technical work was preliminary and inadequate; the unions could not agree on a process to implement the new classes; and the study effort collapsed of its own weight.

It was time to regroup. In what became a second and distinct phase of the overall campaign, management continued to focus on the job classification system, but feminists and unions concentrated on identifying and eliminating inequities between male- and female-dominated jobs. Whereas the voices of women had been muted during the expert's phase, in the second phase the Oregon Public Employees Union mobilized women and involved them in the technical job evaluation activities as well as the political process.

The themes of the second phase of the campaign were justice, dignity, and respect, and the nomenclature shifted from comparable worth to pay equity. Although they were less concerned with the technical aspects of job evaluation, pay equity advocates nonetheless adopted its general thrust by emphasizing the value of women's work. Women exposed how the supposedly neutral "free market" had undervalued their work. They found that child-care workers earned less than workers who tended animals in research labs, that university secretaries earned less than the workers who delivered the mail to the offices, and that social workers earned less than probation officers and computer technicians. They held rallies and hearings and for the first time discussed in public the work they did and how much they earned. Workers who had previously described themselves as "only secretaries" now proudly asserted the value of their work.

This campaign did much to raise consciousness about the demands of "emotional labor"—work that requires women to care for the emotions of clients or to attempt to please customers and patients—and it exposed the invisibility of women's skills.

In addition to women's jobs being undervalued compared to men's positions, women were concentrated in the lowest salary ranges. The union demonstrated that many state workers were so poorly paid as to be eligible for food stamps and housing assistance, adding political strength to the pay equity cause.

The second phase culminated in new pay equity legislation and $22 million in wage upgrades in 1987, despite the fact that the classification overhaul was still not complete. Classification issues drove the first phase, and women were unable to overcome the associated logistical and technical problems. During the second phase, a focus on the undervaluation and low wages of female-dominated jobs allowed advocates to win wage increases for the original job classes. The work on a new classification system was finally complete in 1989, and its implementation led to additional wage increases.

The Impact on Wages

The original task force had found significant gender-based inequities in the state's pay and classification system (Task Force 1985). The state workforce was segregated by gender—80 percent of workers were in male- or female-dominated classes, and women were clustered at the low end of the salary hierarchy. While 62 percent of state employees worked at jobs evaluated at 250 Hay points or less (primarily non-management, semiskilled jobs), over 92 percent of workers in female-dominated jobs were in this relatively low range. The gender wage gap was most pronounced for entry-level jobs, where female-dominated jobs earned on average 32 percent less than male-dominated entry-level jobs.

The first round of pay equity upgrades in 1987 raised wages in selected female-dominated jobs by one or two salary ranges, the equivalent of about 5 to 10 percent. Raises totaling $22.6 million went to about nine thousand state workers, primarily clerical, service, and human service workers. By 1989 the new classification system was complete, and its implementation led to another $32.8 million in upgrades reflecting pay equity and the new personnel system (Oregon Executive Department 1990).

Negotiating new wage rates for hundreds of new job classes strained both management and labor. The state sought to achieve internal equity based on the job evaluation system by tying wages fairly strictly to job evaluation points, setting wages by a "pay line" depicting the average relationship between wages and job evaluation points. The state wanted to freeze wages for jobs that were above the pay line, primarily men's jobs. Unions pushed for wage upgrades for undervalued jobs without wage cuts or wage freezes for other job classes, primarily male jobs.

The overall impact of the campaign was a complete restructuring of the state's classification and compensation system. The original classification system was indeed problematic. In particular, the clerical classifications were huge, general classes that included jobs of varying skill and complexity. Workers in the largest clerical job class, Clerical Specialist, were reallocated to fifty-two different job classes after job analysis.

Wage upgrades were significant for clerical, service, health-care, and human service workers. Most clerical workers moved up two salary ranges, increasing their pay approximately 10 percent. Some clerical workers who had been misclassified moved up even more. For example, the many "secretaries" who were the sole clerical worker in an office became "office coordinators" and moved up six salary ranges, or nearly 30 percent. Similarly, psychiatric aides in the mental health hospitals moved up eight salary ranges, or 40 percent, and other health-care professions also were revalued. Human service workers received upgrades of 15 to 25 percent. One of the most satisfying upgrades, although it affected relatively few workers, was "child care worker," whose wages increased 25 percent.

By the end of the process, all sides declared victory. Management maintained that the new job classification system met the requirements of the original statute, that it was equitable because it was based on a job evaluation system. "Because all classifications are now evaluated using the Hay job evaluation system, there are no classes which can be said to be undervalued" (Oregon Executive Department 1990). This statement is breathtaking from a feminist perspective, because it assumes that job evaluation alone can create equity without revising wages to eliminate inequities.

Unions also declared victory. Workers received two rounds of wage upgrades, and the unions successfully fought off most proposals to downgrade male jobs and freeze incumbent wages, particularly in the trades. During bargaining, unions worked to protect wages in male-dominated classes and weaken the link between the Hay point-factor system and the new salary ranges. They had to struggle against management proposals to lower the salary ranges for "overvalued" jobs. In fact, the new compensation system only loosely followed the job evaluation system, and about one-third of classes ended up in a salary range other than that determined strictly by Hay evaluation (Oregon Executive Department 1990).

Finally, coalition partners were generally positive about the ultimate changes. The Oregon Public Employees Union organized an impressive Pay Equity Action Coalition that pressed for the 1987 upgrades and monitored the final implementation of the job evaluation system. While some feminists were disappointed that wages would not be strictly tied to job evaluation (Acker 1989), the problems inherent in these systems and their gender bias convinced most advocates that a perfect system was unattainable and that women had won a significant victory.

Did the Equity Upgrades Endure over Time?

During the original comparable worth study, one concern of feminists was how the system would be maintained to prevent market forces and discrimination from recreating the gender wage gap (Acker 1989). Indeed, the new system was installed just as the state came under severe budget pressures from ballot measures and initiatives that cut property taxes and transferred more responsibility for public schools to the state. State employee wages were frozen for four years, from 1991 to 1995. After this wage freeze, the main goal of both workers and management was to catch up to the market. Workers wanted cost of living and special market-driven upgrades, and management needed higher wages for recruitment and retention purposes.

Currently, the formal pay policy of the state is guided by statutes, political priorities, attempts to achieve a balance of internal equity (as determined by the Hay job evaluation system), and maintaining parity with market wages and benefits to assist with recruitment and retention, all within a collective bargaining environment with several unions and a limited budget (Oregon Revised Statutes 1998). Union negotiators confirm that the state has a hybrid system that balances internal equity with market relationships, budget, and "other priorities," and the emphasis varies according to political and budgetary developments.

What is the status of pay equity now, nearly ten years after the implementation of the new classification system? Table 7.1 presents data for the OPEU bargaining unit in 1998.[2] Sex segregation remains a key feature of employment in the state system. Over 70 percent of OPEU workers are in classes dominated by one gender. In particular, 72 percent of females work in a job class in which at least 70 percent of workers are women. These figures mirror those of the original task force, which found that 76 percent of women worked in female-dominated jobs. Figure 7.1 shows that women are more concentrated in jobs that are evaluated at relatively low levels—over 62 percent are in jobs with less than 250 Hay points. The large clerical job classes and some service jobs are in this range.

Further analysis of these data confirms that gender remains a significant factor in explaining the wage structure in at least part of Oregon state government. Workers in a female-dominated class would, on average, have a predicted maximum salary of $120 less per month than a male-dominated class at the same point level, a difference of 6 percent for jobs with 200 points. The comparable figure for 1985 was a difference of 9 percent. The wage gap remains largest for entry-level jobs, also echoing the results of the original study. Thus, after controlling for the complexity of the job, women still earn less than men, despite the wage upgrades of 1987 and 1989, although the gap appears to be smaller than before the pay equity initiative.

One interesting finding is that job evaluation points are a better predictor of women's salaries than men's. This implies that male-dominated classes are more influenced by market pressure, while female-dominated classes are more influenced by the job evaluation system.

The Impact of Pay Equity
in the United States and Canada

There were many cases similar to Oregon's, large state-level initiatives that resulted in one-time wage upgrades between 10 percent and 20 percent for selected female-dominated jobs. A review of the impact of pay

TABLE 7.1. Occupational Segregation in OPEU Bargaining Unit, 1998

Gender Composition of Class[a]	No. of Classes	No. of Women	No. of Men	Total Employees
Female dominated	109 (31%)	6,586 (72%)	1,205 (22%)	7,791 (53%)
Male dominated	107 (32%)	298 (3%)	2,393 (43%)	2,691 (18%)
Mixed	126 (37%)	2,230 (24%)	1,949 (35%)	4,179 (29%)
Totals	342	9,114	5,547	14,661

Source: Data provided by Oregon Executive Department, 1998.
[a]A class is dominated if 70% or more of the workers are of one gender.

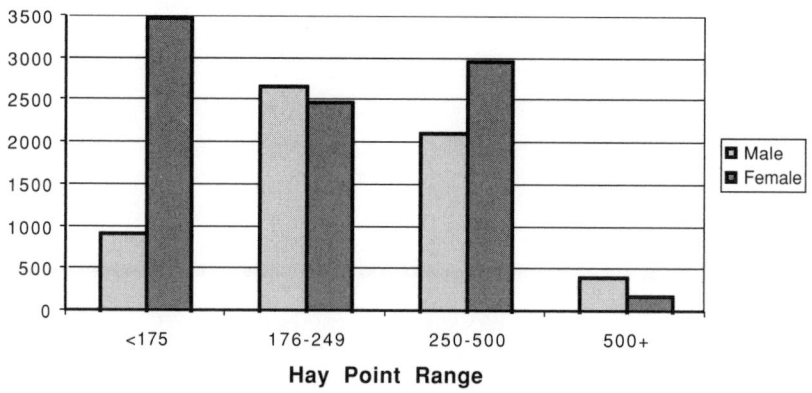

FIG. 7.1. Distribution of workers by Hay points, OPEU bargaining unit. (Date from State of Oregon 1998.)

equity efforts in Canada and the United States confirms that the most common result was wage upgrades of about 20 percent for undervalued jobs but with wide variation (Gunderson 1994). Sorensen (1990) estimated that pay equity raised women's relative wages by 10 percent for Minnesota state employees. Hartmann and Aaronson (1994) studied sixteen states that implemented some form of pay equity and found that the female to-male wage ratio improved in all. The most dramatic improvements occurred in states such as Oregon that adopted comprehensive programs of both classification and wage changes, but these were also relatively expensive. For example, for Oregon, wage upgrades were estimated to total $52.2 million in 1990 dollars, equal to 9.8 percent of total payroll. This is on the high end of the sixteen states studied—only Vermont dedicated more to wage upgrades, at 11.8 percent. The high payroll impact is attributed to the systemic changes undertaken in these states compared with states that targeted pay equity increases to specific jobs and dedicated between 0.1 percent and 3.5 percent of payroll to equity upgrades (Hartmann and Aaronson 1994; see also Gardner and Daniel 1998).

There has been surprisingly little comprehensive analysis of the impact of pay equity in Canada, again due to the decentralized nature of the process. Gunderson (1994) and others maintain that the Ontario legislation that requires all employers to address pay inequities is more effective than the systems in which women must bring a complaint to start the process. For example, in Manitoba, the average wage adjustment was 15 percent, and comparable worth adjustments increased the overall ratio of female to male wages from 0.82 to 0.87. In Ontario, the process was quite decentralized, making analysis of impacts difficult. The Pay Equity Commission there does not collect information on adjustments. However, commission surveys and independent research indicate poor compliance, particularly in the private sector (Gunderson 1994). In the public sector, an estimated 38 percent of women in female-dominated classes received wage increases totaling about 2.2 percent of payroll. In the private sector, where increases were implemented, 18 percent of women received wage increases amounting to 0.65 percent of the payroll.

McDonald and Thornton (1998) confirmed the small impact on women's wages in the private sector in Ontario and also analyzed the compliance issue in qualitative studies of twenty-one firms. They found many instances of noncompliance and manipulation in order to minimize the final wage increases and to get through the requirements of the legislation as quickly as possible. While some respondents cited positive aspects of the process, including both making the firms more aware of internal equity and installing better compensation and classification systems, the majority (mostly managers) emphasized the administrative burden and difficulties with job evaluation.

It is thus very difficult to summarize the impact of the disparate pay equity cases in the United States and Canada. Most observers find wage upgrades for undervalued classes in the neighborhood of 10 to 20 percent in the public sector and smaller upgrades in the private sector. While these upgrades are sizable, they affected relatively few women, even in Ontario. These small impacts seem to confirm the prediction of feminist critics that Canada's pay equity policy excludes women most in need of pay equity and allows too many exceptions and opportunities for manipulation and noncompliance (see Fudge and McDermott 1991).

The Achievements and Limits of Pay Equity

The Oregon case illustrates many of the achievements and disappointments of pay equity that have been noted in other accounts (see particularly Blum 1991; McCann 1994; Figart and Kahn 1997; Evans and Nelson 1989; Feldberg 1984; Hallock 1993).

Achievements in Pay Equity

First, where implemented, pay equity raised wages for female-dominated jobs and low-wage clerical and service jobs. Job evaluation, despite its limitations, identified very consistent gender pay differentials, and informal methods of comparing male and female jobs produced similar results. Wages for female-dominated jobs increased from 10 to 20 percent in most applications, and the emphasis on low-wage jobs in some projects produced broader impacts on people of color and other low-wage workers (Malveaux 1985; Sorensen 1994; Gunderson 1989).

Second, pay equity challenged historical wage patterns and empowered women to improve their status. Unlike affirmative action, which was targeted at individuals, pay equity was a collective reform and affected many more women. Thus it helped generate a social movement among women and created a new cadre of union and social activists. Pay equity was both a product of, and contributed to, the convergence of feminism and unionism in North America. Some pay equity activists came to the struggle as feminists and emerged with a new understanding of class and the necessity for collective action and hence the importance of unions. Others came as union activists and learned the politics of gender and feminism. McCann quotes one union activist: "Our whole local is a women's committee. I learned feminism from my union. It opened up a whole new world for me" (McCann 1994, 120). Thus pay equity helped to merge class and gender interests and provided a vehicle for women to address a key issue, women's pay.

The struggle for pay equity, as with many struggles, transformed the participants. It gave them a new sense of worth, a new political discourse, and heightened consciousness about the workplace. Michael McCann carefully documents the increased empowerment, activism, and leadership of women as a result of pay equity (McCann 1994). The Oregon case certainly confirms his analysis. Low-wage women workers, including clerical workers, had been disenfranchised because of their low status as workers. According to an OPEU activist, "Once we broke the taboo of talking about what people earned and why, women gained confidence and started to organize." They felt liberated by a movement that said they did not have to change jobs in order to earn a living wage.

Pay equity is part of the "new gender politics" that recognizes and values differences between men and women as part of the thrust for equality and solidarity (Milkman 1993; Blum 1991). Pay equity helped union leaders understand that gender matters at the workplace and that women's experience at the workplace is fundamentally different from men's, from training to career opportunities. Women relate to co-workers differently than men, and they often have slightly different goals at work. Recognizing these differences can help activists hoping to organize and empower women. Pay equity has shown us how a focus on the value of women and their work can touch and mobilize women (Hallock 1997; Bronfenbrenner and Juravich 1995). This is perhaps the most important contribution of the pay equity effort—women workers became more active in their unions and workplaces and their workplace networks and demanded fresh attention to discrimination that had depressed their wages and job opportunities.

The Limitations of Pay Equity

Although working women are better off because of the movement for pay equity, the dreams of the early proponents have not been realized. The reform has been limited and constrained, due in large part to technical issues.

First, the actual impact of pay equity on the wage gap has been small, as mentioned previously. Wage adjustments for women have been constrained by budget and political pressures in the public sector and lack of activity or noncompliance in the private sector.

Pay equity often degenerated into a technocratic reform controlled by management interested in changing as little as possible. In Oregon, as in many other cases, management attempted to control the technical process and information, to expand the issue from gender to the entire classification system, to limit participation, to constrain collective bargaining, and to divide men and women with proposals to freeze men's wages. In some cases the process was very divisive and led unions to abandon the reforms.

Perhaps the most problematic aspect of pay equity in North America is its reliance on technical and mainstream job evaluation systems. Early advocates adopted job evaluation in order to document the undervaluation of women's jobs. Unions reluctantly accepted job evaluation, often in a pragmatic attempt to rationalize wage increases or formalize the process so that women could maintain more control (McCann 1994). But in practice it has been fraught with contradictions and problems.

- Feminist scholars have convincingly demonstrated that traditional job evaluation systems are biased toward management jobs and undervalue skills of women, including dealing with people and the demands of emotional labor (Acker 1987; Steinberg 1992). For example, in the Hay system, human relations skill was defined primarily as supervising workers, thus ignoring caregiving skills, and attempts to rectify this omission were overturned by consultants in the job evaluation process. Attempts to improve job evaluation through litigation and activism in Canada have not produced new feminist systems with broad impact.

- Job evaluation is the main way that pay equity became a technocratic reform, often dominated by managers and bureaucrats. In particular, job evaluation turns key political decisions and issues of value into a technical discussion. Questions of rights and values are sidetracked into issues of appropriate technique, leaving workers, according to one union advocate, "intimidated, confused or just plain bored" (quoted in McCann 1994, 202).
- Job evaluation is the key instrument that reinforces hierarchy and meritocracy in the organization (Blum 1991; Acker 1989). Thus while pay equity sets out to critique existing hierarchy and wage determination processes, it ends up adopting a management tool that reinforces hierarchy.
- Job evaluation can thwart collective bargaining. Since the enactment of pay equity, the state of Oregon has attempted to limit collective bargaining by tying wages to job evaluation. The secretary of state went public with "pay line exceptions" and "overpayment" of state workers, and management several times proposed freezing the pay of male-dominated classes. Similar experiences are reported in Canada (McDermott 1991).

Job evaluation reinforces the notion that wages are based on skill and that the solution to the wage gap is to eliminate gender bias in measuring skill or value. But wages are a social construct with deep historical underpinnings relating to class and gender. Thus job evaluation becomes a frustrating exercise because it is presented as a technical tool that has an air of objectivity but is, in reality, a political tool used to define value. The actual process of job evaluation is a far cry from the ideological and political arguments that are promised before the actual study.

The cumbersome and bureaucratic nature of pay equity practice also limits participation. It is an expensive and time consuming process fraught with possibilities for lengthy disputes that leave advocates exhausted and unable to concentrate on other pressing issues.

Many initiatives have attempted to skirt these limitations. On balance, the best pay equity campaigns are those that mobilize women and win wage upgrades without adopting formal job evaluation and new management systems; campaigns that emphasize issues of respect, dignity, and value, thereby bringing together the interests of women as workers and as women (see McCann 1994; Figart and Kahn 1997; NCPE 1989).

It's a New World

How should pay equity advocates proceed at the turn of the new century? The political economy is vastly different in several ways than in the 1980s, presenting challenges to policy and union activism for pay equity (Figart and Kahn 1997; Gregory 1998).

- Economic restructuring and the global economy have put enormous pressure on the labor market and unions. The shift to technology and services, fierce deunionization strategies in key sectors, and the enhanced power of business all change the possibility and urgency for union activity, the main engine of pay equity in the United States.
- Political developments such as the tax revolt, the attack on the public sector, deregulation, and privatization weaken the ability of public sector unions and other advocates to pursue an equity agenda. The progressive movement is also weaker, including the links between the women's movement and the labor movement.
- At the workplace, the nature of the workforce and jobs is changing. There is a new distribution of work whereby some work too many hours while others do not have enough. Job security is much reduced, and more workers are contingent or temporary workers with less formal attachment to a workplace or one employer.
- Union priorities have changed. In the 1980s, unions mobilized women members by organizing around pay equity and other initiatives. Unions now increasingly focus on organizing new members and increasing union density, avoiding expensive representation work such as lengthy pay equity procedures.
- Affirmative action and other antidiscrimination remedies are under attack. The gap between rich and poor continues to widen, exacerbating class differences.

These changes present a sobering picture of the landscape for pay equity. Is it a luxury unions and policymakers can no longer afford to pursue? Do its limitations outweigh the potential benefits in a new political order?

The future of pay equity hinges on both union activity and policy. It is difficult to see how traditional pay equity can be successful in the changed environment. The decentralized approach, tackling firm after firm separately, yields unimpressive results for the magnitude of sweat and tears required. We simply lack the centralized wage setting institutions that exist in many European countries and previously in Australia that can create a wide impact on wages overall.

Further, the biggest issue facing workers in North America is economic restructuring with its associated increase in wage inequality and the working poor. According to the Economic Policy Institute, the share of workers earning low wages has been rising. In 1973, 23.5 percent of full-time workers earned less than the poverty level for a family of four. By 1997, that percentage had grown to 28.6 percent (Mishel, Bernstein, and Schmitt 1999, 136).

The future for pay equity is to broaden the struggle beyond traditional comparable worth. The focus should shift to reducing inequality and improving wages in low-wage jobs through political efforts and collective bargaining.

Politically, there is little legislation pending in the United States that would reduce inequities. The Fair Pay Act in Congress would amend the Equal Pay Act to address pay inequities between dissimilar but equivalent jobs, and it would require employers to submit reports, thereby opening up the wage determination process to public view. The Paycheck Fairness Act would also amend the Equal Pay Act, but less substantially, and in both proposals women would still have to initiate complaints and document discrimination or undervaluation. The National Committee on Pay Equity and Business and Professional Women (BPW/USA) are key coalition partners in these efforts and organize an annual Equal Pay Day. The Working Women's Department of the AFL-CIO also supports this legislation and maintains a web page (<http://www.aflcio.org/women>) on the gender pay gap.

It seems clear, however, from experience in Canada, that policies addressing specific complaints in individual workplaces will have little overall effect. More effective would be policies to boost minimum wages for all workers and reduce inequality.

The key to higher wages through collective bargaining is organizing more workers to expand the reach of collective bargaining and bring up entry-level wages. Unions can follow the example of European unions, which have long emphasized solidarity strategies that reduce inequality by "raising the bottom" and by sharing higher productivity through reduced work hours. In Sweden, for example, wages have been based on concepts of equality and providing a living wage, not on the profitability of individual firms or even industries, although this approach is challenged in the new political economy (Acker 1991). In Canada, unions in British Columbia advocated expanding collective bargaining, raising base wage rates, regulating wages for jobs that have been privatized, and establishing mechanisms for raising wages in problem sectors such as manufacturing and retail trade.

A prominent public sector union recently published a new manual that discusses the resurgence of interest in pay equity and suggests that there are many routes to success, including focusing on the lowest-paid jobs, "starting small" by targeting a few classifications, bargaining flat-dollar rather than percentage wage increases, and using the results of former pay equity studies rather than doing one's own (AFSCME 1998). It also advises activists to "make the most of employer job evaluation studies" by advocating for a bias-free evaluation scheme, analysis of gender issues, no downgrades, and an adequate appeals process. This is sound advice and puts the union in the position of working to improve, but not initiate, formal classification and job evaluation studies.

Another avenue is to address inequities in entry-level wages. This is where the largest wage gap often appears, and equalizing entry-level wages within an organization can have a ripple effect throughout job ladders. Formal job evaluation is not needed; rather, jobs can be compared according to minimum qualifications, education levels, and more informal job valuation methods.

A new emphasis on wage equality is needed in bargaining and advocacy work. One approach could be the reformulation of the family wage into a living wage concept. Indeed, an encouraging development is the proliferation of "living wage campaigns" designed to require public jurisdictions and their contractors to pay more than minimum wages for jobs funded with public dollars.

A key lesson from pay equity campaigns is that women can become a powerful force for change when mobilized to act on issues of justice. Women can be activated through social and economic justice campaigns as well as specific occupational efforts. For example, current social justice campaigns attempt to save social services, expand access to health care or child care, fight welfare reform, and stem the deterioration of jobs and services that are "downsized" from the public sector to the private nonprofit sector. These issues have gender implications— women are central to these issues, and their consciousness about their worth can inform and enliven these campaigns as well as improve women's pay.

Specific occupational campaigns could target child-care, health-care, administrative support, and education jobs. All are dominated by women, and the wages and structure of these jobs reflect the legacy of sexism. Union organizing in these jobs could unite women by providing a vehicle to address the low wages and lack of occupational opportunity and structure associated with female-dominated jobs. Further, advocates can reach out to community allies of social services such as child and health care by emphasizing fair treatment for workers crucial for the provision of quality care (see Cobble 1994; Johnston 1994).

Equal pay is also important to families and therefore legitimately part of the struggle for fair and effective work and family policies. Pay equity advocates often argue that pay inequity leaves families with less than two incomes. Additionally, lower pay means that families have to work longer hours, exacerbating the problem of excessive work hours. Policy and union tactics to reduce the workweek might also benefit women by providing more jobs and allowing for more part-time work.

In sum, then, there are many opportunities to approach the broad issue of pay equity. The common threads in each of these campaigns are the participation of women and the emphasis on economic justice. Women workers will organize around issues that speak to their experience as women and as workers. We have learned this much in two decades of struggle for equal pay.

Notes

1. The following description relies on Acker's analysis, my earlier accounts (Hallock 1990 and 1993), state documents, and interviews with state personnel and union participants.

2. One important caveat is that these data cover about fifteen thousand state jobs in general government and higher education. Excluded from this analysis are management jobs and jobs represented by other unions, including some male-dominated units such as corrections and regulatory agencies. A full pay equity analysis should include all jobs within an organization.

References

Acker, Joan. 1987. "Sex Bias in Job Evaluation: A Comparable Worth Issue." In *Ingredients for Women's Employment Policy,* edited by Christine Bose and Glenna Spitze, 183–96. Albany: State University of New York Press.

———. 1989. *Doing Comparable Worth: Gender, Class, and Pay Equity.* Philadelphia: Temple University Press.

———. 1991. "Pay Equity in Sweden and Other Nordic Countries." In *Just Wages: A Feminist Assessment of Pay Equity,* edited by Judy Fudge and Patricia McDermott. Toronto: University of Toronto Press.

AFL-CIO. N.d. *Ask a Working Woman: A Report on the National Survey for the Working Women's Department.*

American Federation of State, County, and Municipal Employees (AFSCME). 1998. *We're Worth It: An AFSCME Guide to Understanding and Implementing Pay Equity.* Washington, DC: AFSCME.

Blau, Francine, and Lawrence M. Kahn. 1997. "Swimming Upstream: Trends in the Gender Wage Differential in the 1980s." Part 1. *Journal of Labor Economics* 15, no. 1:1–42.

Blum, Linda M. 1991. *Between Feminism and Labor: The Significance of the Comparable Worth Movement.* Berkeley: University of California Press.

Brenner, Johanna. 1987. "Feminist Political Discourses: Radical versus Liberal Approaches to the Feminization of Poverty and Comparable Worth." *Gender and Society* 1, no. 4 (December): 447–65.

Bronfenbrenner, Kate, and Tom Juravich. 1995. *Overcoming Barriers to Organizing Women Workers in the Private Sectors.* Washington, DC: Institute for Women's Policy Research.

Cobble, Dorothy Sue. 1994. "Making Postindustrial Unionism Possible." In *Restoring the Promise of American Labor Law,* edited by Sheldon Friedman, Richard W. Hurd, Rudolph O. Oswald, and Ronald L. Seeber, 285–302. Ithaca, NY: ILR Press.

Evans, Sara, and Barbara Nelson. 1989. *Wage Justice: Comparable Worth and the Paradox of Technocratic Reform.* Chicago: University of Chicago Press.

Feldberg, Roslyn L. 1984. "Comparable Worth: Toward Theory and Practice in the United States." *Signs* 10, no. 2:311–28.

Figart, Deborah M., and Peggy Kahn. 1997. *Contesting the Market: Pay Equity and the Politics of Economic Restructuring.* Detroit: Wayne State University Press.

Fudge, Judy. 1991. "Litigating Our Way to Gender Neutrality: Mission Impossible?" In *Just Wages: A Feminist Assessment of Pay Equity,* edited by Judy Fudge and Patricia McDermott. Toronto: University of Toronto Press.

Fudge, Judy, and Patricia McDermott, eds. 1991. *Just Wages: A Feminist Assessment of Pay Equity.* Toronto: University of Toronto Press.

Gardner, Susan, and Christopher Daniel. 1998. "Implementing Comparable Worth: Experiences of Cutting-Edge States." *Public Personnel Management* 24, no. 4 (winter): 475–89.

Gregory, R. G. 1998. *Women's Pay in a Changing Labor Market.* Paris: OECD.

Gunderson, Morley. 1989. "Male-Female Wage Differentials and the Policy Response." *Journal of Economic Literature* 2:46–72.

———. 1994. *Comparable Worth and Gender Discrimination: An International Perspective.* Geneva: International Labor Office.

Hallock, Margaret. 1990. "Pay Equity Outcomes in the Public Sector: Resolving Competing Interests." *Policy Studies Journal* 18, no. 2:421–32.

———. 1993. "Unions and the Gender Wage Gap." In *Women and Unions: Forging a Partnership,* edited by Dorothy Sue Cobble, 27–42. Ithaca, NY: Cornell University Press.

———. 1997. "Organizing and Representing Women: Lessons from the United States." In *Strife: Sex and Politics in Labor Unions,* edited by Barbara Pocock. Sydney, Australia: Allen and Unwin.

Hartmann, Heidi, and Stephanie Aaronson. 1994. "Pay Equity and Women's Wage Increases: Success in the States, A Model for the Nation." *Duke Journal of Gender Law and Policy* 1:69–87.

Institute for Women's Policy Research (IWPR). 1998. "Stall in Women's Real Wage Growth Slows Progress in Closing the Wage Gaps." Briefing Paper. Washington, DC: Institute for Women's Policy Research.

Johnston, Paul. 1994. *Success while Others Fail: Social Movement Unionism and the Public Workplace.* Ithaca, NY: ILR Press.

Malveaux, Julianne. 1985. "Comparable Worth and Its Impact on Black Women." *Review of Black Political Economy* 14:4–27.

McCann, Michael W. 1994. *Rights at Work: Pay Equity Reform and the Politics of Legal Mobilization.* Chicago: University of Chicago Press.

McDermott, Patricia. 1991. "The Pay Equity Challenge to Collective Bargaining in Ontario." In *Just Wages: A Feminist Assessment of Pay Equity,* edited by Judy Fudge and Patricia McDermott. Toronto: University of Toronto Press.

McDonald, Judith, and Robert J. Thornton. 1998. "Private Sector Experience with Pay Equity in Ontario." *Canadian Public Policy* 24, no. 2:185–208.

Milkman, Ruth. 1993. "Union Responses to Workforce Feminization in the U.S." In *The Challenge of Restructuring: North American Labor Movements Respond,* edited by J. Janson and R. Mahon. Philadelphia: Temple University Press.

Mishel, Lawrence, Jared Bernstein, and John Schmitt. 1999. *The State of Working America 1998–99.* Ithaca, NY: Cornell University Press.

National Committee on Pay Equity (NCPE). 1989. *Collective Bargaining for Pay Equity: A Strategy Manual.* Washington, DC: NCPE.

Oregon Executive Department. 1990. "Executive Branch Report to the Legislative Compensation and Classification Committee: Progress in Implementing a New State Job Compensation and Classification System." Personnel and Labor Relations Division. September.

Oregon Revised Statutes. 1998. Chapter 240.190, 240.235, and 240.656.

Oregon Secretary of State. 1994. "A Review of Personnel Pay Practices." Audits Division.

Sorensen, Elaine. 1990. *Wage and Employment Effects of Comparable Worth: The Case of Minnesota.* Washington, DC: Urban Institute.

———. 1994. *Comparable Worth: Is It a Worthy Policy?* Princeton: Princeton University Press.

Steinberg, Ronnie. 1991. "Job Evaluation and Managerial Control: The Politics of Technique and the Techniques of Politics." *Just Wages: A Feminist Assessment of Pay Equity,* edited by Judy Fudge and Patricia McDermott, 193–218. Toronto: University of Toronto Press.

———. 1992. "Gendered Instructions: Cultural Lag and Gender Bias in the Hay System of Job Evaluation." *Work and Occupations* 19:387–432.

———. 1999. "Measuring Emotional Labor in Job Evaluation: Redesigning Compensation Practices." In *Emotional Labor in the Service Economy,* edited by Ronnie Steinberg and Deborah M. Figart. Annals of the American Academy of Political and Social Science, vol. 561. Thousand Oaks, CA: Sage Publications.

Task Force on State Compensation and Classification Equity. 1985. "Final Report and Recommendations." State of Oregon.

Just Ask: Women's Strengths in Collective Bargaining

Peter Donohue

There is more talk now about workers organizing unions than in fifty years, and more and more, women are doing the talking. Instead of asking what "the union" can do for them, they're listening to one another to figure out what to do themselves.

Women's experiences are increasingly the center of attention for unions, both because of women's increasing numbers in the workforce and because women's strengths in building and maintaining relationships can build and strengthen unions.

Building relationships takes time. In this case, relationships had already been built. The nurses' contract was expiring, and changes needed to be made at the nonprofit community hospital of a small farm and mill town. Mobilizing relationships already in place, nurses talked about their goals and strategies with co-workers and neighbors. Nurses changed the way that bargaining was conducted, demanding and getting a more civil conversation focused on problem solving. The nurses themselves played the major roles in developing union proposals and bargaining for a contract that improved their pay and working conditions.

After discovering how "profitable" their nonprofit hospital was, the nurses were confident that their bargaining goals were responsible and just. They drew on their relationships and asked for help from family, friends, neighbors, government officials, hospital board members, businesses, and the press to persuade the hospital administration to do the right thing without interrupting patient care. On the eve of a threatened strike, the local newspaper endorsed the union's proposals, and the nurses won their contract—all in barely eight weeks.

Key to winning a decent contract and resolution of festering workplace issues was the way the nurses used their existing relationships to build support at work and across the community, supplemented by union research and coaching. The nurses' professional values prioritizing patient care and rejecting the itinerant management's "strictly business" posture found a strong response in the community.

More than management, more than the doctors, more than other staff, the nurses are the hospital of the community, as the poet Wendell Berry defines it.

> By community, I mean the commonwealth and common interests, commonly understood, of people living in a place and wishing to continue to do so. To put it another way, community is a locally understood interdependence of local people, local culture, local economy and local nature. (*Sex, Economy, Freedom and Community* [New York: Pantheon, 1993])

Members of the local community themselves, the nurses understood that their power was their ability to influence rather than to control hospital and community behavior. Their bargaining initiatives were chosen—and sometimes reassessed—both for their leverage at the table and for their impact within the community. As a consultant working with the nurses' union, I participated in and learned from the process too. What follows is the story of a group of small-town nurses who stood up to a successful hospital administration and won.

Background

Silverton, Oregon, is a former wood-products mill town of seven thousand that is still the commercial center for even smaller farm, food-processing, and agricultural-nursery-based villages surrounding it. The town is close enough to the state capital, Salem, to also be the home of a growing number of commuters. The thirty-eight-bed community hospital is far enough from competitors to be residents' primary health-care provider. The hospital recently added a new wing, with a city-backed mortgage that was quickly retired with donations credited to its much-traveled—and very highly paid—hospital administrator's fund-raising acumen.

Silverton nurses are the hospital's best-known public face, caring for local residents through birth, illness, trauma, and death. A core of veteran nurses who have long staffed the hospital's surgery, emergency, delivery, and primary care units are also familiar in town as friends, neighbors, church members, customers, and family. Many nurses are longtime community residents.

The same senior nurses lead the local union, an Oregon Nurses Association chapter representing registered nurses day to day with their employer and in contract negotiations, aided by a union staff representative. The Oregon Nurses Association, like its counterparts in other states, only relatively recently combined the traditional professional development activities that include nurse managers with conventional union functions, including representation of staff nurses through collective bargaining. As elsewhere, this is an uneasy mixture, because the bargaining side's dues subsidize other association activities often conducted with nurse managers against whom staff nurses bargain.

At Silverton, the experience of the veteran registered nurses (RNs) is invaluable for the more transient doctors and is vital for new grad, temporary, and "registry" nurses that the hospital employed frequently to fill the empty shifts resulting from its cost-cutting policy of short staffing. In profitable surgery and emergency units, next to impossible to staff with registry nurses, the hospital counted on double twelve-hour shifts by regular RNs. One nurse, a bargaining committee member during contract negotiations, was often called upon for double shifts, although she officially worked part-time!

Her story and those of others exemplify the nurses' ruefully admitted codependency in caring for others at the expense of their own health. The hospital was ready to exploit the nurses' dedication to their jobs, knowing they were reluctant to say no to caring for patients and additional income. Many nurses would regularly staff extra or extended shifts, despite knowing that their acquiescence enabled hospital management to maintain a policy of inadequate staffing, especially in certified specialties.

Without an adequate number of nurses certified in some specialties, managers struggled to implement hospital nursing directives. The nursing director, not a Silverton resident, was always under pressure from the hospital president to contain patient care costs. Nurse managers have come and gone often, leaving frequent vacancies, so that senior RNs regularly had to step in to schedule and direct patient care.

The results of a prebargaining survey confirmed that understaffing was among the Silverton Nurses Association's biggest concerns in renegotiating the contract that was expiring after two years. Linked to staffing concerns was the hospital's refusal to provide paid time off or to make retirement contributions for hours worked beyond regularly scheduled shifts. Even though benefits were low—the retirement contribution was a miserable $100 per month, only $36,000 for thirty years of full-time employment—the hospital lacked any incentive to increase staffing. It relied instead on regular overtime, especially in emergency, surgery, and delivery units where registry nurses are available only at high premiums, if at all.

After supporting a building drive for the hospital's new wing by settling for minimal wage increases in the expiring contract, the nurses were irate over management's plan for nurses to pay for increases in health insurance premiums. Still more aggravating was that contractually negotiated educational benefits were being used for "educational" junkets of nonunion managers, while nurses were denied funding for recertification courses.

During preparation for bargaining, the association staff representative, anticipating other demands, recruited me as an economic consultant to help with Silverton's negotiations. Their proposals ready, the bargaining committee wanted help developing a contract strategy, research, and coaching. I focused our research on nurses' pay and benefits at comparable hospitals and the hospital's overall financial condition, because of the hospital's claim of limited resources during the previous negotiations as well as during the new-wing fund drive.

Interestingly, the hospital's nonprofit IRS filings over the past five years (see table 8.1) told a different story.

1. Net revenues were up from $0.5m to $2.14m;
2. net worth had risen in each of the past five years (11, 19, 43, 39, and 23 percent); and
3. funds available for any purpose (including paying nurses) had grown each year (11, 20, 43, 39, and 12 percent) and now totaled over $18 million.

A one-page summary of this information assured the nurses on the bargaining committee of the hospital's ability to meet their proposals' costs. It also made many angry at the way the hospital management had misrepresented the hospital's overall financial condition in previ-

TABLE 8.1. Forms 990 Highlights

Year	Line 18 Year Excess	Line 21 Change in Net Assets	Line 59 Change in Total Assets	Line 67 (Line 74*) Unrestricted Assets Change	Schedule A William Winter's Pay	Schedule A William Winter's Benefits
1995	$2,139,097	23%	11%	12%	$134,404 (+40%)	$147,328 (plus)
1994	$2,599,294	39%	70%	39%	$95,740	?
1993	$1,982,569	43%	26%	43%	$109,002	?
1992	$750,946	19%	20%	20%	$119,251	?
1991	$546,614	11%	21%	11%	$77,661	?

Source: Author's computations of IRS filings

Year Excess = Annual Revenues – Annual Expenditures, i.e., a nonprofit's "profits"

Net Assets = Total Assets – Liabilities, i.e., net worth

Unrestricted Assets = funds available for any purpose a non0profit chooses

ous bargaining. The realization that the hospital president had received more than a 40 percent raise, from $96,000 to $134,000, and another $147,000 in deferred compensation at the same time infuriated the nurses even more.

In stark contrast, while nurses' starting pay was comparable to pay elsewhere, wages for nurses with ten or more years at Silverton had fallen further and further behind (see fig. 8.1), and the hospital's monthly retirement contribution was far below benefit levels elsewhere. Compensation practices aggravated staffing difficulties; encouraged turnover, jeopardizing patient care; and exploited veteran RNs' commitment to patient care.

A "Do-It-Yourself" Counterstrategy

Upset by the evidence that they enabled the hospital's strategy, the nurses' bargaining committee and I developed a counterstrategy of "Do It Yourself" to realize the nurses' goals by drawing on their strengths in bargaining, at work and in their community. The strategy was for the nurses themselves to handle professional issues at the bargaining table, serve as liaisons with nurses not involved directly in the bargaining and other co-workers, and make the vast majority of outside contacts with members of the hospital's board, local officials, and the press.

In bargaining, each committee member presented the proposals, arguments, and evidence about which that individual was most confident. Other committee members would offer evidence or arguments, but new or modified proposals were discussed together before

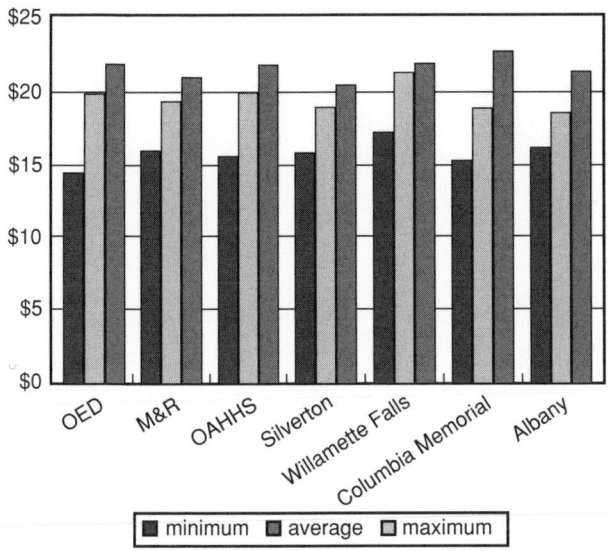

FIG. 8.1. The longer registered nurses stay at Silverton Hospital, the farther and farther their hourly wage rates fall behind those of their counterparts at other Oregon hospitals. (Data from Oregon Employment Department; Oregon Nurses Association.) Minimum, average, and maximum refer to nurses' pay schedule.

being presented to hospital management negotiators. As the consultant, I made the case for general wage increases.

Another of my functions was to block the hospital attorney's attempts to direct the bargaining process. The attorney clearly hoped to operate as he always had, to undermine nurses' sense of competence at the bargaining table and to plow through the contract in lawyerly language, wearing the nurses out with procedural questions and legalistic language about work rules—which govern issues such as scheduling practices—so that they would have little energy or confidence left to address pay issues.

The hospital's attorney started by grumbling about the committee's size. He bridled at the committee's resistance to discussing work rules before taking up wage and benefit issues. His "table manners" had to change, at the insistence of the nurses' bargaining committee, which would not tolerate hectoring or belittling. The nurses requested that the nursing director prevent any such unprofessional conduct toward fellow hospital employees.

The hospital's attorney also attempted to prevent the nurses from directing their proposals to change nursing practice to the hospital nursing director, who had a close working relationship with the same senior nurses who now faced her across the bargaining table. The nurses' strategy was to make the nursing director, not the hospital attorney, discuss all nursing proposals and to promote concrete problem solving, rather than legalistic haggling.

Changes in bargaining ground rules went beyond the bargaining table, to encompass greater involvement of nurses not on the bargaining committee than in the past. With a larger bargaining committee than previously, more nurses talked to more co-workers about bargaining issues while at work. The union held shift-change rallies to communicate new developments, proposals, and strategies. Nurses on the bargaining committee were responsible for creating and implementing strategies, as well as sharing them with nurses and other staff on duty.

The one-page summary of the hospital's overall financial condition that we had pulled together was circulated widely in the hospital. It also made its way around Silverton and the surrounding communities, as nurses talked with family, friends, neighbors, businesspeople, teachers, and others concerned or curious about what was happening at the hospital. We had spent some time early on talking with local newspaper reporters about why nurses were not happy with the situation at the hospital. Public interest jumped when the local papers then were ready to recount details of hospital finances and the nurses' proposals after each union press release. Negotiations became a community issue, not just a private concern at the hospital.

The importance of the battle for public opinion was grasped late by the hospital president. After regular and extensive front-page coverage in local daily and weekly community newspapers, the hospital spokesperson insisted that there was no reason for public concern—even after the nurses had filed the federally mandated ten-day notice of a potential strike. But what went on at the hospital was a community concern, fueled by nurses sharing their own perspectives and experiences.

The hospital president was an itinerant hospital administrator and, like the nursing director, lived out of town. Already remote from staff and daily hospital operations, he refused to meet with the nurses, even as the strike deadline approached. This may have been his standard operating procedure, but it worked against him in the eyes of the public as the nurses' press releases regularly highlighted his distance from the community.

The hospital president's remoteness compelled nurses and other community residents to ask the hospital board of directors to intervene. Though handpicked by the president, board members lived in Silverton or communities nearby. The board included the Silverton school superintendent, local bankers, realtors, insurance agents, the largest local employer, a nurse, a senior staff doctor, and a minister. All board members were known by sight to nurses at the hospital. Many were acquaintances or neighbors; almost as many were friends; and some were family. Though reluctant to become involved in the negotiations as a board, most directors were in fact involved with nurses personally and were uncomfortable when nurses and others asked them to help. Meanwhile the newspapers cranked up their coverage of the bargaining.

At the bargaining table, on the job, and in the community, the nurses linked the hospital's robust financial condition with nurses' efforts and the justice of their proposals, asking the community for fairness at their community's hospital.

Making It Happen

Besides differences over ground rules, the initial bargaining session annoyed nurses when, after the nurses had provided their proposals, the hospital attorney declined to do so, saying that the hospital never provided its proposals at the first session—despite having demanded proposals from the union even before negotiations began.

A week later, the nurses' committee handed over new proposals to hospital negotiators. Skimming them, the attorney reacted angrily when he saw that each wage proposal was increased. He accused the nurses of bad-faith bargaining, saying that the union proposals were supposed to go down, not up. But without any hospital proposals, the committee doubted their own bad faith. They told the attorney that bargaining would be like using a credit card: if the hospital did not produce proposals now, a settlement would cost more later.

To spur negotiations, the nurses held an on-site evening shift-change rally before the third scheduled bargaining session. At the rally nurses were urged to report unsafe staffing situations to state hospital regulators. To highlight the nurses' goal to radically increase the hospital's miserly $100 a month retirement contribution, nurse-designed buttons were distributed, asserting that "Nurses Deserve to Retire, Too!"

Hospital negotiators failed to make proposals on wages and benefits at the third session. The nurses' committee balked, saying that without economic proposals from the hospital, they would not discuss other issues. They did not want to be trapped into wearing themselves out before addressing money questions. Irritated, hospital negotiators left to caucus, returning three hours later with wage and benefit proposals. Meeting separately to review hospital proposals, the union committee was jubilant. Real discussion had begun.

Success in changing the bargaining ground rules encouraged fifty-one of seventy nurses to participate in the next shift-change rally. Elation was mixed with anger, as nurses beyond those on the bargaining committee discovered the facts of the hospital's unexpected financial well-being and the president's $281,732 pay. The nurses decided to post the five-year summary of hospital finances prominently around the hospital and to continue to repost it as it was removed by managers. A group of volunteers drafted a letter relating nurses' concerns to board members, asking them to urge the president to come to the bargaining table. Copies of this letter were faxed to local newspapers.

The following day the bargaining committee met with hospital negotiators, amid rumors that the president, irate over disclosure of his pay, had verbally blistered the nursing director for providing hospital's IRS filings—legally public information—to the committee. But after one half-hour discussing "language" items such as scheduling practices, hospital negotiators failed to offer a retirement proposal, provoking the committee to end negotiations, saying that hospital negotiators should think over the nurses' determination. The nurses had things to do other than sit at the bargaining table.

The bargaining committee feared that the hospital would claim an impasse and call for official mediation, undercutting the union's strategy of building support at the hospital and in the community. The nurses developed a "climb-down strategy" of union concessions and planned visits to members of the board of directors and other community members. They sent out another press release, headed "Care for the Caregivers," that resulted in a front-page article in the next day's state capital newspaper. One step discussed, but that nurses were unwilling to take, was to refuse extra shifts, which would have shut down particular hospital departments and exposed the hospital's policy of deliberate understaffing.

Also at the strategy session, nurses talked over their desire for more information on the hospital's financial situation. Earlier, the committee had requested public information about the hospital's finances. Rather than comply, the hospital's attorney had complained about another request for also-public information about the hospital foundation and the city health-care-financing authority that had backed the mortgage for the new wing with local property tax receipts.

Members of the bargaining committee, with other nurses along, went to the hospital foundation's executive director to track down some of this financial information. The director was panicked by the nurses crowding into her office and refused to provide them with the foundation's IRS filings detailing the foundation's connections with the hospital, despite the fact that these are legally required to be available for public inspection. She blurted out that the hospital president had ordered her not to show the IRS filings to the nurses and insisted that the records had to be obtained through the hospital's attorney negotiator.

Word of the foundation's refusal to share public documents spread around the hospital. When the nurses visited the city's health-care-financing authority, they discovered that the hospital's state-mandated current annual report was not available—or even on record with the state attorney general's office that monitored the hospital's state-tax-exempt status. The hospital's labor attorney was appreciative when I called to alert him that the hospital president's gag order jeopardized the hospital's federal- and state-tax-exempt status and quickly agreed to get us copies of these public records.

Widening Discussion

Excitement filled the room at the next week's shift-change meeting, which almost every nurse attended. The news coverage in the capital daily and the local weeklies had heightened awareness about negotiations both at the hospital and throughout the surrounding communities. The doctors' executive medical committee was meeting to draft a letter urging the president to prevent a strike, and some doctors were wearing the nurses' buttons. Unless hospital negotiators made a retirement proposal at next day's session, the nurses agreed that a strike-authorization vote would be held immediately.

Before the session began, the hospital's attorney handed over the foundation's IRS 990s and the health-care-financing authority's state filings. He warned me to be careful with the contents, a puzzling remark at first since the union had long before obtained copies from the IRS. But a quick review showed that these copies included donor lists that had been removed from the IRS-provided copies. Now the nurses had the opportunity to tell prospective donors about the hospital's abundant resources less than two months before the hospital president's next fund-raising drive.

The hospital attorney had proposed that nurses pay all premium increases for health insurance or accept a flat $300 monthly payment to provide their own health insurance. But there would be no retirement proposal available until the president returned to review it later that day. While caucusing to consider the health insurance proposals, committee members quickly recognized that both hospital proposals meant lower take-home pay for nurses within two years.

The hospital attorney returned to the bargaining table, still without a retirement proposal, and put forward a general wage increase labeled "the going market rate increase." This proposal did not even bring Silverton nurses' pay up to the average among comparable hospitals nearby and failed to correct the current practice of leaving senior nurses far behind their counterparts elsewhere. Three hours later, still without a retirement proposal, discussion turned to the related problem of paid time off being earned only on scheduled hours worked, instead of all hours worked.

Careful not to risk impasse, the committee offered its climb-down financial proposals as a small step in good-faith bargaining. After twelve hours at the bargaining table, the hospital's attorney shook his head incredulously, saying that the union's climb-down offers were "way over market." As the session ended, he was reminded that the hospital was a tax-exempt community facility and that union proposals reflected community values. The attorney allowed that he was beginning to believe that the market really did not matter to the nurses.

Staying the Course

The next day the nurses posted one of two hard-hitting posters—replicated in figure 8.2—reminding people of the president's hypocrisy in pleading for nurses to accept minimal raises while taking the highest pay of any hospital president in the state. The poster showed what percentage of the president's annual pay it would take to cover the union proposals to improve the pay and benefits of seventy nurses for two years.

But many nurses objected to the poster's aggressive tone and to another that played off an earlier "good work" memo from the hospital to the nurses that had been presented in the form of a "check." The check had been inscribed "Thanks a Million to the Silverton Nurses" for helping the hospital to set financial records the year before. The nurses' poster relabeled the check "Thanks a Million—Not!" But the committee quickly learned that these posters made some other nurses uncomfortable. The bargaining committee had to be more careful not

HOW MANY WINTERS IS THAT?

William Winter got $134,404 in pay, and $147,328 in benefits or $281,732 total pay in 1995, according to Hospital IRS filings.

How many Winters would it take to pay 70 Silverton Hospital Nurses:

• 6% more wages? [Hint: in 1995 William Winter got a 40% raise.]

70 x $36,000 (avg.) x 6% = $151,200 or 0.43 OF A

• 4% more retirement? [Hint: in ONE year William Winter got almost THREE TIMES what a Nurse gets working full time for THIRTY YEARS.]

70 x $36,000 x 4% = $100,800 or 0.35 OF A

IMPROVING 70 NURSES' PAY & RETIREMENT WOULD COST $252,000 —NEARLY $30,000 LESS THAN WILLIAM WINTER WAS PAID IN ONE YEAR!

FIG. 8.2. How many Winters is that? (Data from author's computations of IRS filings.)

to let bargaining table frustrations push them out too far ahead of other nurses not at the table.

Three days later, barely a month after bargaining began, negotiations resumed. We developed an endgame spreadsheet for monitoring proposals and agreements to use at the table and to show nurses where issues stood. Progress had been made in resolving pay differentials for overtime, holiday, call-in, and extended shifts, but discussion turned acrimonious over the nursing director's abuse—called "outright theft"—of union-negotiated educational benefits, as these had been given to nursing managers not in the union but denied to nurses pursuing professional development.

Following a lunch break, the hospital attorney mischievously challenged the nurses to show whether the nurses currently had any health insurance, since the contract had expired. Adjourning to find out the facts, the committee warned that if insurance coverage was missing, all of the nurses' wage and benefit proposals would be increased. At the following session two days later, the committee reminded hospital negotiators that the health insurance plan was in place through the following year, and the question was withdrawn.

At that evening's shift-change meeting, committee members were admonished not to do "mean things"—like the more aggressive posters—that undercut the nurses' professional dignity. Then the nurses authorized an open letter/press release, titled "The Time for Silence Is Over," that called for the board of directors to speak up. A silent demonstration at the board's meeting was planned, and two days later, a majority of the nursing staff, with their families and supporters, stood quietly outside the meeting. Board members skulked in through the back door to avoid reporters and photographers, who put the story on the front page of the capital's daily.

Community supporters redoubled efforts to meet with board members individually and distributed another open letter/press release, headed "It Just Won't Do," that chided the board for its failure to intervene with the president. Strike preparation escalated. The nurses made plans to boycott a hospital-sponsored picnic and to refuse to staff the hospital's booth at the annual Silverton Days celebration, while readying their own blood-pressure testing station that would be next to the hospital booth. Police, firefighters, and emergency medical technicians announced that they would not take patients through the nurses' picket line if the nurses were to strike.

That evening bargaining resumed, with the nurses' committee insisting on more nighttime sessions. More information was demanded about whether hospital accounting of late federal Medicaid payments had been treated as income payments or as unpaid liabilities that diminished the hospital's appearance of financial well-being. When hospital negotiators failed to offer new pay and benefit proposals, the committee caucused, then canceled negotiations to prepare instead for a strike-authorization vote and to wait for a hospital proposal as the strike deadline approached.

The nurses' filing of a strike notice with the Federal Mediation and Conciliation Service charged the atmosphere. On the eve of the strike vote, the local newspaper published a front-page-banner headline story and an editorial cartoon endorsing the nurses' efforts (see fig. 8.3). Communicating through the mediator, hospital negotiators suggested the hospital might agree to a settlement that the committee had previously indicated they could recommend to nurses for ratification once the hospital made it in writing. In the interim, a strike vote carried 59–2 but was postponed for ten days pending the hospital offer.

Later the committee recommended—and the nurses ratified—an agreement that included three annual 4 percent wage increases, an

FIG. 8.3. Cartoon published in Silverton newspaper. (From *Silverton Appeal Tribune,* August 14, 1997. © Syd Stibbard. Reprinted by permission.)

increase in the retirement contribution from $100 to $500 monthly, no health insurance premium increases, and union control of educational benefits. Nonscheduled work still does not earn additional paid time off, but nurses can refuse unscheduled shifts.

Conclusion

Silverton nurses' "overnight success" in achieving their bargaining goals came through making their contract the community's concern. Ties with other staff, neighbors, friends, and family members were mobilized quickly. Nurses' collaborative work skills, well developed from customarily taking charge on the job, let me help nurses do it themselves, rather than to substitute for them. Our research high-lighted the strength of the nurses' case and the leverage they had at the bargaining table. The hospital's robust financial condition was linked to nurses' efforts and prior sacrifices. Staffing problems were linked to substandard pay for senior nurses and retirement benefits. Simple explanations of the issues were shared at work and with neighbors, which bolstered the nurses' confidence and embarrassed the hospital administration.

With some coaching, the nurses figured out how to use their strengths and opportunities to advantage. More important, as I always reminded them, getting a contract depended not on which side exerted more pressure but on which side could endure more. Hospital management never had a chance.

PART 3

Moving Women into Higher-Paying Work

9

Promoting Women's Economic Progress through Affirmative Action

M. V. Lee Badgett and Jeannette Lim

The Need for Affirmative Action

Women's inferior position in the labor market is obvious by all available measures, such as women's lower wages and lower-status jobs. One common explanation for these differences is that women experience discrimination in employment—employers treat men better than equally qualified women. Discrimination can have two effects on women's wages. It can exclude women from higher-paying jobs, and it can result in women being paid less than men doing the same job. Equalizing earnings would require addressing both problems.

In theory, policy has addressed both discrimination issues. Outright discrimination is patently illegal. The Equal Pay Act of 1963 outlaws paying women less than men when they hold the same job, and Title VII of the 1964 Civil Rights Act forbids the use of sex to determine wages, hiring, promotion, or other employment decisions. A woman who believes an employer has treated her unfairly based on her sex can file a complaint with the Equal Employment Opportunity Commission (or a state version of the federal agency), which will investigate complaints and will sue employers who appear to be guilty of discrimination. Studies suggest that these laws have contributed to small but noticeable improvements in earnings and occupational attainment for women (Beller 1977, 1979, 1982) and for people of color.

Even after thirty-five years of enforcement, however, these laws appear to have been insufficient for removing more than a portion of economic inequality. Two general reasons have been offered. The first is that generations of inequality and other social processes might have reduced the ability of women and people of color to compete with white men for jobs. Fewer years of education, different college majors, inferior schools, and other social pressures might have hindered the progress of disadvantaged groups.

The second reason is that an individual-complaint-driven enforcement process has some obvious problems. Complaints tend to be personally costly to file. Discrimination is not always obvious to a job applicant. A female applicant may have been turned away because someone else was more qualified or because the employer preferred to hire a man—but the woman who did not get the job might never know which happened. Employers might believe and say that they are acting fairly even when their decisions are driven by an unconscious bias. Certain job requirements might be applied equally to all job candidates but might not be necessary, such as a requirement for physical strength in a desk job. Affirmative action was designed to address both sets of issues.

Like many topics of fervent political debate, however, affirmative action as a policy tool for reducing labor market inequities is often misunderstood. In 1965 President Lyndon B. Johnson gave affirmative action meaning in his Executive Order 11246, which required affirmative action by companies doing business with the federal government. In its origins, affirmative action embodied some notion of making extra efforts to locate, recruit, and train disadvantaged workers who might not otherwise be hired, practices often referred to as "soft" affirmative action.

As the intractability of many forms of bias and the difficulties of assessing employers' intentions became more obvious, increasingly people started using the actual results of employers' hiring practices to identify the points in a hiring process that unfairly weeded out women and people of color. Results-oriented affirmative action, described more fully in the next section, means that if companies are hiring fewer women than they should given the availability of qualified female candidates, then they must develop goals for hiring and a timetable for meeting those goals over the next few years.

Although affirmative action does not typically focus on wages and salaries, such programs are likely to result in greater equalization of women's and men's wages. Actually paying women less than men in exactly the same job is relatively rare, studies show, but shutting women out of high-paying occupations and high-paying companies appears to be more common. Research suggests the primary causes of women's lower wages are that women are employed in lower-paying occupations and work for lower-paying employers (Groshen 1991; Petersen and Morgan 1995). While some women might choose lower-paying occupations voluntarily (perhaps because those jobs provide more flexibility for meeting family responsibilities or because women are socialized to prefer certain kinds of jobs that are traditionally low paying), there is no obvious reason why they would prefer to work in lower-paying firms, suggesting that discrimination plays a role in creating this pay disadvantage.

To see how affirmative action might increase women's wages in light of those patterns, consider the results of a 1996 study by economist David Neumark and some of his students. The researchers matched up pairs of men and women, who were given resumes equivalent in experience and then separately applied for jobs waiting on tables at Philadelphia restaurants. Some of the restaurants were fancy, high-priced eating establishments; others were low-priced diners; and some fell in between in terms of prices charged. If employers were hiring without regard to sex, then the man and woman in each pair should have had the same chance of being offered a job at each restaurant. However, Neumark found that 48 percent of the male applicants received job offers from the high-priced restaurants but only 9 percent of the female applicants did. In the low-priced restaurants, the opposite pattern occurred, and 38 percent of the women but only 10 percent of the men were offered jobs.

Although the study did not directly compare the wages of men and women who already worked for the fancy restaurants, let us suppose that they were, in fact, equal. What impact does the employment discrimination observed have on the wages of men and women who are waitpersons? Since the fancy high-priced restaurants generated the highest tips, employment discrimination also caused wage inequality between men and women, because men were hired into high-paying jobs and women into low-paying jobs.

If the expensive restaurants were required to implement an affirmative action plan that included a utilization study, their managers would probably find that the proportion of women hired was vastly lower than the proportion of women in their applicant pool and lower than the proportion of women who were already waitpersons in the Philadelphia area. Over time, as normal turnover occurred and as the businesses grew, the restaurants could meet their goals by hiring more women than they had been hiring before the implementation of the affirmative action plan. As more women got jobs in these restaurants, perhaps by leaving their jobs waiting on tables at less expensive restaurants, the average earnings of women would also rise relative to men's earnings in Philadelphia.

That example illustrates the potential for affirmative action to increase women's earnings. The remainder of this chapter examines the actual record of affirmative action in improving women's labor market position. The following section outlines which employers and how many employers must have affirmative action plans. The next two sections describe the impact of affirmative action, based on qualitative in-depth studies of a few companies and quantitative studies of many firms. In the final section, we explore and recommend policies that would push affirmative action to live up to its potential.

Mandated Affirmative Action Plans

Employers that are legally required to implement an affirmative action plan fall into one of three categories: (1) federal contractors, (2) government agencies, and (3) employers that have been ordered by the courts to do so or have signed a consent decree as a result of a lawsuit. Some employers also voluntarily adopt affirmative action policies. In this section, we will outline the basis for the mandates and their respective regulations.

Federal Contractors

Executive Order 11246, as amended, requires contractors and first-tier subcontractors with federal contracts of $50,000 or more and at least fifty employees to produce written affirmative action plans. The Office of Federal Contract Compliance Programs (OFCCP), the government agency charged with ensuring the contractors' adherence to the executive order, describes an affirmative action plan as "a set of specific and result-oriented procedures to which a contractor commits himself to apply every good faith effort" (OFCCP 1980).

Federal contractors are required to conduct a utilization study to determine whether there are any discrepancies between the representation of women and minorities in their workforce and in the labor force available to them. If women and people of color are underrepresented in the firm, the employer must (1) eliminate discriminatory practices and (2) take affirmative action, such as targeted recruiting and training, to correct the deficiency. Contractors must set hiring goals and timetables for meeting these goals. The focus of affirmative action plans is on outcomes; underrepresentation is considered evidence of barriers to equal employment opportunity.

An important point is that goals and timetables are different from the rigid quotas that are often the topic of debate around affirmative action. In fact, the OFCCP regulations stipulate that "Goals may not be rigid and inflexible quotas which must be met, but must be targets reasonably attainable by means of applying every good faith effort to make all aspects of the entire affirmative action program work" (OFCCP 1980).

The OFCCP periodically audits selected firms for adherence to their programs. To avoid sanctions federal contractors only need to demonstrate that they have made a "good faith effort" to reach their goals. These audits involve reviewing the contractor's personnel, payroll, and other employment records, as well as the contractor's workforce analysis, utilization analysis, and goals for underutilized groups. The contractor's policies and progress toward achieving goals are judged against a "reasonableness standard." The equal opportunity specialist assigned to audit the firm also looks into any complaints made against the contractor to the Equal Employment Opportunity Commission (EEOC), state and local fair employment agencies, and the Veterans Employment and Training Service (U.S. Department of Labor 1999; Turner 1990). If the contractor does not comply with the executive order, the firm could face debarment, that is, be declared ineligible for any future government contracts (U.S. Department of Labor 1999). While affirmative action mandated by federal contracts does not cover a large number of companies, many of these companies are very big, so that the contracts apply to about 20 percent of the nation's labor force (Reskin 1998).

Government Agencies

Executive Order 11246 also called for affirmative action in federal agencies by directing them to "promote the full realization of equal opportunity." The 1972 Equal Employment Opportunity Act reinforced the executive order by requiring federal agencies to take "positive steps" to achieve equal employment opportunity. These positive steps resemble the affirmative action policies expected of federal contractors, such as the development of equal employment opportunity goals, plans of how to achieve those goals, and recruitment efforts to diversify job candidate pools.

During the 1990s approximately 3 million federal employees were covered by these regulations (Reskin 1998). In addition, many state and local agencies are also subject to their own executive orders or statutes mandating affirmative action. In 1989, at least thirty-five states and the District of Columbia had such laws (Hill and Jones 1993).

Court-Ordered/Consent Decrees

A third set of employers is required to have affirmative action programs either because they have been found guilty of discrimination or because they have negotiated a court-approved settlement in response to a charge of discrimination. In this instance, a court may require a firm to hire specific proportions of women or minorities. That is, a court-ordered affirmative action program or a consent decree can mandate quotas. However, the use of quotas can only be a temporary remedy for a specific job and cannot completely block employment or promotion of members of the majority group.

Voluntary Affirmative Action Programs

Many employers voluntarily implement affirmative action programs. There are a variety of reasons why an employer might do this: (1) a firm might have once been a federal contractor or hope to be a contractor in the future; (2) a firm might have an affirmative action plan to try to prevent lawsuits; (3) the employer may value a diverse workforce either because it gives the firm a competitive edge or because it is a desirable social goal; or (4) there may be a "spillover" effect from mandated affirmative action plans within the same industry. That is, mandated affirmative action programs may contribute to the development of an industry norm encouraging all firms within the industry to have an affirmative action plan. Also, because a mandated affirmative action plan may have resulted from improper employer practices that are common within an industry, other firms in the industry have a greater incentive to adopt an affirmative action program to protect themselves from lawsuits. Voluntary programs run the gamut from advertising as an affirmative action employer to basing part of a manager's compensation on his or her record of recruiting, hiring, and promoting individuals from underrepresented groups. Reskin (1998) presents estimates that about one-fifth of U.S. workers are employed at firms with some form of voluntary affirmative action policy.

Qualitative Evidence of
Affirmative Action's Impact

In this section, we will consider how affirmative action policies attack barriers to integrating occupations by examining three case studies that provide concrete details of affirmative action policies and their effects. In order to understand the rationale behind the affirmative action policies discussed in these case studies, we need to first think about what kinds of barriers to desegregation affirmative action policies need to overcome. Barriers can arise in different stages of the employment process, including the recruitment of job applicants, the hiring process, and job promotions.

The first barrier is the absence of women in the pool of applicants for male-dominated jobs. Employers often rely on informal, word-of-mouth advertising, which tends to produce a pool of candidates that resembles the current set of employees since people often have friends and acquaintances of their own gender or race (Braddock and McPartland 1987). Also, if an occupation has traditionally been dominated by white men, white women and people of color might be discouraged from applying because they have been socialized away from that occupation, lack (or lack access to) the necessary skills or training, and/or have pessimistic expectations for successful employment (Pettigrew and Martin 1987; Deaux and Ullman 1983).

Another barrier to occupational integration is biased hiring procedures. One source of bias is employers' use of stereotypes in their evaluation of job candidates. Employers who have little time or few resources to gather outside information about an applicant may rely on what they perceive to be true, on average, about a group to judge its individual members. Stereotyping is a common way that people organize how they think about individuals, and so the stereotype is an easy and familiar, although unfair, way to form judgments. For example, an employer may assume that women are not good management material because the employer stereotypes women as nonassertive, timid, too emotional, or perhaps not willing to "go all out" for the company because of family responsibilities. In this way, sexist stereotypes damage women's labor market position. Another way hiring procedures may be biased is by using qualifications that are not tied to job performance but that favor a particular group, such as unnecessary educational requirements that favor whites or, as we will discuss subsequently in the case of the steel industry, unnecessary physical requirements that favor men.

Once hired, women often face difficulties in advancing up the pay scale beyond an entry-level position. Employers sometimes exclude women from pivotal positions that provide crucial training and access to career ladders. Also, the same biases and stereotypes that affect the hiring of women can enter into the evaluation of an employee's job performance and potential to advance successfully. Finally, women may be put at a disadvantage in their ability to perform well in their jobs if male co-workers' hostility or indifference to women isolates them from informal networks that provide important sources of information and support. Golf outings, for example, often provide social settings in which business tips are shared, contacts are made, and agreements reached. If female co-workers are not invited, they will be locked out of the informal business forums that help foster a career.

This brief overview of the different kinds of barriers to women moving into male-dominated occupations points to some affirmative action policies that are straightforward and can be monitored, such as recruiting through community outreach to women's organizations. However, barriers to integrating occupations are also formed by subjective biases that are not easily addressed or easily monitored. Ultimately, the only concrete gauge for the presence or absence of barriers is whether women's employment shares and occupational distribution reflect their representation in the labor force with respect to skills and availability. For that reason quantitative goals and timetables are important. The case studies that follow reveal how three firms have confronted these challenges.

Craft Occupations in Steel

Deaux and Ullman (1983) provide a detailed study of two midwestern integrated steel plants from 1965 to 1980, covering the period during which nine major steel companies and the United Steelworkers of America signed a consent decree with the federal government. The impetus for the decree was the mounting number of court cases brought against the steel companies and the United Steel Workers of America (USWA) charging that their seniority policies and employment were discriminatory (Ichniowski 1983). The decree directed the steel companies to analyze the minority and female representation in each craft occupation. If representation of women and minority groups was found to be disproportionately low, the companies had to establish goals to increase their numbers. Further, to achieve these goals, the decree stipulated that 50 percent of new transfers into craft occupations had to be members of a minority group or female. One of the plants in the study was a signatory to the consent decree. The other plant, although not a signatory to the consent decree, accepted conciliation agreements with the EEOC that required that 20 percent of its new hires be women. Thus, both plants were required to increase their female employment shares, particularly within craft occupations that were among the highest-paid blue-collar positions in the steel industry.

The steel mills overwhelmingly employed men. In 1976, men made up 91 percent of the two plants' total employment. Craft occupations were even more homogeneous: men's share of craft employment was 99.6 percent. In the face of such a clearly male-dominated occupation and industry, several barriers stood in the way of integrating crafts.

The steel plants' main affirmative action policy tool focused on recruitment. The traditional sources of recruitment were through apprenticeship programs and trade schools that were dominated by men; referrals into apprenticeship programs had historically been provided from father to son or uncle to nephew. Consequently, women faced two barriers: restricted access to training and restricted access to information about job opportunities. In addition to these barriers, women were (and still are) traditionally socialized away from jobs that require the use of tools and machines. A clear example of this can be seen in the past policy of many middle schools that required girls to take home economics and boys to take metal shop or woodshop. Consequently, women did not typically seek the job skills required for craft occupations in industrial settings.

One plant opened a separate training school specifically for minority and female students; the school's enrollment was 50 percent minority and/or female. These minority and female students were primarily recruited through a Comprehensive Employment and Training Act program that provided a minimum wage for the students while they were in training. The USWA negotiated to fill the other half of the school's enrollment with current employees. This training facility provided a nontraditional source of craft training that supplied over 100 women for craft positions over five years, many of whom were new to the industry.

The other plant hired an outside nonprofit recruiting agency to identify and recruit prospective female and minority apprentices. These individuals received training that upgraded their skills and prepared them for the apprenticeship entry exams. Approximately 10 percent of the nonemployee graduates of the training program (i.e., those who were not current steel employees in noncraft positions) were placed in craft positions. Around two-thirds were hired into the plant, which put them in a position to bid for craft positions as openings occurred. The success of these programs, however, was contingent on the availability of job and apprenticeship openings in the plants' craft positions. As the number of openings declined due to a downturn in the U.S. steel industry, so too did the ability of the programs to introduce qualified women into the profession.

In these two plants specially targeted training and outreach programs contributed to the placement of women into high-paying blue-collar craft jobs. The mandates requiring specific hiring goals for women and minorities probably helped to work against possible biases in hiring such as an implicit requirement of physical strength favoring male candidates. Whether such a qualification was actually tied to job performance is unclear since the plants had not determined the level of physical strength required for each occupation nor were applicants required to demonstrate a particular level of physical strength.

From 1976 to 1979 the number of women in craft employment rose from 0.4 percent to 2.2 percent in the two midwestern steel plants. While women were still a very small minority in crafts, this change reflected a sevenfold increase in the number of women in these jobs. However, the importance of the economic conditions in which affirmative action policies operate is made clear in this case study. During the period in which the consent decree was signed and the recruiting efforts were implemented, employment in the two plants was expanding. After 1979, employment in the steel industry fell, and the impact on women's share of steel jobs was significant. Seniority policies in layoffs dictated that those with the least seniority were the first to be laid off; that is, women were the "last hired, first fired." The percentage of women in steel dropped from 9 percent in 1979 to 7.1 percent in 1980, back to the level of representation they had in 1970.

AT&T

In 1973, AT&T signed a consent decree with the EEOC that included a settlement amounting to $15 million in back pay, $23 million for pay adjustments, and a new promotion pay policy for nonmanagement jobs. The decree was the outcome of a series of hearings before the Federal Communications Commission (FCC) initiated by the EEOC; by 1970, the EEOC had received over two thousand charges of discrimination against the company.

The EEOC's central charge against AT&T concerned sex discrimination. A 1971 EEOC study of Bell companies in the thirty largest urban areas found almost complete segregation of men and women: 92.4 percent of all employees in major job categories were concentrated in classifications filled by 90 percent or more of people of the same sex. Women mostly held low-paying jobs such as operator, clerk, service representative, and first-level manager.

This description of the AT&T case draws from a series of studies based on the documents written for the AT&T hearings compiled in *Equal Employment Opportunity and the AT&T Case* (Wallace 1976) and a follow-up study conducted by Northrup and Larson (1979). The affirmative action plan approved in the consent decree involved the setting of goals for minorities and women in each of fifteen major job classifications, along with two goals for men in operator and clerical positions. The goals, based on the relevant labor pools and projected job opportunities, were to be reached through intermediate targets set at one-, two-, and three-year intervals.

In order to meet these targets several new procedures were put in place. First, the upgrade and transfer program replaced a system that provided numerous opportunities for subjective judgments to enter the hiring and promotion process: qualifications necessary for each job were unclear; job descriptions were vague; and the interview process was ill defined. The new program required management to inform all employees of all nonmanagement job opportunities, the requirements for those jobs, and the application procedures. The program also established "transfer bureaus" in each Bell company to centralize personnel decisions and to support employees' efforts to seek out opportunities to transfer and advance. The centralization of personnel decisions for entry-level nonmanagement jobs increased the likelihood of a consistent hiring process and prevented managers within departments from practicing favoritism.

Second, the seniority criteria were modified to compensate for seniority advantages given to men who had virtually exclusive access to particular departments under the old system. For example, women and minorities who wished to transfer into a semiskilled craft position in which they were underrepresented could compete on the basis of their company-wide seniority and basic qualifications with men who had equivalent departmental seniority. Similarly, for some jobs "affirmative action overrides" were used to promote members of protected groups at higher percentages than their representation in the labor pools. In order to facilitate the higher proportions of promotions, an affirmative action override would be used to bypass the "most senior" criterion used in the selection process.

In 1975, a supplemental agreement was reached after the Bell companies had been found to be noncompliant—they had only reached 51 percent of their intermediate goals. Joint reviews by the federal government and AT&T found the recruitment efforts and use of affirmative action overrides to be deficient. The supplemental agreement stipulated that a fund be created to finance several programs, including management training to determine job requirements for second- and third-level management jobs and an exploration into the effectiveness of sensitivity training. The agreement also called for an increase in monitoring, allowed companies to prorate their hiring targets to other Bell companies with more job openings, and shifted the emphasis from attaining goals to demonstrating good faith efforts.

Thereafter, the Bell companies achieved at least 90 percent of their goals. Over the life of the consent decree (1973–79) the occupational distribution of women and men at AT&T improved. Women increased their presence in official and managerial positions from 24.6 percent to 29.1 percent, in sales positions from 37.6 percent to 44.9 percent, and in craft positions from 11.4 percent to 22.6 percent. While black and Latina women gained more proportionately in these more desirable occupations, white women made the most gains in absolute numbers. Women also decreased their concentration in low-paying clerical positions from 94.1 percent to 88.9 percent.

Xerox

For the Xerox Corporation the impetus for change came formally from the OFCCP's requirement that federal contractors implement an affirmative action policy. Additional pressure came from a series of events, including two race riots in 1964 and 1967 that took place in Rochester, New York, where Xerox's headquarters was located, and a 1971 class action suit charging Xerox with racial discrimination. In response to these events, the chairman of the board, Joseph C. Wilson, and company president, Peter McColough, took an unusually strong stance in support of affirmative action policies by sending a letter to all the Xerox managers declaring the corporation's commitment to affirmative action. McColough backed up this statement with financial resources: he designated $1 million to be used to form and implement affirmative action programs.

In 1972, in compliance with OFCCP requirements, Xerox developed an affirmative action plan that included numerical targets based on labor force availability. The strategy of Xerox's affirmative action programs relied on improving management skills in working with a diverse workforce, diversifying entry-level hiring to integrate jobs at all levels, keeping lines of communication open between management and protected groups through caucuses (employee associations for underrepresented groups such as African Americans, women, and Latinos/as), and making the paths to promotions transparent. The details of Xerox's programs presented here are based on a study conducted by Sessa (1992) and observations from Barry Rand (1996) on his experience as one of Xerox's top black executives.

At first, management training relied on a program called Management Awareness Training and Education Seminar that appeared to be successful in raising managers' awareness of their own biases but was criticized because it did not provide them with the skills to deal with these biases. A second training program, developed in 1975, the Management Practices Program, focused on modeling appropriate behavior for managers. Managers were instructed on how to listen to and communicate with employees, as well as how to interact with employees regardless of differences in race, culture, or gender. The importance of such training is suggested by research conducted by social psychologists that demonstrates how racial stereotypes and biases can influence the level of uneasiness with which blacks and whites interact (Pettigrew and Martin 1987). This, in turn, can affect the ability of the manager to supervise and counsel an employee, as well as the employee's overall job performance.

The Pivotal Job Concept, initiated in 1972, was developed to integrate entry-level jobs in a way that would lead to integrating upper-level jobs. Key positions leading to senior management jobs were identified and targeted for minority and female recruitment.

Not all of the changes within the corporation were initiated by management. African American employees, frustrated with the inhospitable environment and social isolation they experienced at Xerox, formed caucus groups to provide support networks and professional development and to advocate for African American employees. Women and Latino\a employees subsequently formed caucus groups to address their own particular needs. As well as providing different kinds of assistance for their group members within the given workplace environment, the caucuses were able to cause changes in the workplace itself. African American caucus groups played a role in getting Xerox to implement a nationwide job-posting system. The Hispanic Association for Professional Advancement worked with the company to develop separate targets for each minority group. The caucus groups lobbied to make public the list of employees eligible for promotion and their ratings according to the Management Resources Process, a career development tool that evaluates and counsels middle-level managers. The caucus groups not only provided a mechanism for retaining employees but also acted as a kind of internal "policing" body; the caucus groups were able to monitor the experience of their group members and pursue relevant changes within the corporation that supported and expanded its affirmative action policies.

Several new procedures were instituted to formalize the promotional practices and make them transparent to all employees. For example, the Panel Interview process outlined how an employee could find out the necessary requirements for a particular managerial position and then demonstrate his or her qualifications for that position by requesting a Panel Interview.

To motivate the managerial staff, affirmative action was added to the performance appraisals of line managers in 1975. Up to 15 percent of a manager's appraisal depended on the manager's efforts to recruit, hire, and promote minorities and women; merit increases in managers' pay depended on these performance appraisals.

This strategy has proven slow but has produced some results. In 1984, Xerox assessed the progress it had made in the past ten years. While goals were met for minorities and women in entry-level positions, goals for women in upper-level and executive positions were not. The progress of women into top executive positions appears to be very gradual: in 1991 senior executives were 17 percent minorities and 8.5 percent women; in 1996 35 percent were women or minorities or both (Xerox 1999). Even so, minority representation at Xerox reflects that of the U.S. labor force, and in 1990, Xerox was named one of the best companies for women because of its aggressive affirmative action program (Konrad 1990). In contrast to the layoff policy discussed in the steel case study, Xerox implemented a layoff policy that would conserve the diversity of its workforce. Affirmative action gains that were made possible when Xerox's labor force was expanding were preserved as its labor force contracted in 1981.

The reader should keep in mind that in these three cases, the employers had a powerful incentive—an immediate threat of legal sanctions—to create and actively enforce affirmative action plans. Two of the three case studies involved companies that had been ordered by the court to implement an affirmative action plan. (Xerox was partly motivated by a lawsuit and partly motivated by its contractor status but did not have a court-ordered affirmative action plan.) Such a court-ordered decree only comes after a court case has been brought against a company and the company has agreed to settle the case through such an agreement. Other firms not under this kind of legal scrutiny have strong incentives to avoid such vigorous pursuit of affirmative action. The efforts required for affirmative action add to the employer's expenses, especially in recruiting costs and a significant time commitment of human resources staff. Also, an affirmative action policy may cause friction among current employees who are hostile to changing the status quo. And, of course, the employer may simply not agree with the goals of affirmative action or may not perceive any problems with his or her own employment practices. Firms may implement some kind of affirmative action program to avoid lawsuits, but their implementation will not be scrutinized by an outside party unless the firm has a contract with the federal government. Federal contractors, who are occasionally audited, only need to demonstrate "good faith efforts" rather than carry out a specified program or meet specific goals mandated by the courts. Legal sanctions in the three case studies served to counterbalance firms' tendency to simply do "business as usual."

Quantitative Evidence of Affirmative Action's Impact

Assessing the impact of affirmative action on women nationally is a difficult research task. Researchers do not usually have access to detailed information about what goes on within individual companies, and we need data collected from many companies that are representative of all companies to make generalizations about the policy's impact. As a result, studies of affirmative action that seek conclusions about affirmative action in general, as opposed to affirmative action at a particular workplace, as in the previous section, are limited to certain kinds of questions. Even with these limits, such studies indicate that affirmative action has resulted in clear gains for women, particularly for African American women.

The main source of data on many companies is the EEOC. All private companies with more than one hundred employees and federal contractors with more than fifty employees are required by law to report the race and gender composition of their workforce, broken down into eleven occupational categories. Most of the studies of affirmative action have used those data to compare federal contractors, who are required to develop and carry out affirmative action plans, with companies that are not federal contractors. As noted previously in the section "Mandated Affirmative Action Programs," though, some noncontractors might voluntarily adopt an affirmative action plan or might have had one imposed by a court. In that case, the comparison studies will underestimate the impact of affirmative action.

Employment and Occupational Effects

At least eight studies have made such comparisons to see whether companies that are required to have affirmative action programs have a higher proportion of female employees or of men of color than do noncontractors. Other studies of the federal contractor compliance program have measured the existence of an affirmative action plan less directly by using more aggregated measures of federal contracts within an industry. The studies measure the impact of contractor status on employment, on occupational status, and on wages of women and people of color. (For a more complete review of these studies, see Badgett and Hartmann 1995.)

Because of differences in statistical methods and in time periods studied, the studies do not show a consistent pattern. The most consistent beneficiaries of affirmative action in these studies are African American men. Their shares of employment grew faster in contractor firms than in noncontractor firms, at least through the 1970s. The work of Jonathan Leonard, an eminent researcher of affirmative action's employment effects, shows that the employment of African American women and Asian and Latino men has also received a boost from affirmative action. While the impact is positive, it is not large.

In general, most of these studies find little positive effect of affirmative action on white women, and some studies actually find a negative contractor effect on white women. One notable exception is a recent study by Harry Holzer and David Neumark (1999) of employers in four large cities. Holzer and Neumark find that companies that use some form of affirmative action in recruiting or hiring are more likely to hire a white woman but are not more likely to hire a woman of color. The ambiguous finding for white women from the earlier studies is puzzling because in the economy as a whole, white women's relative wages have risen and their unemployment rates have fallen greatly relative to white men, suggesting much more economic progress for white women than for African American men and women. Since affirmative action for women was added to the executive order on affirmative action in 1968, white women have entered the labor force in massive numbers, increasing their employment greatly among both contractors and noncontractors. Perhaps the flooding of labor markets with white female applicants prompted both contractors and noncontractors to discriminate less and hire more white women than before, an effect that would swamp the relatively small effects of affirmative action observed for African American men and women. The Holzer and Neumark study might find different outcomes than earlier studies because of conditions specific to the four cities that their data came from or because of the later time period examined.

While increases in employment are a positive outcome of affirmative action, the quality of jobs is also important. The positive effects found in studies comparing firms' employment in 1974 and 1980 are not limited to either blue-collar jobs or white-collar jobs. Leonard (1984a) finds that affirmative action increased the occupational status of white women and of men and women of color. Their shares of employment increased in managerial and professional jobs as well as in blue-collar jobs.

Finally, one study of women's probability of quitting a job showed that women's quit rates were lower in industries with high levels of federal government purchases and with lots of compliance reviews (Osterman 1982). This suggests that affirmative action creates work environments or wages and terms of employment that are more hospitable to women, who are then less likely to quit.

Factors Influencing the Success of Affirmative Action

Several factors have increased the effectiveness of affirmative action for women and people of color. First, the quantitative studies demonstrate that compliance reviews have a positive and independent effect on the shares of women and people of color beyond the positive effect of simply being a contractor. As mentioned earlier, the OFCCP in the U.S. Department of Labor periodically audits firms for adherence to their affirmative action programs. This simple form of policy pressure— monitoring—appears to increase the vigor with which companies implement their affirmative action programs, even when the OFCCP imposes no sanctions.

Second, implementing goals and timetables also appears to increase the affirmative action effort of companies, increasing the proportion of black women hired (Leonard 1985). When firms find that they are underutilizing certain race and gender groups in the available labor pool, they are supposed to use the labor pool data to create employment goals for different race and gender groups and a timetable for meeting those goals. This has been one of the most controversial aspects of affirmative action, with opponents claiming that goals and timetables constitute quotas for hiring that force employers to set aside certain jobs for women and people of color. Leonard found, however, that the "goals are not being fulfilled with the rigidity one would expect of quotas" (Leonard 1985, 18).

A third factor also influences affirmative action's effectiveness. Whether a firm is growing or shrinking in total employment matters. Contractor firms that are growing disproportionately hire a higher share of women and people of color (Leonard 1984b). In other words, affirmative action works largely by increasing the share of new jobs for women and people of color, not by a displacement of white men in existing jobs.

Finally, a broader indicator that the strength of the enforcement effort matters is evident from comparisons of employers' outcomes in the 1970s with those in the 1980s. Little doubt exists that enforcement effort dropped when President Ronald Reagan, an ardent opponent of affirmative action, took office in 1980. The number of compliance officers at the OFCCP was cut from 735 to 430 in Reagan's first two years in office. And although the number of compliance reviews increased during his two terms in office, the higher number of reviews resulted in fewer debarments and much smaller back pay awards for far fewer people (Anderson 1997). (Back pay awards went back up in the Bush administration.) When Jonathan Leonard measured the influence of affirmative action on employers' workforces in the early 1980s, he found that a firm's contractor status no longer increased the proportion of minority or female workers, a finding that he ascribes to the reduced enforcement effort (Leonard 1990).

Conclusions and Recommendations

These reviews of the quantitative evidence from most of the companies using affirmative action and the qualitative evidence from several key case studies all suggest that affirmative action can and does increase the employment prospects of women, although the changes that have been observed tend to be small. Given this history, how can affirmative action be used to further improve women's current position? Public policy clearly matters in two ways, from a national perspective and from a company-level perspective.

First, from a national perspective, affirmative action plans tend to be more effective when companies are growing. Companies are more likely to be growing when the economy is in an upswing. Thus the government can promote affirmative action by promoting a strong and growing economy.

Second, from the company perspective, the federal government can play a different role. Expanding the affirmative action requirement to cover all companies, not just those that are federal contractors, would likely increase the employment prospects and relative wages of women. A less dramatic policy change would be to increase government efforts to enforce the existing contractor program. In 1996, Bergmann estimated that the OFCCP could only review each workplace under its jurisdiction once every thirty-eight years if it continued at its annual rate of 4,000 compliance reviews of 150,000 contractors. Another indicator of the government's weak enforcement efforts is indicated by the fact that by 1996, only 41 firms had been debarred since 1972 (Bergmann, 1996). Of these debarments, four involved large corporations that were reinstated as contractors within three months. Adding compliance review officers, implementing more frequent and regular reviews, and fully using all available sanctions, such as debarment, would be likely to increase the urgency with which firms undertake affirmative action efforts.

The record also shows, however, that affirmative action alone is not strong enough to equalize men's and women's wages. At the usual rates of job turnover it would be many years before even a perfectly unbiased hiring process would result in equal distributions of men and women across high-paying occupations and companies. This suggests that affirmative action is a necessary, but not sufficient, policy tool for achieving economic progress for women in the United States. But is affirmative action worthy of the political effort necessary to defend it in today's political climate? We argue that it is: the evidence shows that affirmative action is an effective—and, indeed, the only—tool designed for proactively and systematically breaking down employer-specific barriers to women's employment in high-status and high-paying jobs.

References

Anderson, Bernard E. 1997. "Affirmative Action Policy under Executive Order 11246: A Retrospective View." In *Civil Rights and Race Relations in the Post Reagan-Bush Era,* edited by Samuel L. Myers Jr. Westport, CT: Praeger.

Badgett, M. V. Lee, and Heidi Hartmann. 1995. "The Effectiveness of Equal Employment Opportunity Policies." In *Economic Perspectives on Affirmative Action,* edited by Margaret C. Simms. Washington, DC: Joint Center for Political and Economic Studies.

Beller, Andrea H. 1977. "EEO Laws and the Earnings of Women." In *Proceedings of the Twenty-ninth Annual Winter Meeting.* Madison, WI: Industrial Relations Research Association.

———. 1979. "The Impact of Equal Employment Opportunity Laws on the Male-Female Earnings Differential." In *Women in the Labor Market,* edited by Cynthia B. Lloyd, Emily S. Andrews, and Curtis L. Gilroy. New York: Columbia University Press.

———. 1982. "Occupational Segregation by Sex: Determinants and Changes." *Journal of Human Resources* 17, no. 3:371–92.

Bergmann, Barbara R. 1996. *In Defense of Affirmative Action.* New York: Basic Books.

Braddock, Jomills, and James McPartland. 1987. "How Minorities Continue to be Excluded from Equal Employment Opportunities." *Journal of Social Issues* 43, no. 1:5–39.

Deaux, Kay, and Joseph C. Ullman. 1983. *Women of Steel: Female Blue-Collar Workers in the Basic Steel Industry.* New York: Praeger Publishers.

Groshen, Erica L. 1991. "The Structure of the Female/Male Wage Differential: Is It Who You Are, What You Do, or Where You Work?" *Journal of Human Resources* (summer): 457–72.

Hill, Herbert, and James E. Jones, Jr. 1993. *Race in America.* Madison, WI: University of Wisconsin Press.

Holzer, Harry, and David Neumark. 1999. "Are Affirmative Action Hires Less Qualified? Evidence from Employer-Employee Data on New Hires." *Journal of Labor Economics* 17, no. 3:534–69.

Ichniowski, Casey. 1983. "Have Angels Done More?" *Industrial Labor Relations Review* 36, no. 2:182–98.

Konrad, Walecia. 1990. Cover story: "Business Week's Best Companies for Women." *Business Week,* August 6, 49–55.

Leonard, Jonathan S. 1984a. "Employment and Occupational Advance under Affirmative Action." *Review of Economics and Statistics* 66, no. 3:377–85.

———. 1984b. "The Impact of Affirmative Action on Employment." *Journal of Labor Economics* 2, no. 4:439–63.

———. 1990. "The Impact of Affirmative Action Regulation and Equal Employment Law on Black Employment." *Journal of Economic Perspectives* 4, no. 4:47–63.

———. 1985. "What Promises Are Worth: The Impact of Affirmative Action Goals." *Journal of Human Resources* 20, no. 1:1–20.

Neumark, David. 1996. "Sex Discrimination in Restaurant Hiring: An Audit Study." *Quarterly Journal of Economics* 111, no. 3:915–41.

Northrup, Herbert R., and John A. Larson. 1979. *The Impact of the AT&T-EEO Consent Decree.* Philadelphia: University of Pennsylvania.

Office of Federal Contract Compliance Program (OFCCP). 1980. *OFCCP Affirmative Action Guidelines.* Washington, DC: Bureau of National Affairs.

Osterman, Paul. 1982. "Affirmative Action and Opportunity: A Study of Female Quit Rates." *Review of Economics and Statistics* 64, no. 4:604–12.

Petersen, Trond, and Laurie Morgan. 1995. "Separate and Unequal: Occupation-Establishment Sex Segregation and the Gender Wage Gap." *American Journal of Sociology* 101, no. 2:329–65.

Pettigrew, Thomas, and Joanne Martin. 1987. "Shaping the Organizational Context for Black American Inclusion." *Journal of Social Issues* 43, no. 1:41–78.

Rand, A. Barry. 1996. "Diversity in Corporate America." In *The Affirmative Action Debate,* edited by George E. Curry. Reading, MA: Perseus Books.

Reskin, Barbara. 1998. *The Realities of Affirmative Action in Employment.* Washington, DC: American Sociological Association.

Sessa, Valerie I. 1992. "Managing Diversity at the Xerox Corporation: Balanced Workforce Goals and Caucus Groups." In *Diversity in the Workplace,* edited by Susan E. Jackson and associates. New York: Guilford Press.

Turner, Ronald. 1990. *The Past and Future of Affirmative Action: A Guide and Analysis for Human Resource Professionals and Corporate Counsels.* New York: Quorum Books.

U.S. Department of Labor. 1999. *The Facts on Executive Order 11246.* Employment Standards Administration, Office of Federal Compliance Programs, U.S. Department of Labor, Washington, DC. Available at <http://www.dol.gov/dol/esa/public/regs/compliance/ofccp/aa.htm>. Accessed on September 10.

Wallace, Phyllis. 1976. *Equal Employment Opportunity and the AT&T Case.* Cambridge, MA: MIT Press.

Xerox Corp. 1999. *Diversity at Xerox.* Available at <http://www.xerox.com/go/xrx/about_xerox/...xerox_detail.jsp?view=editorial&id=11163>. Accessed on September 13.

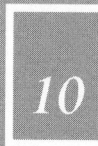

Great Work If You Can Get It:
Women in the Skilled Trades

Barbara Byrd

From the mid- to late 1970s, women were encouraged to enter construction craft occupations as one of many attempts to reduce occupational segregation and raise women's incomes. During the 1980s and 1990s, though, the daunting obstacles facing women in the construction industry were increasingly documented by scholars and confirmed by women construction workers themselves. Today, with women still representing only 2 percent of all skilled construction workers, this strategy for raising women's incomes seems risky at best. Nevertheless, labor organizations, advocacy groups, and others continue their efforts to gain access for women to construction craft jobs, and projects designed to recruit and keep women in the trades flourish in some parts of the country.

The trades have much to recommend them to low-income women workers. The entry requirements of these jobs are modest: most construction apprenticeship programs require simply a high school diploma or GED, a valid driver's license, and good physical condition; a few require high school algebra and/or geometry. Employment tends to be seasonal and cyclical, but earnings are high enough to tide one over during the lean times. Especially in the unionized trades, workers are often eligible for group health and retirement plans. The possession of craft skills allows one to travel to other parts of the country to work if desired. Finally, craft workers can take great pride in the skill involved in and the durability of their work.

But very few women work in the construction trades. In 1998, women made up approximately 2 percent of construction craft workers, as shown in table 10.1. In a few trades, such as painters and glaziers, women made up between 4 percent and 5 percent of all workers; in most other trades, such as carpentry, electrical, and plumbing, women represented less than 2 percent of the workforce.

These figures reflect the enormous barriers to women's participation in construction occupations. Nevertheless, a small number of determined women have persisted in their efforts to break into and remain in the trades. Recently, their efforts have been given a boost by a number of public and private initiatives. The main purpose of this chapter is to consider the more promising of the initiatives to increase women's share of work in the trades, with an eye toward assessing the policy implications of different efforts.

TABLE 10.1. Women as a Proportion of the Construction Workforce, 1998 (in thousands)

Occupation	Total Employed	Women as Percentage of Total
Construction trades	5,594	2.0
Supervisors	755	1.3
Construction trades, except supervisors	4,839	2.0
Brickmasons and stonemasons	195	1.2
Tile setters	63	1.0
Carpet installers	135	1.6
Carpenters	1,346	1.2
Drywall installers	180	2.2
Electricians	806	1.9
Painters, construction and maintenance	590	4.7
Plumbers, pipe-fitters, and steamfitters	531	.9
Concrete and terrazo finishers	83	.4
Glaziers	54	4.4
Insulation workers	55	6.4
Roofers	241	.8
Structural metalworkers	63	1.5
Sheetmetal workers	127	4.1
Cabinetmakers	89	5.5
Operating engineers	245	2.2
Helpers, construction	122	3.6
Construction laborers	821	4.5

Source: U.S. Department of Labor, Bureau of Labor Statistics, *Employed Persons by Detailed Occupation, Sex, Race, and Hispanic Origin* (1999).

This chapter will present the data on women's employment in construction occupations and on earnings in construction as compared to those in jobs that are typically held by women. It will briefly review the barriers that still face women in the construction trades. It will then consider promising efforts to reduce these barriers, examining pre-apprenticeship training, apprenticeship program recruitment and retention efforts, the work of women's advocacy groups in the trades, and the efforts of building and construction trades unions. It will also look at the special importance of systemwide partnerships among construction industry stakeholders. Illustrative examples will be drawn from experiences in the Portland, Oregon, and Seattle, Washington, metropolitan areas. The chapter will conclude with an assessment of the potential of these efforts to substantially affect the employment of women in the trades.[1]

The Numbers

Much has been written about occupational segregation and its impact on women's earnings. Though the past twenty years have seen a rapid increase in female employment in some previously predominantly male occupations, especially those in fast-growing categories such as managerial and professional jobs, women are still very much concentrated in lower-paid clerical, service, and retail positions. Men still hold nine out of ten jobs in the precision production, craft, and repair category, which includes construction occupations.[2] As the figures in table 10.1 show, women have made few inroads into these trades.

In jobs where women are concentrated, wages tend to be lower than in comparable jobs where men predominate. For those female-dominated occupations in which no more than high school graduation is required, for example, cashiers, nursing aides, waitresses, and salesclerks, wages are typically $300 per week or less (see table 10.2). In contrast, table 10.3 gives wage rates for male-dominated occupations. The lowest weekly wage in the construction trades is $335 for construction helpers, which is an entry-level position for those with no prior experience or training. For the skilled trades, the lowest weekly wage is $402 for painters, and the highest is $643 for electricians. Clearly, especially for women without college degrees, there is a substantial monetary incentive to train for skilled construction occupations,

TABLE 10.2. **Employment and Earnings of Women in the Twenty Leading Occupations of Employed Women, 1998**

Occupations	Employed Women (in thousands)	Percentage of Women	Women's Median Weekly Earnings[a] $
I. Occupations typically requiring high school graduation or less			
Secretaries	2,868	98.4	430
Cashiers	2,367	78.2	259
Nursing aides, orderlies, attendants	1,703	89.0	308
Bookkeepers, accounting and auditing clerks	1,604	93.0	426
Waitresses	1,079	78.3	282
Salesworkers	967	68.3	287
Receptionists	960	95.5	351
Machine operators	915	32.2	347
Cooks	873	40.9	259
Investigators/adjusters (excluding insurance)	793	75.6	431
Janitors and cleaners	777	34.8	292
Fabricators, assemblers, and handworkers	693	33.1	347
Hairdressers and cosmetologists	693	90.8	313
Textile and apparel machine operators	688	72.1	285
II. Occupations typically requiring a college degree			
Managers and administrators	2,287	29.8	666
Sales supervisors and proprietors	1,890	40.0	449
Registered nurses	1,879	92.5	734
Elementary school teachers	1,639	84.0	677
Accountants and auditors	941	58.2	618
Secondary school teachers	697	56.9	698

[a]Wage and salary for full-time workers.
Source: U.S. Department of Labor, Bureau of Labor Statistics, Women's Bureau (1999), February.

If the jobs for which women train are unionized, the rewards are even greater. The limited research on this topic confirms that the benefits of union membership for women in all occupations include higher pay, pay that more closely approaches that of males in the given occupation, and increased job stability.[3] In 1997, union membership among construction workers was approximately 19 percent, higher than union density in the labor force overall, which is approximately 14 percent.[4] If we consider that the wage differential between union and nonunion jobs in the precision, craft, and repair category is approximately 45 percent,[5] and that union jobs generally carry with them access to health insurance and pension benefit plans, the financial incentive for women to seek unionized jobs is even more compelling. Moreover, women appear to fare better in union apprenticeship programs than in nonunion programs. Of all women construction apprentices who entered an apprenticeship between 1989 and 1991 and completed their training and achieved journey-level status by 1995, 92 percent came from union programs. Women in union programs were 17

TABLE 10.3. Median Weekly Earnings of Full-Time Workers in Construction Occupations, 1998

Occupation	Median Weekly Earnings ($)
Construction trades	543
Supervisors	708
Construction trades, except supervisors	520
Brickmasons and stonemasons	573
Carpet installers	476
Carpenters	490
Drywall installers	493
Electricians	643
Painters, construction and maintenance	402
Plumbers, pipe-fitters, and steamfitters	593
Concrete and terrazo finishers	483
Roofers	441
Structural metalworkers	583
Sheetmetal workers	584
Cabinetmakers	531
Operating engineers	570
Helpers, construction	335
Construction laborers	390

Source: U.S. Department of Labor, Bureau of Labor Statistics, *Median Weekly Earning of Full-Time Wage and Salary Workers by Detailed Occupation and Sex* (1999).

percent more likely to complete and 21 percent less likely to drop out relative to their peers in the nonunion programs.[6]

Clearly, to the extent that the answer to the gender pay gap is occupational desegregation, then women's entry into construction occupations is worth some effort.

The Barriers

The barriers are many, but they arise from two root causes: most women have not been socialized for jobs in the trades, and too many male construction workers and supervisors do not want them there. To make the matter more difficult, government agencies have, for the most part, failed to aggressively enforce affirmative action requirements.

Women are rarely socialized for blue-collar work. They are generally not expected to work outdoors in inclement weather or to perform heavy and dangerous manual labor,[7] nor are they expected to do so in predominantly male environments. To some degree, women have internalized society's expectations of their future job prospects. But women overcome their socialization to take jobs in other previously male-dominated occupations, including working as doctors and lawyers and even in the military. Why has construction been so much more impervious to their entry?

The barriers are exacerbated in construction because of the unique nature of the industry. Entry to the trades is often informal, though young workers increasingly enter formal apprenticeship programs as a means of learning a trade.[8] Marc Silver found that almost two-thirds of the workers he surveyed learned their trade on their own or by working side by side with a friend or relative, though this was less true for younger workers.[9] Construction workers change jobs frequently, rarely working long for any particular employer, and jobs are typically found by word of mouth. Even in unionized construction, where workers are sent out to jobs from the union hiring hall, the better-connected workers or those who have established their competence with particular contractors tend to have a much easier time finding and keeping jobs. Each trade has thus developed its own informal network of job seeking and upward mobility. Women are, for the most part, not included in these networks.

Young men not only expect to be able to perform manual labor but are often given opportunity to do such work. In addition to taking shop classes in school, young men from construction families work with their fathers or other male relatives when they are young; on summer jobs and part-time while in school; and in entry-level "helper" or laborer positions when they enter the industry. In this way, young men supplement their early socialization with actual on-the-job learning and become familiar with the material conditions of the job and its cultural expectations. They learn how jobs are acquired, become familiar with particular contractors, and begin to build the web of informal relationships that will provide future access to opportunities and to advancement in the trade. When they enter an apprenticeship program, many are already working in the industry. Their expectations tend to be relatively accurate, and their physical conditioning tends to be good.

Not many young women have the opportunity to work with their families on building projects as they are growing up. Their part-time and summer jobs are much more likely to be in clerical or sales work. Thus even if they decide that they are interested in a trade, they may not know where to begin—how to learn the rudiments of the trade, to obtain entry-level jobs, to act once they are on the job, to prepare for the physical demands of the work. Some of this is changing, of course. For example, more young women today enroll in woodshop and related classes that were closed to them fifteen years ago. Girls' participation in organized athletics has increased, thanks to Title IX enforcement as well as cultural shifts, and so some girls are in better physical condition than in the past. But until young women have actually worked in a construction job, they may underestimate the difficulties involved, both physical and emotional.

Any woman who has tried to enter a construction trade has been confronted with the argument that women cannot do this kind of work because it is too physically demanding for the female physique. And clearly, strength and endurance are crucial to doing many kinds of construction work. However, weight lifting and other physical fitness training can go a long way toward building the necessary muscle mass for women. Pre-apprenticeship programs increasingly stress this conditioning; apprenticeship programs have begun to target recruitment for women workers to city soccer clubs and other athletic venues, where physically fit women are likely to congregate. Any woman who wants to enter the trades should take this need for conditioning into account.

In addition, working smarter can sometimes take the place of working harder, and this has benefits for male as well as female workers. Though most construction occupations do require considerable upper body strength, mechanical lifting devices are now more readily available and more accepted on the job. Newer and lighter-weight materials have taken the place of older, heavier woods and metals. And there is a growing awareness of the need to take precautions on the job: male workers are increasingly unwilling to wear out their own bodies by the time they are in their fifties, and so they are more likely to scrutinize traditional work practices. As the construction industry grows more competitive, and contractors push for greater productivity, construction unions and some contractors have increased their attention to safety, including investigating ergonomically sound tools and work practices.[10] This increased attention to safety will make it easier for men as well as women to handle the physical demands of construction jobs.

Even when women want to do the work and are physically fit, and even after they have negotiated the hurdles to finding work, they are frequently unwelcome on the job. Many women find themselves the only females on the job site, though in some trades and on some large sites this is gradually changing. The overwhelmingly male environment often results in stereotyping women workers, giving them the worst jobs in order to get them to quit or giving them only the light jobs, so that they do not get well-rounded on-the-job training. Sexual harassment is widespread. A recent study by a Chicago tradeswomen organization found that

> Sexual harassment in various forms is a fact of working life for almost all tradeswomen. Complaints include sexual assault, being touched in sexual ways, working around "pin-ups" of naked and nearly naked women, and unwanted sexual remarks, including comments on appearance. Women tell of co-workers spreading vile rumors and of playing "pranks" such as putting condoms on their car aerials. Women report threats of physical harm and many prefer to work in areas with several workers. They also complain of other, more subtle forms of sexual harassment, including being stared at constantly. (Chicago Women in the Trades, *Breaking New Ground* [1992], p. 12)

In addition, women routinely report a range of other problems. One is the general "culture of disrespect" on the job that takes the form of crude language, insults, and physical violence. Another is the lack of clean, private toilet facilities for women. Women also find that the construction environment is not family friendly: time cannot be taken off to care for sick children or parents due to the time pressures of construction projects. More fundamentally, women apprentices frequently find themselves relegated to the drudge work, receiving less crucial on-the-job training than male apprentices. Sometimes, in a misguided attempt to be considerate, male co-workers give women all the easiest jobs, not realizing that this prevents them from learning their trade.[11]

The culture of the construction work site is universally and persistently male.[12] Some scholars attribute the hostility of male construction workers toward female "interlopers" to the threat these women pose to their male identity.[13] Male construction workers' self-worth, these researchers explain, is tied to their ability to do skilled work, and earn a high wage, in an occupation that is physically demanding and dangerous. These men may feel the "hidden injuries of class"[14] in the larger world, but their position at the top of the hierarchy of wage-earning jobs for men is a source of great pride and esteem. The entry of women into the all-male domain of construction can thus represent not only competition for jobs but more fundamentally a challenge to identity. The result, as Susan Eisenberg (*We'll Call You If We Need You: Experiences of Women Working Construction* [Ithaca, NY: Cornell University Press, 1998]) has so eloquently described, is that work in the trades has taken a great personal toll on many of the women who have entered. It is also the reason so many women have left.

In some ways, the construction culture has changed little over the past two decades. On the other hand, some employers and some apprenticeship programs have made special efforts to recruit and retain women workers. And in any trade, the women can tell you who the "good employers" are—which jobs have foremen who set a decent example for the treatment of female workers.

One source of pressure on employers to become "good employers" is the threat of discrimination lawsuits. Researchers agree, however, that the impact of affirmative action and equal opportunity legislation has been minimal in the construction industry. For one thing, women seldom take discrimination or harassment claims to court. Litigation is an expensive, lengthy process, and jobs in construction tend to be short term anyway: dissatisfied workers, both male and female, simply look for other work rather than fighting a particular employer. A few lawsuits have forced changes in apprenticeship selection procedures, but these are notable for their rarity.[15] State and federal registered apprenticeship programs are supposed to be monitored for affirmative action compliance, but it is extremely rare for an apprenticeship program to lose its certification or even to be put on probation for failing to increase its proportion of women.

Therefore, it is not surprising that federal goals and timetables for hiring women and attracting women to apprenticeship have had minimal impact. The original federal regulations, enacted in 1978, stated that female apprentices should number 6.9 percent of all apprentices by 1981. For the first few years, the percentage did rise—from 1.7 percent in 1976 to 3.7 percent in 1979.[16] In 1989–91, however, women still averaged only 4.4 percent of all construction apprentices.[17]

In part, this dismal performance must be laid at the door of the federal government itself. Enforcement of goals and timetables on federally funded construction projects has been insignificant. Even the most visible projects show only partial attainment of goals. Even where progress is made under a particular court order, there is little lasting impact. The high attrition rate of women in construction often means that many women who get their start on a public project fail to stay in the industry after the project ends.

Finally, the fragmented nature of the construction industry itself accounts for some of the failure of affirmative action to have an impact. There were approximately 2 million construction businesses operating in the United States in 1992, with huge firms competing against one-person operations in the same market.[18] The competitive pressures on these firms, the attrition rate of the smaller firms, and the cyclical nature of the construction economy all mean that consistent, long-term attention to affirmative action enforcement may be much more difficult than in more stable occupations and industries.

Now, however, since the late 1990s, there are signs of renewed efforts to open the construction trades to women and keep them open. There is new scholarly attention to the issue.[19] There is grant money available for model projects, so that tradeswomen's advocacy groups and others now have the funds to start up pre-apprenticeship and related programs.[20] Some unions and employers, apprenticeship programs, and community organizations have come together to attempt to address the problem in a systematic way. A few large-scale construction projects, whether voluntarily or under court order, have made special efforts to recruit women.[21] The issue has also increasingly been addressed in the mainstream media in connection with stories about the "skills shortage" in the construction trades.[22]

These efforts tackle one or more of the barriers outlined previously—women's lack of socialization and preparation for construction jobs, their absence from the informal construction jobs network, the hostile culture of the construction work site, and the problem of isolation experienced by the handful of women who have entered the skilled trades. The remainder of this chapter reflects on a number of the most promising programs, most drawn from experiences in the Pacific Northwest of the United States.

Getting Them Interested: Attracting Women to the Trades

Because women tend to lack specific knowledge of construction jobs, recruitment efforts are crucial. In the short run, this means that employers, apprenticeship programs, and others who wish to increase their access to qualified women applicants must reach out to women in a variety of settings to inform them of the benefits of and opportunities in the trades. In the longer run, it means that from middle school on, young women must be exposed to the option of careers in the skilled trades. Whether long or short run, recruitment efforts must first overcome stereotypes of construction work, for example, that it is only for those who are not smart enough for college and that construction is not any place for a woman.

Traditionally, recruitment efforts in the construction industry have taken the form of attendance at high school or community college career fairs; speaking engagements in high school vocational classes; and other similar sporadic, short-term approaches. In practice, few women are recruited via such activities. To reach women in particular, recruitment must be specifically targeted to female audiences. Effective recruitment of women demands a strategic approach.

Tradeswomen advocacy groups provide some of the best examples of sophisticated, strategic, ongoing recruitment efforts. For example, the Oregon Tradeswomen Network, among its many activities, conducts a regular outreach program that includes speaking engagements in the schools, an annual Women in the Trades Fair, and a newly initiated summer camp for girls. These activities have grown out of an effort to build relationships with local middle and high schools and with apprenticeship programs, government agencies, and community-based organizations interested in jobs for low-income women and minorities. The speakers program, staffed by Oregon Tradeswomen Network's paid staff and volunteers, strategically targets high schools that are more vocationally oriented and concentrates time and energy on those schools. Volunteers are trained to make lively, hands-on presentations based on their own trades. Staff cultivates relationships with interested counselors and teachers, resulting in regular requests to speak. The network recently expanded these efforts by hosting a weekend summer camp for fifteen middle school girls.

Finally, the Oregon Tradeswomen Network takes advantage of its relationships with schools, apprenticeship programs, and employers to host an annual Women in the Trades Fair. Employers and apprenticeship staff are encouraged not only to set up literature tables and demonstrations but to create hands-on workshops in which participants may use some of the tools and materials of the trade to create simple, useful objects. At the most recent fair, workshop attendees built birdhouses at the carpenters' workshop, tool holders with the sheet metal workers, and trivets with the tile setters. Women apprentices from the various trades facilitated the workshops, serving as role models. On the first day of the fair, several dozen high schools brought 450 young women in groups of 4–30 to the fair. A number of schools had to be turned away due to lack of space. On the second day, 400 adult women attended, lured by a widespread publicity campaign among community-based organizations, community colleges, and both free and paid media coverage. Apprenticeship directors interviewed after the fair were well pleased, estimating that small but significant numbers of women showed a realistic interest in the trades.

Outreach to young women in schools, trades career fairs for women, and other such efforts are crucial to overcoming traditional social experiences for women and women's lack of exposure to blue-collar work. They are essential for raising the consciousness of women in any given community about opportunities in the trades. Unfortunately, they are also time consuming and labor intensive, given the relatively small numbers of women whose participation in such programs results directly in their entering the trades. As a more focused form of recruitment, the creation of direct pathways from low-income work and welfare to construction jobs is necessary. The programs described in the next section attempt to meet that need.

Getting Them Ready:
Preparation for Apprenticeship

For many years, attempts have been made to assist women entering the trades by providing them with a kind of remedial education and orientation to blue-collar work. If women cannot break into the industry due to their lack of previous experience and unfamiliarity with the world of construction, then it is crucial to address these gaps in knowledge. Pre-apprenticeship or preparation-for-apprenticeship programs attempt to substitute for the familiarization with the trades that boys often gain while growing up. They typically provide training in basic skills, trade-specific skills, and strength building and sometimes also pay wages during training. In addition, such programs offer support, networking opportunities, and assistance with entry into registered apprenticeship programs. Sometimes they are set up just for women, though increasingly they are designed for economically disadvantaged groups, including low-wage and unemployed workers of both sexes and all races.

Such programs have been funded by the Job Training Partnership Act or other federal work-related sources. Frequently they are operated from community and technical colleges, though sometimes they are set up by other agencies, such as the Job Corps, advocacy groups, and joint apprenticeship programs. They typically extend from six months to a year.

The challenges facing these programs are not only to provide the kinds of training outlined previously but also to work with trainees to assure that they are job ready, that they have a valid driver's license, adequate transportation, and child care if needed. Most important, if the graduates are to move from preparation for the trades into the trades occupations themselves, the program staff must establish relationships with employers and apprenticeship training committees.

A successful example of a pre-apprenticeship program is Apprenticeship and Nontraditional Employment for Women and Men (ANEW), which was established in 1980 in Seattle. This program trains economically disadvantaged workers for jobs in construction, manufacturing, and warehouse trades. It faces added challenges since its mission was broadened to include low-income males as well as females in 1998. Applicants are heavily screened for motivation and the ability to work in physically demanding jobs. Approximately 80 women and men per year enter a five-month, full-time program, receiving training in math, blueprint reading, and related classroom subjects, along with shop work in carpentry and other trades. In addition to trades training, they take fitness and job readiness classes and are provided with individual support for child care and other needs. The program has served 1,400 women and 31 men, with a completion rate of 80 percent and a placement rate of 65 percent, stunning figures that attest to the strength of the program. Fifty percent of the graduates enter the construction trades, including 30 percent who are placed in registered apprenticeship programs.

A recent survey of fourteen Seattle pre-apprenticeship programs found that somewhat over half the participants were eventually placed in apprenticeship programs or other family wage jobs in the building and construction trades. The key elements of successful programs, such as the one described earlier, included aggressive outreach, careful screening of applicants for physical fitness and other criteria, the capacity to address the job readiness issues facing the economically disadvantaged, and an active job placement component. The study also identified typical problems of such programs, including uncertain funding, complexity of procedures, and lack of organic connection to apprenticeship programs or other job sources.[23]

Another pathway to work in the skilled trades is work in related but unskilled occupations. Women are increasingly seeking out "helper jobs" in construction and highway repair. Positions in parts supply stores and related retail outlets also function as pathway employment to construction trades jobs. This kind of work gives women exposure to the culture of the workplace, the tools and terms of the trade, and the demands of employment in a male-dominated occupation while at the same time providing the earnings that many need to support themselves and their families. It allows women to observe the work of skilled tradespeople, to meet or talk with them, and to hear about apprenticeship and other opportunities informally from co-workers and supervisors. Thus women are able to ease their way into the word-of-mouth, informal construction jobs network.

Some unions and apprenticeship programs now use these kinds of opportunities purposefully, as a part of their strategy to recruit more women workers. In Portland, for example, women who apply to the union electricians' (NECA/IBEW) apprenticeship program and do well on the written aptitude test, but who are not accepted into the program due to their lack of experience, are counseled to register with the union for available "electrician's helper" jobs. A year or two of this work experience not only gives them a better understanding of the trade but also gives them a leg up if they reapply to the apprenticeship program, once they have demonstrated their determination to work in the trade as well as their ability to handle the difficulties they will face. An increasing number of women admitted to this apprenticeship program have worked at least a year in one of these "helper" positions.

The Sheet Metal Training Center in Portland operates a slightly different kind of pre-apprenticeship program, in which those interested in apprenticeship work for a year at entry-level wages—approximately $10 per hour in 1999—until they qualify for regular apprenticeship, which often requires their taking additional math or science classes. The advantage of this program, as with the electrician's helper jobs, is that participants "work out of the hall," receiving dispatches from the union hiring hall to employers with openings. In both cases, training directors report that efforts to steer women into these helper-type jobs has resulted in increases in the number of women entering the regular apprenticeship program.

Keeping Them Working and Learning: Retention Efforts

Once women have been recruited to apprenticeship programs and construction jobs, the next problem is keeping them there. Women working in construction and enrolled in apprenticeship programs are more likely than men to leave, especially during their first year. Though good data are sparse, one recent study of women in federal Bureau of Apprenticeship and Training apprenticeship programs indicated that women's graduation rates were 10 percent lower than those of men.[24] Efforts to increase the number of women in the trades must therefore consider retention as well as recruitment practices. Retention activities can take the form of direct support of women workers, individually or in groups. Retention efforts can also consist of practices that create more female-friendly environments. The sections that follow highlight examples of these kinds of activities.

Support Groups and Mentoring

Direct support encompasses a range of activities, from peer support groups at apprenticeship training centers, to the support work conducted by tradeswomen advocacy organizations, to a variety of formal and informal mentoring programs.

Peer support groups for women apprentices can be crucial in overcoming the isolation of being the only woman at the work site or in the apprenticeship class. Many new apprentices experience difficulties in their first year of work and training. New apprentices in every trade are expected to do the most routine and least rewarding jobs, such as moving materials, cleaning up, or digging holes; and they sometimes experience a kind of testing by the seasoned workers that can take the form of practical jokes and other forms of hazing. For new female apprentices, this experience is exacerbated by male reactions to their presence on the job, which can range from mild surprise to outright hostility. On a daily basis, new female apprentices must deal with unfamiliar work, unfamiliar tools, and an unfamiliar and often unwelcoming environment. This may include sexual harassment in its many guises, as well as discriminatory treatment in work assignments and layoff.

Many women who have worked as apprentices report that their isolation meant that they had no other women with whom to compare notes. They had no yardstick by which to measure the treatment they received. If they experienced severe difficulties and dropped out, they felt it a personal failure. On the other hand, those women lucky enough to have female co-workers or to know other women in their apprenticeship program were able to talk over these experiences and realize that "it was nothing personal." They could support each other with sympathy, advice, and encouragement when times got especially rough.

Women entering construction have always sought out other tradeswomen for this kind of support. This, in fact, is what led to the creation of tradeswomen advocacy groups around the country, including the Oregon Tradeswomen Network and Washington Women in the Trades. As more women entered particular trades, support groups within a union or an apprenticeship program emerged, either spontaneously or with the support and assistance of union or training staff. The International Brotherhood of Electrical Workers' Minority Caucus, which includes women, is an excellent example of how such support groups have grown and become institutionalized.

Another, newer form of support, similar to the journey worker/ apprentice model, is one-on-one mentoring. Mentoring means close contact between a new worker and an experienced one, where advice, sympathy, and concrete assistance are offered as needed to assist the new worker over the initial hurdles of the job. One of the best-documented efforts to provide systematic mentoring services for women and people of color in the construction trades is the Trades Mentor Network, a program originally established in 1991 by the Worker Center of the King County Labor Council, AFL-CIO. The Trades Mentor Network began as a pilot project in cooperation with the unionized carpenters', painters', and electricians' apprenticeship programs in Seattle to reduce the attrition rates of women and minorities. With large-scale public construction projects at the Port of Seattle increasing the demand for women and minority workers,[25] a consortium of unions, vocational educators, apprenticeship coordinators, and community service organizations was able to secure more stable funding from the Office of Port Jobs.

The success of the Trades Mentor Network's program rests in part on its requirement for twenty-four hours of training for mentors as well as careful follow-up. Mentors are journey-level craft workers who are matched with apprentices from their own craft. They are expected to maintain regular contact with the apprentice, to provide a sympathetic ear, to refer the apprentice to community support services if necessary, and to assist with job-related difficulties and other problem solving. Network staff monitor the relationships, assuring that mentors carry out their commitment to stay connected with the apprentice for the three to five years of the apprenticeship. A study of the effects of the impact of mentoring on women apprentices, conducted five years after the program began, documented a decline in their dropout rate from 50 percent in 1991 to 12 percent in 1996.[26]

Though peer support and mentoring have been shown to reduce the attrition rate of women from construction apprenticeship, these programs do little directly to change the hostile culture in which these women frequently find themselves. It is to this effort that we now turn.

Creating Female-Friendly Work Environments

The most difficult approach to bringing women into the trades is to tackle the work environment of the construction job site itself. There is widespread agreement that the construction industry's culture and the attitudes of male supervisors and male journey workers are extremely difficult to change. For one thing, contractors have little motivation to change. Because prevailing stereotypes about women hold that women cannot physically handle the work, and because so few contractors have employed female employees to challenge these stereotypes, contractors feel they are taking risks by hiring women. They cite the risk that women cannot work hard enough and fast enough to meet productivity standards and the risk that because of their physical limitations, they will be more likely to incur injuries. This is not to say that there are not employers willing to give women a chance in the trades. Some of these employers happen to be women themselves, with a background in the trades and a commitment to mentoring their sisters. Some are men with unique personal histories that make them more open to the employment of women in their industry. These contractors, however, are the exceptions that prove the rule.

There are two sources of pressure on contractors that compel them to change. One is community pressure. More likely to be addressed to the hiring of minority workers, community pressure, including lawsuits in some cases, has proven to be effective in increasing the hiring of minority workers on construction sites in minority communities.[27]

The primary incentive to hire women is felt by contractors who are subject to affirmative action requirements—in particular, contractors or subcontractors involved in public projects that fall under the jurisdiction of the Office of Federal Contract Compliance or state and local statutes. Thus it is no surprise that it has been on large public construction projects that the biggest efforts have been made to recruit women laborers, apprentices, and journey-level workers. The fact that these opportunities are, by their nature, of limited duration can be a drawback. Women hired for particular projects may be unable to find work once the project is over. On the other hand, work on such projects provides many women with their first exposure to construction work, their first real job in the trades, the opportunity to enroll in an apprenticeship program, and the beginnings of the self-confidence that can take them through a three–five year training program and into the world of the skilled craft worker. These large projects, too, can provide models for other smaller or private sector contractors looking for ideas on diversifying their workforce. Women's experience on these projects can help overcome stereotypes about their ability to do the work among foremen, co-workers, and others. Finally, governmental agencies, contractors, and community organizations that recruit and work with women on these large projects gain valuable knowledge about ways to overcome the barriers to women in the trades.

In 1992, an advocacy group called Chicago Women in the Trades published its recommendations for "model construction worksites."[28] The organization described these model work sites as large construction projects (defined as those with budgets over $75,000,000) with ambitious numerical goals for work hours for women; oversight of efforts to recruit and retain women; partnering with community groups, government agencies, and schools; pre-apprenticeship training and on-site orientation for women; clear policies on sexual harassment; training for supervisors and craft workers; support services; separate toilets and locker facilities for women; placement of more than one woman on a crew; and women in supervisory positions. A follow-up study documented the implementation of some of these recommendations at six sites, but it pointed up the necessity for goals that are high enough and well enough enforced to make a real difference.[29] Though a few projects, like the Century Freeway in Los Angeles, have been compelled by law to increase female and minority presence on the job, the examples of construction sites that have implemented even a majority of the preceding recommendations are few. Further, the bulk of such projects are large scale and in the public arena. Unfortunately, smaller projects and most of the work done by the many small contractors and subcontractors in the private sector of the industry rarely reflect any such efforts.

Again, the role of government in enforcement of affirmative action requirements is an important issue. While some local governments, such as Seattle and Chicago, have demonstrated that inroads can be made via aggressive enforcement of goals for minority and female hiring, many projects do not set goals that are high enough, nor do they effectively monitor outcomes. The federal government has had even less impact, because its enforcement tends to be weak or nonexistent. Typically, projects are reviewed for having met goals only after they are substantially complete,[30] and penalties are rarely imposed on noncompliant contractors.

Partnerships

Because the barriers to women's participation in construction are complex and multifaceted, some of the most promising and innovative programs are those that bring together a wide range of organizations and individuals with a stake in the issue. A number of these efforts are systemwide rather than limited to a specific apprenticeship program or construction project.

Partners in systemwide collaborations typically include governmental entities, unions, contractors and developers, apprenticeship programs, community organizations, educational institutions, and women's advocacy groups. Such partnerships have a number of benefits. They allow for economies of scale: no single partner has to "reinvent the wheel," and all benefit from combined activities and shared support services. They facilitate the movement of women from general outreach activities to job readiness training to apprenticeship to journey-level employment. And at their best, as successful collaboration builds mutual trust and confidence, over time they replace miscommunication and scapegoating with good working relationships among the partners. In this section, two such systemwide partnerships will be described—one that has been in place for a number of years and one that has just been developed.

Perhaps the best is Port JOBS in the state of Washington. A major construction boom in Seattle in the 1990s gave impetus to efforts to extend the benefits of growth to women, minorities, and disadvantaged residents of the metropolitan area. In 1993, the Office of Port JOBS was created. Port JOBS is a partnership between the Port of Seattle; the City of Seattle; King County; the King County Labor Council; the AFL-CIO and its Worker Center; and other labor, business, and community-based organizations and education and training providers. It seeks to create employment and training opportunities for disadvantaged job seekers, with a particular focus on women and minorities.

In 1994, the Apprenticeship Opportunities Project was established by Port JOBS staff to focus on employment in the building and construction trades. The project has had great success: it reports that six months after placement, 80 percent of female and minority apprentices are still working, and 60 percent of the apprentices placed since the project began operations are still working in 1999. Successful partnerships are the key to its success. Project staff focus on recruitment and placement, while other partners provide support services. For example, the Trades Mentor Network (discussed previously) sets up mentoring for new workers. ANEW (also discussed previously) offers its program of pre-apprenticeship training and intensive individual counseling and assistance to remove barriers to employment. Finally, a host of union apprenticeship programs provide training and support. The project has broadened its scope beyond the port and has now signed agreements with three major private developers. As a result of this activity, the percentage of women in construction apprenticeship in Washington State has grown to be one of the highest in the country.[31]

A key feature of Washington's program is the creation of apprenticeship "set-asides"—the reservation of a specified percentage of work hours for apprentices and, within that, a specified percentage for women and minorities. Such set-aside programs have been developed for the city of Seattle, King County, the port, and the three large private developer partners mentioned previously. The goal is 15 percent of the labor hours on construction projects of over $1 million to be worked by apprentices, and between 1994 and 1998, the actual combined apprentice utilization rate on the eighty-eight participating projects has been 14.6 percent, representing the work of 2,200 apprentices.[32] The affirmative action goal for the port in 1996 for women was 10 percent, and the actual apprentice and journey-level female participation was 13 percent. For the city of Seattle, the goal was 11 percent female, with an actual rate of 10 percent. For King County, the goal has been set at 25 percent female. Given the demographics of the typical construction project, these numbers are impressive.

Elements crucial to the success of the Washington efforts include a labor movement willing to make major efforts to recruit and retain women and minorities; a booming construction economy featuring some major long-term construction projects; and an active state apprenticeship agency staffed by professionals with experience in the construction trades, including a female director who is the former apprenticeship director for Seattle's joint electrical apprenticeship program. A history of successful partnering on smaller projects, as well as continuing pressure from low-income community advocates, has further enhanced the ability of stakeholders in the city and county to develop pathbreaking programs.

In Portland, a group of over fifty private and public partners came together in 1998 to form the Oregon Construction Workforce Alliance, a loosely knit umbrella group whose mission is "to increase and improve access, recruitment, training, graduation, and retention of women and minorities into construction trade careers through state-approved apprenticeship programs." The economic, social, and political environment in Portland is quite different from that of Seattle, and nonunion construction has a larger presence.

In Portland, as in many parts of the country, community-based organizations that work with low-income clients and women have historically had troubled relationships with construction contractors, unions, and apprenticeship programs. A legacy of past discrimination as well as a host of mutual misunderstandings colors present-day attempts to build working relationships. Though minorities are better represented in the trades today, they are still underrepresented in the most highly skilled trades. Mistrust of construction unions and contractors continues to characterize the attitudes of many in minority communities. For their part, some unions, contractors, and apprenticeship training staff feel that community training advocates misunderstand the apprenticeship system, underestimate the qualifications necessary to perform construction work, and refer few applicants. No one feels entirely comfortable with government agencies, given their control over the distribution of public funds and projects, as well as their power to monitor compliance with equal opportunity rules and regulations.

In part, the Oregon Construction Workforce Alliance resulted from public reaction to a 1996 analysis of the disparate representation of women and minorities in the construction industry, which also brought some reluctant acknowledgment of the problem from key players. Meanwhile, the state apprenticeship agency conducted compliance reviews of apprenticeship programs for the first time in ten years, putting pressure on these programs to account for their low rates of female and minority entry and graduation.

These developments eventually brought both union and nonunion apprenticeship programs and contractors to the table. The Oregon Tradeswomen Network, community groups, the community college, the City of Portland, and Multnomah County joined with them to sign an official partnership agreement. Unfortunately, funding has been difficult to secure, and Portland's Construction Alliance has not succeeded in involving private developers. Without these two key components, it will be difficult to proceed. On the other hand, the stakeholders have begun through their regular meetings and discussion to support small projects, to participate in small grant-funded activities, and to build the kind of trust that will be necessary for larger projects to unfold.

Such collaborative efforts are crucial. Pre-apprenticeship programs can train their clients, but without connections to apprenticeship programs and contractors, they cannot place them. These same apprenticeship programs and contractors need the close community ties represented by many pre-apprenticeship and service provider organizations in order to recruit nontraditional workers. And all these players need the cooperation of government to secure funding for their efforts and to assist in leveling the playing field by enforcing civil rights laws. The lesson here is that each agency, each community organization, each union, and each apprenticeship program must work in concert with others to assure opportunities for women. No single initiative will succeed without being able to draw on the expertise and resources of all these potential partners.

Conclusion

Those concerned with increasing the number of women in construction craft occupations can learn much from the experiences described in this chapter about activities and programs that might work in their own areas. But, while all the efforts described previously are promising, their impact on widespread and persistent barriers to women in construction has been small, and the cost of many of the programs is enormous relative to the numbers of women affected. The significance of women's entry into the skilled trades as a strategy for raising women's incomes is thus, as yet, not great.

Without question, stronger enforcement of equal employment opportunity laws is a necessity. Since the federal government has failed to do this in the construction industry, the problem has been left to state and local jurisdictions. These jurisdictions have tools at their disposal, should they choose to use them. Cities and counties have public construction projects to let out for bids; state apprenticeship agencies have a responsibility to enforce affirmative action among apprenticeship programs; and state transportation agencies have the ability to set affirmative action goals and timetables for their own highway construction projects. Willingness to take strong action is not widespread in state and local governments, however, making federal enforcement efforts absolutely crucial.

It is equally clear that government action alone is unlikely to solve the problem of limited employment of women in an industry as fragmented and cyclical as construction. Therefore this chapter stresses voluntary cooperation among construction employers, unions, apprenticeship programs, training providers, tradeswomen advocacy groups, and others from the community, in combination with governmental action, as the best avenue for lasting change.

Some hope may be drawn from new leadership among organizations that were, in the past, hostile to women's participation in the construction trades. In particular, the participation of some unions and union apprenticeship programs in recruiting and retaining increasing numbers of women workers is encouraging. For now, this leadership is limited to a minority of organizations, but signs of change are apparent.

Construction occupations are obviously not for every woman. But for those who are given the opportunity to enter and to succeed, the rewards are enormous—not only a living wage but the intrinsic satisfaction of practicing a skilled craft. The point of affirmative action for women in the trades is not to open them to all women but to make them accessible to the women whose desire to work with their hands, willingness to take on the rigors of a physically demanding occupation, and ability to handle the construction culture are strong. For these women, construction work is a viable—and perhaps the best—way to narrow the pay gap between female and male workers.

Whether a critical mass of women in construction occupations can be reached is still in question. There are hopeful signs but no general upward swing in the percentage of women working in the industry. What we do have is a better understanding of what will be necessary to gain women jobs in the trades and to help them keep those jobs, and that is a step in the right direction.

Notes

1. This chapter will not focus on the issue of women who own their own construction firms, who comprise fewer than 10 percent of all construction contractors. Though construction firm ownership may be a viable path to higher earnings for women workers, and though women contractors do experience some of the same discrimination that women craft workers face, nevertheless their situation poses a somewhat different set of problems. Not all women construction contractors have worked in the trades, for example, and the problems they face are likely to include the difficulties of female small-business ownership in general. These problems are certainly worthy of consideration, but they cannot be addressed in this chapter in sufficient detail.

2. Barbara H. Wooten, "Gender Differences in Occupational Employment," *Monthly Labor Review* (April 1997): 15–24.

3. Richard B. Freeman and Jonathan S. Leonard, "Union Maids: Unions and the Female Work Force," in *Gender in the Workplace,* edited by Clair Brown and Joseph Pechman (Washington, DC: Brookings Institution, 1987).

4. U.S. Department of Labor, Bureau of Labor Statistics, *Employment and Earnings* (January 1998).

5. U.S. Department of Labor, Bureau of Labor Statistics, *Median Weekly Earnings of Full-Time Wage and Salary Workers by Union Affiliation, Occupation, and Industry, 1998* (1999).

6. Bunseli Berikeli and Cihan Bilginsoy, "Do Unions Help or Hinder Women in Training? Apprenticeship Programs in the U.S.," manuscript, 1998, 11. University of Utah.

7. This perception that women are not suited for difficult manual labor is belied by the fact that many traditionally female occupations in workplaces such as hospitals, laundries, and canneries require great strength and expose women workers to numerous safety hazards.

8. Studies of the construction industry document this trend: Herbert Applebaum, *Royal Blue: The Culture of Construction Workers* (New York: Holt, Reinhart and Winston, 1981); Daniel Quinn Mills, *Industrial Relations and Manpower in*

Construction (Cambridge, MA: MIT Press, 1972); Marc L. Silver, *Under Construction: Work and Alienation in the Building Trades* (Albany, NY: State University of New York Press, 1986).

9. Silver, *Under Construction,* 112.

10. Billy Gibbons and Steven Hecker, "Integration of Ergonomics into a Construction Safety and Health Program," *Proceedings of the Thirteenth Triennial Congress of the International Ergonomics Association,* Finnish Institute of Occupational Health, Helsinki, 1997; Susan Moir and Brian Buchholz, "Emerging Participatory Approaches to Ergonomic Interventions in the Construction Industry," *American Journal of Industrial Medicine* 29 (1996): 425–30; Scott Schneider, "Implementing Ergonomic Interventions in Construction," *Applied Occupational and Environmental Hygiene* 10, no. 10 (1995): 822–24.

11. The hardships women face in the construction trades are described in numerous firsthand as well as scholarly studies. For example: Norma Briggs, *Women in Apprenticeship—Why Not?* Manpower Research Monograph 33, U.S. Department of Labor, Manpower Administration, 1974; Susan Eisenberg, *We'll Call You If We Need You: Experiences of Women Working Construction* (Ithaca, NY: Cornell University Press, 1998); S. Harlan and B. O'Farrell, "After the Pioneers: Prospects for Women in Traditionally Blue-Collar Jobs," *Work and Occupations* 9 (August 1982): 271–98; J. Hedges and S. Bemis, "Sex Stereotyping: Its Decline in Skilled Trades," *Monthly Labor Review* (May 1974): 14–21; Jean Reith Schroedel, *Alone in a Crowd: Women in the Trades Tell Their Stories* (Philadelphia: Temple University Press, 1985); Lynn Shaw, "Women Union Electricians," Master's thesis, California State University, Long Beach, 1996; Kath Weston, "Production as Means, Production as Metaphor: Women's Struggle to Enter the Trades," in *Uncertain Terms: Negotiating Gender in American Culture,* edited by Faye Ginsburg and Anna Lowenhaupt Tsing (Boston: Beacon Press, 1990).

12. Briggs, *Women in Apprenticeship;* Chicago Women in the Trades, *Breaking New Ground* (1992); Jeffrey W. Riemer, *Hard Hats: The Work World of Construction Workers* (Beverly Hills, CA: Sage Publications, 1979); Applebaum, *Royal Blue;* Silver, *Under Construction.*

13. Irene Padavic, "The Re-Creation of Gender in a Male Workplace," *Symbolic Interaction* 14, no. 3 (1991): 279–94; Weston, "Production as Means, Production as Metaphor."

14. The notion that male blue-collar workers experience internal conflict due to their working-class status was first described by Richard Sennett and Jonathan Cobb in *Hidden Injuries of Class* (New York: Norton, 1973).

15. In one of these rare but notable cases, an apprenticeship selection procedure in the San Francisco Bay Area was challenged and overturned because of its adverse impact on female applicants to the program. The case took twenty-two years to resolve. See a description of the case in "Positive Outcomes," *Tradeswomen* (fall 1996): 7.

16. Roslyn D. Kane and Jill Miller, "Women and Apprenticeship: A Study of Programs Designed to Facilitate Women's Participation in the Skilled Trades," in *Apprenticeship Research: Emerging Findings and Future Trends,* edited by Vernon Briggs and Felician Foltman (Ithaca, NY: New York State School of Industrial and Labor Relations (NYSSILR), Cornell University, 1981), 91.

17. Berik and Bilginsoy, "Do Unions Help or Hinder Women in Training?" table 1, 21. This figure represents the situation only in those states under the juris-

diction of the federal Bureau of Apprenticeship and Training. Recently released figures from the National Association of State and Territorial Apprenticeship Directors, which reflect the situation in states with their own apprenticeship legislation, confirm that women's presence in construction apprenticeship remains between 5 and 6 percent in these states.

18. Gerald Finkel, *The Economics of the Construction Industry* (New York: M. E. Sharpe, 1997).

19. See, for example, Eisenberg, *We'll Call You If We Need You;* Shaw, "Women Union Electricians."

20. An important example is WANTO (Women in Apprenticeship and Non-Traditional Occupations). This grants program was initiated in 1994 by the Department of Labor's Women's Bureau to promote and support women and their employers and labor unions that are seeking to increase the participation of women in apprenticeship and other better-paying nontraditional occupations. The grants that have been awarded have supported a wide variety of projects and have provided a welcome source of funding, in particular to tradeswomen advocacy groups.

21. The Century Freeway Project in Los Angeles is one of the best known among these projects. Goals and timetables for the hiring of women and minorities were established by court order because of the freeway's imminent destruction of low-cost housing stock in its path.

22. For example, Dirk Johnson, "As Construction Booms, Builders and Unions Court New Workers," *New York Times,* March 12, 1999.

23. *Preliminary Review of Seattle–King County's Apprenticeship and Pre-Apprenticeship System,* March 1998, sponsored by Office of Port Jobs; the Worker Center–King County Labor Council, AFL-CIO; and the University of Washington's Northwest Policy Center.

24. Women's completion rate in the union construction programs is 32 percent and in the nonunion programs 16 percent. Men's completion rates in union programs are 43 percent and in nonunion programs 27 percent. Berik and Bilginsoy, "Do Unions Help or Hinder Women in Training?" table 2, 22.

25. The increased demand was brought about in part by apprenticeship utilization agreements negotiated by the Office of Port Jobs and in part by the voluntary setting of goals by project partners.

26. Jeanne Arvidson, "The Trades Mentor Network," Ph.D. diss., Oregon State University, 1997.

27. See, for example, Ray Marshall and Robert Glover, *Training and Entry into Union Construction,* U.S. Department of Labor, Manpower Administration, Manpower Research and Development Monograph 39, 1975.

28. Chicago Women in the Trades, *Breaking New Ground,* 26–27.

29. Chicago Women in the Trades, *Building Equal Opportunity* (1995), 38.

30. Ibid.

31. Apprenticeship Opportunities Project, *Program Manual* (1999), 10.

32. While exact figures are not available for all states, the median for percentage of females in apprenticeship appears to be in the 4–6 percent range. Washington State's figure is 14 percent for 1998. Figures are from the National Association of State and Territorial Apprenticeship Directors, "Registered Apprenticeship Survey," June 1999; and the "1998 Annual Report" of the Washington State Apprenticeship and Training Council, April 1999.

Is Teaching More Girls More Math the Key to Higher Wages?

Catherine J. Weinberger

Science and engineering occupations are among the highest paid in the U.S. economy. Employment in these occupations is predominantly male and requires more than the average amount of coursework in mathematics. Are young women unable to enter science and engineering occupations because they do not know enough math? Are women prevented from filling other well-paid jobs because of inadequate math preparation? Could the gender differential in economic outcomes be substantially reduced if more girls learned more math?

Given the current opportunity structure, both girls and boys who learn more math do tend to have better labor market opportunities later in life. But this does not mean that the gender gap in earnings could be eliminated by teaching more girls more math. The key to this apparent contradiction is understanding one of the most important lessons in the study of public policy: an action that tends to improve the earnings of an individual will not necessarily have the same effect on the earnings of a large group of people.

In this chapter we describe what is known about the complex relationships between gender, math, and labor market outcomes. We perform a simulation showing that U.S. women, as a group, would fare somewhat better if they knew as much math as men. We then describe how occupational structures have changed over the past thirty years, as gender differences in mathematics education have decreased and as other barriers to the career development of women have fallen. We conclude that continued improvement of gender equity in math education is likely to have modest effects on income but that other policies have a greater potential to improve the economic well-being of U.S. women.

Historical Context

Gender disparities in precollege mathematics preparation were once taken for granted. Just as few girls participated in organized athletics, few girls were trained in mathematics and science. Until relatively recently, even the most academically and socioeconomically privileged young women had little math preparation. In 1974, Lucy Sells wrote a paper observing that, among girls admitted to the elite University of California Berkeley campus, 92 percent did not have enough high school math preparation to qualify them for most college majors. At first, this paper was not deemed important enough to publish (Tobias 1978). After further research and publicity, however, the issue of insufficient math preparation as a barrier to economic achievement became a major policy issue (Sells 1978; Tobias 1978, 1990). The American Association of University Women (AAUW) has released several highly publicized reports on gender equity in education, broadening the base of support for policy action (AAUW 1991, 1999).

Because most schools are not segregated by sex, increasing the gender equity of mathematics preparation is often a matter of encouraging, or requiring, girls to enroll in existing classes within the schools they already attend. Reducing inequities of mathematics preparation by socioeconomic status, race, and ethnicity is more challenging because schools are more highly stratified along these dimensions. Advanced mathematics courses with highly qualified teachers are not currently available at many high schools serving poor or minority students (Jones 1984, 1987; Oakes 1990). Even within high schools, traditional systems of "tracking" tend to assign the slightly more advanced students to the best teachers. This custom contributes to maintaining the status quo of students from less affluent homes and students of color having less access to high-quality math education (Oakes 1990; Eccles 1997). Despite these traditions, levels of high school math education are increasing for all groups of students, and intergroup differences in math preparation are diminishing (NCES 1995).

Barriers to women's educational opportunities in science, math, engineering, and medicine have become much more porous than they once were. Many women I have met or read about faced barriers that were humiliating, limited their career development, and left lasting emotional scars. Each of the women I am about to describe remembered, verbatim, what was said to her during her ordeal.

My grandmother wanted to be a doctor. As a college senior in the 1920s, she received special permission to take a medical school course that she was particularly interested in. However, she was asked to leave the class when no other women enrolled.

In the 1950s my friend Shirley excelled in science and math during high school and easily passed the pre-med hurdles in college, only to be advised that she would never be accepted into a state medical school she could afford because only one woman would be admitted per year—a space that was reserved for the daughter of a doctor or someone so unattractive that there was no risk that she would marry and leave the profession.

In the 1960s, Betty Friedan completed writing *The Feminine Mystique* and decided to pursue a Ph.D. The classic book that would later be credited with igniting the women's movement had not yet been published and was still unknown. Its author was denied entry to the graduate program in social psychology on the basis that she would not have the mastery of statistics that was required. She protested, "But I used statistics throughout the book," to which the baffled chair responded, "Well, my dear, what do you want to bother your head getting a Ph.D. for, anyhow?" (Friedan 1983).

A 1970s college graduate was a math major until she went to her professor to ask about a homework problem. She was told that if she needed help, she should not be a math major.

In the early 1980s I worked with a talented African American engineer who had just dropped out of a very prestigious graduate school. She was greeted on the first day of a new class by the professor's telling query, "What are *you* doing here?"

Today, girls and women are legally entitled to an educational environment free of discrimination or sexual harassment. But these legal protections are meaningful only if people work to ensure that schools follow through. One such person is Dr. Vinetta C. Jones. Once denied entry to a middle school algebra class, she now works with school districts to promote a systemwide commitment to preparing and expecting every child to learn algebra (Matthews 1997).

In the early 1970s boys outnumbered girls in upper-level high school mathematics classes by a four-to-one ratio (Tobias 1978). Since the mid-1980s more girls than boys have taken high school math at every level but calculus, where girls are not far behind (NCES 1997). Since the 1980s, the trend has been toward greater numbers of high school students, both boys and girls, taking upper-level math. Among 1982 high school seniors, 38 percent of boys and 37 percent of girls completed algebra II (NCES 1995). By 1992, the numbers had risen substantially to 54 percent of boys and 58 percent of girls (NCES 1995). Over the 1982 to 1992 period, remaining differences across racial, ethnic, and socioeconomic groups continued to decrease.[1]

At every level, from junior high school through college, girls tend to earn higher grades in math classes than do boys (Kimball 1989; Bridgeman and Wendler 1991). Nevertheless, girls' scores on standardized math tests remain somewhat below those of boys (Kimball 1989; Rosser 1989; Hyde, Fennema, and Lamon 1990; Byrnes and Takahira 1993; NCES 1994; Hyde 1997). Gender differences in math test scores are largest among those with the highest scores (Benbow and Stanley 1980, 1982; Hedges and Nowell 1995). But differences in math test scores cannot fully explain the low numbers of women in technical careers: young women are less than half as likely as young men with equally high math test scores to pursue a bachelor's degree with a major in engineering, mathematics, computer science, or physical science (Weinberger 1999a, Shaumen and Xie 2000). The proportion of technical college degrees conferred on women increased substantially during the 1970s and early 1980s but did not grow between the mid-1980s and mid-1990s (NCES 1997). If women pursued technical degrees at rates comparable to men with equally high math test scores, women would be earning about two-fifths, rather than one-fifth, of technical college degrees (Weinberger 1999a).

Studies of why so few college women choose technical college majors describe both subtle and overt social pressures to conform to gender norms (Tobias 1978, 1990; Betz and Hackett 1981, 1983; Hall and Sandler 1982; Lunneborg 1982; Eccles 1987; Ware and Lee 1988; Seymour and Hewitt 1994; Arnold 1994; Hanson 1996; Lapan, Shaughnessy, and Boggs 1996; Hyde 1997; Betz 1997; Leslie, McClure, and Oaxaca 1998; Badgett and Folbre 1999). These pressures are often internalized as personal preferences or as unrealistically low perceptions of ability. Recent work by Claude M. Steele and others demonstrates that simple reminders of widely held stereotypes that women, African Americans, or non–Asian Americans are not good at math can actually impair cognitive functioning. This effect is observed even in mathematically competent and confident women (Steele and Aronson 1995; Steele 1997; Spencer, Steele, and Quinn 1999; Aronson et al. 1999).

Despite these barriers, many women successfully complete college degrees in technical subjects and enter professional technical occupations. Currently in the United States, 60,000 women are employed as pharmacists, 150,000 as medical doctors, 200,000 as engineers, and 440,00 in computer science or mathematics occupations. The women in these professional technical occupations earn, on average, $880 per week, compared with only $680 per week for all women employed full-time in professional or managerial occupations and only $460 per week for all women employed full-time (U.S. Bureau of Labor Statistics 1999).[2]

Research on Math Preparation and Labor Market Outcomes

Policy interest in math equity is based on the observation that many well-paid job opportunities require knowledge of math. Of course, scientists, engineers, and doctors must learn math. Knowledge of math also improves employment opportunities for those taking civil service or military qualifying exams (Sells 1978; Tobias 1978). Math tests are required for graduation from many two-year college programs; for admission into most bachelor's degree programs; and for entrance into graduate school in seemingly unrelated fields, including law schools and business schools. The cognitive skills associated with strong math test scores are useful in a wide range of occupations. Within some occupations, people with stronger math skills are more productive but earn no more than their co-workers who know less math (Bishop 1992). Along many different career paths, better math preparation leads to more occupational options, higher productivity, and higher earnings (Sells 1978; Murnane, Willet, and Levy 1995; Grogger and Eide 1995; Murnane and Levy 1996).

In research studies, an individual's mathematics knowledge is measured either by the score on a standardized test of mathematics or by the number of math courses taken. Obviously, these measures are related: math test scores tend to increase with the number of high school or college math courses taken (Jones 1984, 1987; Angoff and Johnson 1990), and they increase more if the teacher has taken more college math classes (Monk 1994; Goldhaber and Brewer 1997). On average, later earnings are higher for individuals with either more math coursework or higher math scores. Interpretation of these studies is complicated by the fact that students who learn more math might also differ in other ways; their higher earnings may be partially due to factors unrelated to learning math. Studies estimating how earnings increase with the number of math courses tell us something about the effect of policies to increase course requirements. Studies estimating how earnings increase with math scores may provide a better control for the fact that individual students might realize different educational and economic benefits from the same number of courses—because they have different teachers, because they are in different types of math classes, or because they have different amounts of talent or prior knowledge.

The most thorough study of the relationship between mathematics coursework and later earnings finds stronger effects for women than for men (Levine and Zimmerman 1995).[3] Girls who take more math classes during high school do tend to earn more as adults than comparable girls who take fewer. However, this relationship is not particularly strong. The primary effect on earnings is to increase the probability that a girl will pursue a technical college degree and career. There appears to be little economic benefit of taking math for girls who do not go on to college or who pursue a nontechnical career path. Overall, Levine and Zimmerman (1995) estimate that "if girls took the same amount of math and science in high school as boys, the wage gap would be reduced by no more than about one percentage point."[4] Among the full-time, year-round workers studied in Levine and Zimmerman's sample, women who completed high school would continue to earn about 83 percent of what men earned, even if they took as many math courses.

There is considerable evidence that young women with strong high school math test scores have higher average earnings later in life (Bishop 1992; Grogger and Eide 1995; Murnane, Willett, and Levy 1995). Again, at least part of the explanation is that individuals with higher mathematics test scores are more likely to pursue college degrees in high-paying technical fields (Wise, Steel, and MacDonald 1979; Fiorito and Dauffenbach 1982; Blakemore and Low 1984; Angoff and Johnson 1990; Hanson 1996).

Women with technical college majors earn more than female college graduates with other college majors but less than men with the same college major (Polachek 1978, 1981; Daymont and Andrisani 1984; Rumberger and Thomas 1993; Eide 1994; Hecker 1995, 1998; Brown and Corcoran 1997; Weinberger 1998, 1999b). The gap in wages between men and women with the same college major appears during the first year after college graduation, before gender differences in labor force participation are a factor (Weinberger 1998, 1999b). By midcareer, gender differences are dramatic. For example, among midcareer college graduates who work full-time, median annual earnings are above $40,000 for men who majored in engineering, math, computer science, pharmacy, physics, accounting, economics, chemistry, business, nursing, architecture, biology, geology, political science, and psychology. For similar women, earnings are above $40,000 only for those who majored in economics, engineering, pharmacy, architecture, computer science, nursing, and physical therapy.[5] While choosing a technical college major improves the chances of a high-paying job for both men and women, men face a much wider range of high-paying career options.

What If More Girls Learned More Math?

While the existing research paints a picture of high school mathematics preparation increasing the likelihood that a girl will have higher earnings later in life, it is difficult to visualize exactly how math education affects a young person's future or the overall distribution of earnings. The examples that follow illustrate how high school math preparation and technical college coursework affect later labor market outcomes.[6] The first example shows the full range of occupational outcomes for girls, and for boys, who earn very high math scores in high school. The second example simulates what might happen to average labor market outcomes if girls learned as much math as boys. The third example shows how the occupational distributions of men and women changed over time as girls learned more math and as other barriers to women's occupational attainment diminished.

Example 1: What happens to people who had very high math test scores in high school?

Most people believe that those who excel in math in high school go on to become doctors, engineers, and computer programmers. Many do. However, the relationship is not as strong as most people believe it to be.

Table 11.1 shows the occupations of 32-year-old men and women who had very high math test scores as high school seniors. "Very high" is defined to be above the median score of white men who later completed college degrees in engineering. By this definition, 12 percent of the men and 6 percent of the women have very high math scores. In table 11.1, the occupational distributions of men and women with very high scores are compared to the occupational distribution of the entire high school class.

Both men and women who had very high math scores in high school are more likely than their high school classmates to become doctors or to become engineers, scientists, or computer programmers. High scoring men and women are also more likely to enter a highly skilled profession, such as accountant, architect, economist, lawyer, librarian, or psychologist.[7] In addition, high scoring men, but not women, are overrepresented among managers. High scoring men are overrepresented among Ph.D. college professors, and high scoring women are overrepresented among non-Ph.D. college instructors.

It is very interesting to note that women who had very high math scores as high school seniors are overrepresented among schoolteachers. This is a statistic that defies common misconceptions. While it is true, as is often repeated, that teachers tend to have lower average test scores than other college graduates (Schlechty and Vance 1982; Weaver 1983; Manski 1987; Hanusheck and Pace 1994), many young women with very high math scores enter and remain in the teaching profession.[8]

Similarly, women who had very high math scores as high school seniors are heavily overrepresented in nursing and other health-related occupations, such as physical therapist or pharmacist. High scoring women are much more likely to become nurses than to become doctors.

Finally, strong math performance is no guarantee of occupational attainment. More than a quarter of employed men and one-fifth of employed women who had very high math scores as high school seniors are, at age 32, employed in sales, clerical, craft, unskilled labor, or service occupations. The average hourly earnings of the high scoring women in these occupations are remarkably low—virtually the same as the earnings of average scoring women with no college degree (see table 11.2).[9]

Example 2: How much difference might more math education make?

Gender equity of math education is a noble goal in and of itself. Mathematics used to be considered one of the humanities, a subject to be studied for the sake of personal enrichment. But how much will it affect the bottom line of women's economic security? This is impossible to know with certainty. However, by running a simulation, we can make an estimate of the maximum effect to expect from math equity alone.

In this example, we simulate a world in which there are more women like the women with higher math test scores. Technically speaking, we weight the high scoring women until the distribution of women's scores is just like that of men.[10] This procedure (described in the technical appendix, which follows) is a bit like cloning the high scoring women to make more of them. We can then observe the distri-

TABLE 11.1.   1986 Occupational Distributions of Men and Women Who Had Very High Mathematics Test Scores during the 1972 Senior Year of High School Compared with the Occupational Distribution of the Entire Senior Class (percentage of group in each occupation)

	1972 Seniors with Very High Math Scores		
	Men	Women	All 1972 Seniors
Engineer, scientist, computer specialist, mathematician	18	7	4
Physician or other health diagnosing	6	2	1
Nurse or other health providing	1	10	3
Ph.D. college professor	1	0	0
Postsecondary instructor (no Ph.D.)	1	5	1
Teacher (preschool through high school)	3	7	3
Highly skilled professional	12	11	4
Other professional	4	4	2
Managerial	20	13	14
Skilled technician	3	5	3
Sales	8	2	5
Clerical	3	7	14
Skilled trades	6	1	9
Less skilled labor or service occupation	8	5	16
Full-time mother	0	12	11
Student only	1	5	1
Other voluntary withdrawal	3	4	4
Unemployed	2	1	4
Sample size	577	324	9,118

bution of women's occupations in this simulated world, where girls learn as much math as boys.

Given equal math test scores, women are less likely than men to pursue technical college degrees (Weinberger 1999a). We therefore also reweight the women who are college graduates, until the resulting distribution has approximately the same math scores and the same distribution of college majors as those of the men. We can then compare existing economic outcomes with estimates of what economic outcomes might look like in a world where women learned the same amount of math as men in high school and then pursued the same college majors as men do.

One limitation of this method is that it can only tell us what might happen if there were more women like the high scoring women—not what might happen if more of the lower scoring women learned math. If the higher scoring women are better employees partly for reasons other than their math skills, then simply teaching math will not produce as large a gain in hourly earnings as is estimated in this way. A second limitation is that this method assumes a relatively large increase in the number of workers with math skills but no adverse effects on the wages of mathematically skilled workers. For both of these reasons, this simulation probably overstates the potential improvement in wages resulting from gender equity of math education.

The results of this analysis are reported in table 11.3. The first column shows means for men in the real world; the second column shows means for women in the real world; the third column shows means for

TABLE 11.2. 1986 Hourly Earnings of Full-Time Workers by Sex, Occupation, Mathematics Test Scores during the 1972 Senior Year of High School, and Education

	Men	Women
All full-time workers	12.70	9.50
By high school math scores and employment in a professional, managerial, or technical (PMT) occupation		
Very high math scores and PMT occupation	16.20	13.60
Very high math scores and non-PMT occupation	13.60	8.60
Lower math scores and PMT occupation	13.60	11.00
Lower math scores and non-PMT occupation	11.40	8.00
By education level		
Bachelor's degree or higher	15.10	11.90
Less than bachelor's degree	11.50	8.40
Sample size	3,276	2,404

women weighted to have the same high school math scores as men; and the fourth column shows means for women weighted so that math skills—both math scores and college majors—are the same as for men. The means of math test scores, college completion rates, and the representation of women with technical college majors are all, of course, higher for the "math-enhanced" women in the third and fourth columns.

As we already know, women are less likely than men to be employed in the labor force and less likely to work full-time if employed. These gender differences are unaffected by simulated improvements in math skills: with or without math skills, only about 73 percent of the women are in the labor force at age 32, and of those, only about 78 percent work full-time in paid employment. Fully 95 percent of the men are in the labor force, and 96 percent of those work full-time. After simulated gains in math skills, women spend just as much time in unpaid activities. They may be more productive in some of these activities (e.g., helping with homework) but will not earn more as a result.

About 70 percent of both the men and the women are married. Simulated changes in the math preparation of women have virtually no effect on the marital status of women. Nearly one-third of the women are reliant on their own earnings at age 32. In addition, many of the married women are likely to become self-supporting at some time in the future.

Gender differences in earnings are reported for full-time workers only. Among full-time workers, the men in this sample earn an average of $12.70 per hour, while the women average $9.50—only 75 percent of what the men earn. When the women's sample is weighted to have the same math skills as the men's sample, women's average hourly earnings increase to $10.20, or 80 percent of what men earn. There is an effect on the wage gap, but it is relatively small. No more than one-fifth of the earnings gap between women and men working full-time might disappear if women had the same math skills as men.

For the majority of the population with no college degree, gender equity in math has almost no effect on the gender wage gap. The average hourly earnings of men with no college degree employed full-time are $11.50, compared to $8.40 for women, 73 percent of what men earn. When the women's sample is weighted to have the same math test scores as the men's sample, women's average hourly earnings increase only to $8.60, or 75 percent of what men earn. Most of the effect of math on earnings is through increasing the probability of pursuing higher education and of choosing a technical college major.[11] Among full-time workers with no college degree, less than 8 percent of the gen-

TABLE 11.3.   Simulated Effects of Increasing Women's Math Skills on Selected Labor Market Outcomes (1986 labor market outcomes of 1972 high school seniors)

	Men	Women		
	Actual	Actual	Weighted to Match Men's Math Scores	Weighted to Match Men's Math Scores and College Majors
Mean 1972 math score	14.2	12.1	14.2	14.2
Proportion with any college degree	0.34	0.28	0.34	0.34
Proportion with technical college degree	0.05	0.01	0.02	0.05
Proportion in labor force	0.95	0.73	0.74	0.73
Proportion employed in full-time jobs	0.96	0.78	0.78	0.79
Proportion married	0.69	0.70	0.70	0.68
Hourly earnings of full-time workers	12.70	9.50	10.00	10.20
Hourly earnings of full-time workers with college degree	15.10	11.90	12.20	12.60
Hourly earnings of full-time workers with no college degree	11.50	8.40	8.60	8.60
Occupation (percentage of group with this occupation or activity)				
Engineer, scientist, computer specialist, mathematician	6.6	1.7	2.2	3.6
Physician or other health diagnosing	1.7	0.3	0.5	0.6
Nurse or other health providing	0.9	4.7	5.6	3.6
Ph.D. college professor	0.2	0.1	0.1	0.1
Postsecondary instructor (no Ph.D.)	0.4	0.6	0.9	1.2
Teacher (preschool through high school)	1.9	5.0	5.4	3.4
Highly skilled professional	5	3	4	5
Other professional	2	2	3	3
Managerial	19	9	10	11
Skilled technician	4	3	3	3
Sales	6	4	4	4
Administrative support (clerical)	5	22	20	20
Skilled trades	16	1	1	1
Less skilled labor or service occupation	21	12	10	10
Active military duty	1	0	0	0
Full-time mother	0	21	20	20
Other voluntary withdrawal from labor market	6	6	6	7
Unemployed	4	3	3	3
Sample size	4,327	4,791	4,791	4,791

der gap would be eliminated by equalizing math achievement. For those with no college degree, fully 92 percent of the gender wage gap must be addressed through policies other than math equity.

The gender wage gap among college graduates is more strongly affected by improvements in math skills. Male college graduates average $15.10 per hour. When the women's sample is weighted to have the same math skills as the men's sample, the average hourly earnings of female college graduates employed full-time increase from $11.90 to $12.60, or from 79 percent to 83 percent of what men earn. Among full-time workers with college degrees, equalization of math scores and college major choices reduces the wage gap by one-fifth. While improvements in math skills are likely to increase the wages of women with college degrees, these improvements in skills cannot close the gender gap.

Simulated changes in math have little effect on the occupational distribution of women. In the math-weighted sample, more women do enter science, engineering, and managerial occupations and other skilled professions, and fewer women end up in clerical and less skilled positions. However, the changes are marginal. When women's math skills are simulated to match men's, fewer than 10 percent of all women move from one sector of the occupational distribution to another. Women remain greatly overrepresented in teaching and nursing—in fact the numbers of women in teaching and in nursing increase with simulated increases in math scores alone. This is further evidence that lower math ability is not what keeps women in these vital occupations. Simulating changes in math skills has absolutely no impact on the proportions of women in skilled technical or craft positions. Increasing the numbers of women with training in mathematics may improve productivity in some occupations but is not likely to dramatically change the kinds of jobs women do. Policies to value women's work have much greater potential for increasing the incomes of U.S. women.

Example 3: Occupational changes before and after gender equity in high school mathematics

The analysis described previously relies on data from 1986, the only large data set with both academic test scores from the senior year in high school and earnings data at age 32. It is likely that the labor market opportunities of women have changed since 1986. To see how much they have changed, we compare the occupational distributions of the 1986 sample of 32 year olds who completed high school in 1972 with a 1999 sample of 31–33 year olds who completed high school in the mid-

1980s. We also compare these with occupational distributions for a 1970 sample of 31–33 year olds who completed high school in the 1950s. We refer to the 1986 32 year olds as the 1972 senior cohort, since that is the year they completed high school. Similarly, we refer to the 1970 32 year olds as the 1956 senior cohort and to the 1999 32 year olds as the 1985 senior cohort.[12]

The results can be seen in table 11.4. Over the period 1970 to 1999, there was a dramatic decline in the proportion of 32 year old women engaged only in unpaid work such as full-time child rearing, which fell from 55 percent to 22 percent. There was a corresponding increase in the representation of women in many occupations. Women's representation grew substantially among scientists and engineers, physicians, managers, skilled technicians, sales personnel, and skilled trades workers.

Although the 1985 senior cohort (1999 32-year-old women) had a much more solid foundation of high school mathematics than the women in either of the earlier cohorts, the entry of women into several traditionally male occupations increased much more quickly between 1970 and 1986 than during the 1986 to 1999 period. This is true for scientists and engineers, managers, skilled technicians, and the skilled trades and is true whether we look at the numbers of women in these occupations or at the proportions of employed women in these occupations.[13] Differences in high school mathematics cannot be responsible for keeping the women of the 1956 senior cohort out of these jobs, since the gender differences in math were also present for the 1972 senior cohort. The 1985 senior cohort enjoyed continued opening of occupational opportunities. But it is not clear that this opening was due to changes in math skills, since the entry of women to many traditionally male occupations went more slowly for this more mathematically educated cohort.

As women continue to enter traditionally male occupations, there is also a remarkable stability in the occupational distributions of 32-year-old women between 1986 and 1999. Between the two later cohorts, there is absolutely no change in the proportion of women employed in science or engineering occupations (1.7 percent in both years). It is possible that more women are now engaged in science and engineering careers but have been promoted up to management. Many changes are visible: the proportion of women employed as physicians increased from 0.3 percent to 0.7 percent. This change involves a small number of women but is a large change in the gender composition of the profession. There are also visible increases in the fraction of women employed in skilled technician (2.8 percent to 3.8 percent), sales (4.0 percent to 6.2 percent), and skilled trades (1.4 percent to 1.8 percent) occupations. A large increase in the proportion of women employed in managerial professions (from 9.3 percent to 15.0 percent) is tempered by the continued scarcity of women at higher levels of management (Reskin and Roos 1990) and by the assignment of managerial job titles to positions that were formerly classified as clerical (Reskin and Padavic 1994).

Women's participation in some traditional activities is now lower: fewer women are employed in teaching (5.0 percent to 4.4 percent) and nursing (4.7 percent to 3.9 percent), and the proportion of women engaged only in unpaid work continued to fall, from 27 percent to 22 percent. However, despite changing opportunities for women, about half of all 32-year-old women are currently engaged in traditionally female activities, including unpaid child rearing, clerical work, teaching and nursing.

TABLE 11.4. Occupational Distributions of 32-Year-Old Men and of 32-Year-Old Women with at Least 12 Years of Education for Three Cohorts of High School Graduates

	1956 High School Seniors, 1970 Occupations ($n = 45,356$) (%)		1972 High School Seniors, 1986 Occupations ($n = 9,118$) (%)		1985 High School Seniors, 1999 Occupations ($n = 5,112$) (%)	
	Men	Women	Men	Women	Men	Women
Engineer, scientist, computer specialist, mathematician	7.3	0.3	6.6	1.7	6.8	1.7
Physician or other health diagnosing	1.4	0.1	1.7	0.3	1.1	0.7
Nurse or other health providing	0.5	2.3	0.9	4.7	0.4	3.9
School teacher	3.1	4.9	1.9	5.0	1.4	4.4
Other professional	10.0	3.2	7.8	6.4	4.8	3.6
Managerial	12.9	1.4	18.7	9.3	19.4	15.0
Skilled technician	3.5	0.6	4.2	2.8	3.4	3.8
Sales	7.6	2.1	6.0	4.0	5.9	6.2
Administrative support (clerical)	7.0	17.3	5.0	21.7	5.5	17.6
Skilled trades	17.3	0.6	16.3	1.4	17.2	1.8
Less skilled labor or service occupation	24.5	10.6	20.6	12.2	25.9	16.1
Voluntary withdrawal from labor market	3.1	55.1	5.6	27.3	5.2	21.9
Unemployed	1.7	1.6	4.6	3.4	3.0	3.2

Despite large improvements in mathematics preparation, the occupations of 32-year-old women in 1999 look much more like the occupations of women in 1986 than like the occupations of men in 1999.

Limitations of Math Equity as a Tool to Raise Women's Incomes

For the small group of women who complete college degrees in technical fields, investing heavily in mathematics-intensive education is an effective strategy for high later earnings. However, fewer than 5 percent of all U.S. workers are employed as doctors, scientists, engineers, or computer programmers. Learning math improves the chances that an individual woman will get one of these scarce and potentially remunerative jobs, but this strategy simply cannot have a significant impact on the earnings of all women.

Even the few highly trained women cannot expect economic outcomes equal to those of men. Women with technical skills are not exempt from earning lower wages than equally experienced men with the same amount and type of education (Ferber and Kordick 1978; Vetter 1979; Jagacinski 1987; Strober and Arnold 1987a; Zuckerman 1992; Bielby 1992; Haberfeld and Shenhav 1990; McIlwee and Robinson 1992; Hampton and Heywood 1993; Hecker 1995; Weinberger 1998, 1999b; Ferree and McQuillan 1998; Schiebinger 1999). While overtly exclusionary policies are no longer as prevalent as they once were, gender differences in labor market outcomes among scientists and engineers are as large as gender differences in the labor market as a whole (Bielby 1992).

Social scientists in economics, sociology, and psychology are all working to understand the complex processes that lead to women's lower earnings. One factor is that women in technical jobs are subject to the pervasive cultural norms and expectations about women's roles as helpers and caregivers. Anecdotal evidence suggests that when technical jobs are filled by women, the job description can change to include a requirement to provide nurturing and caregiving (see "Women in the Comics," which follows). For example, when men are employed as computer systems managers, their job is to keep the computers running. A woman in the same occupation can also be expected to help the users feel comfortable with the technology and to console frustrated users.[14] Women who are employed as systems analysts are more likely than men to spend their working hours helping customers and less likely to be involved in managerial decision making (Donato 1990). Women who are doctors are more accommodating to their patients than are male doctors (Tannen 1994). When female college professors fail to be nurturing, feminine, and available outside of class hours, students give lower teaching evaluations despite forming higher estimations of the professors' technical competence (Schiebinger 1999). Women who are on the faculty at research universities are expected to serve on more committees and to be better teachers than their male colleagues (Tack and Patitu 1992; Park 1996; Schiebinger 1999). Unfortunately, the time spent in this way interferes with time for research and therefore with opportunities for promotion (Tack and Patitu 1992; Park 1996).

Women in the Comics

Even in the comics, women with technical skills are expected, or choose, to use them to nurture and help people. In the strip *Dr. Katz*, a woman comes to the psychologist for career counseling and proclaims, "I teach remedial math and I'm wondering where I could do the most good." Rather than work to clarify her goals and motivations, the doctor recommends the express checkout line. The character June of *Rex Morgan* is a very competent nurse who often goes far beyond the line of duty to help people. The character Deanna of *For Better or Worse* recently completed her degree in pharmacy and signed on as a medical volunteer in Honduras with the comment, "How often do you have the chance to make a difference in someone's life?" And Dr. Burber of *9 Chickweed Lane*, a tenured biology professor, was recently instructed by her department chair, "I don't want you to change the content. Just try looking a bit more reassuring—smile a little."

Often these gender-normed expectations are explicit in job descriptions. Within a given technical occupation, women are more likely to be hired into jobs that require both technical and people skills (Reskin and Roos 1990). But even when women and men are hired into exactly the same job, expectations differ. Bielby (1992) argues that women scientists might behave in ways that accommodate the expectations of their colleagues, sometimes without even being aware of being influenced in this way.

If women did their jobs differently but were paid as much as men, then we might simply celebrate what women bring to technical occupa-

"For Better or For Worse." © UFS. Reprinted by permission.

"If she were an engineer, would they stop expecting tissues?"
("Dilbert." © UFS. Reprinted by permission.)

tions as new opportunities for women open up. In practice, those who help and nurture on the job tend to be valued and paid less (England et al. 1994; Kilbourne et al. 1994; England and Folbre 1999). If job descriptions change when women fill them, is it ever really possible to move women into men's jobs?

There are other reasons to believe that increasing the number of technically trained women might have a limited ability to raise women's wages. As has been discussed in other chapters of this book, jobs that are predominantly filled by women tend to have lower pay than predominantly male jobs that require similar levels of skill (Treiman and Hartman 1981; Sorensen 1989; England et al. 1994; Kilbourne et al. 1994; Bellas 1994, 1997). Historically, when the proportion of female workers in an occupation has risen, relative wages have fallen. This occurred for clerical workers at the turn of the century (Davies 1982; Cohn 1985); bank tellers at midcentury (Strober and Arnold 1987b); and, more recently, for pharmacists, news reporters, insurance adjusters, bartenders, and bus drivers (Reskin and Roos 1990). As women entered these occupations, employers adjusted wages downward toward those paid for other women's jobs. Greatly increasing the numbers of women trained for professional technical occupations could very well result in decreasing the earnings of all workers in those occupations, including and especially the women.

Finally, it is possible that some employers currently advertise for individuals with strong technical training simply because it is a legal way to maintain a predominantly male applicant pool. If so, then policies to increase the number of women with technical training will not guarantee women access to these high-wage jobs. Another loophole will surely be found to fill desirable positions with men if, in fact, employers would prefer men in these jobs.

Among all U.S. women, gender equity in math education can have, at best, a small effect on gender equity in U.S. incomes. Previous research indicates that gender equity in high school math preparation might have reduced the gender wage gap among those in their late twenties by no more than 1 percent (Levine and Zimmerman 1995). The simulation described in this chapter estimates that gender equity in high school math education and college major choices might have improved the later earnings of women, working full-time at age 32, from 75 percent to 80 percent of what men earned. However, even this modest effect is probably overstated. Simple laws of supply and demand suggest that large increases in the number of people with mathematics training are likely to diminish the economic value of math in the labor market; as any skill becomes more abundant, its price falls unless demand for the skill rises even faster than the supply.[15] Hence, teaching many more girls more math will tend to reduce the economic return associated with knowledge of math.

Given the tendency for women to be paid less than men with the same skills, the knowledge that math skills might be valuable because they are relatively scarce or because men have them, and the fact that women spend more time engaged in activities where they receive no compensation for their skills, policies to significantly increase the number of women who know math have a limited potential to increase women's incomes. This analysis suggests that policies designed to value the work done by women, and enforcement of laws to protect women from discrimination in hiring and promotion, will continue to have an important role in improving women's incomes.

Conclusion

Math education opens the doors to many educational and career opportunities. As increasing numbers of young men and women enroll in college, high school mathematics preparation is becoming important to a larger proportion of the population. It is simply wrong to make that preparation unavailable to large segments of the population, for instance to girls and to students in poorly funded school districts. In fact, increasing numbers of students, both girls and boys, are studying math in high school. There is an important role for policy to ensure that all students have access to well-educated math teachers and understand the importance of math for maintaining future career options.

Women with strong high school math preparation are more likely than other women to enter technical careers but are less than half as likely as men with the same math test scores to choose technical college majors. Among college-educated women who do pursue careers in technical fields, earnings are high, relative to the earnings of other women. This strategy effectively raises the wages of a small number of women but is limited by the fact that fewer than 5 percent of all U.S. workers are employed in technical occupations—we simply cannot all become scientists and engineers. A further limitation is that women earn less than men, even among scientists and engineers.

In the larger labor market, high school math preparation is only a first step toward occupational attainment and is no guarantee of high later earnings. This is especially true for women. Among women with very strong high school math preparation, more wind up as teachers than as engineers or doctors. One-fifth of women with very strong high school math test scores land in very low-status jobs, earning no more than women who entered the labor market with weak math preparation. Yet, on average, mathematically trained women tend to earn more than other women.

How much of the gender gap in wages is due to gender differences in math skills? The results of my mathematical simulation suggest that if women had the same math skills as men, but had labor market opportunities and career paths typical of women, the gender gap in wages would be reduced but not dramatically. Simulated increases in women's math skills have no effect on either the proportion of women working in paid employment or the proportion working part-time. Among those with no college degree, improving the math skills of girls has almost no effect on the 25 percent wage gap. Among those with college degrees, those who know more math earn substantially higher wages. Simulated gender equality in both precollege math preparation and college major reduces the gender gap in wages from 21 percent to 17 percent among college graduates employed full time. Among all women employed full-time, the pay gap is reduced from 25 percent to at 20 percent. Simulated math equity reduces earnings inequality, but more than 80 percent of the gender pay gap among full-time workers is due to other factors.

These simulations probably overstate the potential economic effect of policies to improve gender equity of mathematics education. If technically trained individuals are valued in the labor market because they are relatively scarce, or because most of them are men, then a large increase in the number of technically trained young women is likely to diminish the earnings advantage associated with mathematical training.

Historically, the largest gains in young women's occupational attainment occurred before many learned upper-level high school math. Many careers were simply closed to women for reasons other than math preparation. Conversely, gender equity of high school math education will not necessarily open career opportunities to women. But as more high-status jobs become accessible to women, women who know more math might be better prepared to fill them.

With or without high school mathematics preparation, large numbers of highly educated women fill valuable but undervalued roles in our economy, including teaching, nursing, and mothering. Policies to insure the economic security of women who perform these jobs are vital to the health of our economy.

I do encourage every girl and boy I know to learn as much math as possible.

Girls who learn more math can certainly expect to have more educational and career opportunities in the future. When they go to work, women with technical skills can expect to earn more, on average, than other women.

However, teaching more girls more math can not insure the lifelong economic security of U.S. women. Policies to ensure equity of educational opportunities must be joined by policies to ensure that women will be rewarded for all of the work that they do.

Data Appendix

Examples 1–3 all use data from the National Longitudinal Study of the Class of 1972. This study is used because it follows individuals from the 1972 senior year of high school through 1986 and because all participants were given a standardized math test as high school seniors. The Cognitive Test of Mathematics had twenty-five questions, with one point given for each correct answer and a 1/3 point penalty for incorrect answers.

All estimates are weighted using weights provided with the data set to control for differential sampling, response, and attrition rates. These weights are constructed so that weighted estimates are representative of a cross section of 1972 U.S. high school seniors.

Example 1 uses the sample of 4,327 men and 4,791 women with both scores from the 1972 math test and information on 1986 activities. Table 11.1 is based on all 9,118 observations. Table 11.2 is based on the subset of 3,276 men and 2,404 women who were full-time workers in 1986 and for whom hourly earnings were reported.

Among white men who earned an engineering, math, computer science, or physical science bachelor's degree by 1979, the median score on the Cognitive Test of Mathematics was 22 1/3 . The 577 men and 324 women with "very high" scores described in Example 1 have scores greater than 22 1/3.

Example 2 uses the full sample of 15,860 students who took the 1972 math test to determine score frequencies for men and women. College major frequencies similarly make use of all observations with these data available. (See the technical appendix, which follows, for a description of how the weights were constructed.)

After the weights were created, the simulations reported in table 11.3 used the same sample of 9,118 that was used in table 11.1. Full-time hourly earnings are based on the same subset used in table 11.2.

The 1986 occupational distributions described in table 11.4 again use the sample of 9,118 used in tables 11.1 and 11.3. The 1970 data are from an IPUMS (Integrated Public Use Microdata Series) extract of the 1970 census ($n = 45,356$). This extract is representative of all individuals who were ages 31–33 in 1970 and who had at least twelve years of education. The 1999 tabulations were computed by the U.S. Bureau of Labor Statistics Ferret System based on all individuals in the March 1999 Current Population Survey who were ages 31–33 and who had at least 12 years of education ($n = 5,112$).

Technical Appendix: Description of Weighting Procedure to Simulate Equal Distributions of Math Skills

In Example 2, weighted averages of women's labor market outcomes estimate what labor market outcomes might be in a simulated world with more women like the higher scoring women and fewer women like the lower scoring women. The simulated effect on earnings cannot tell us exactly what would happen if more women knew math but can give us a ballpark estimate. The weighting procedure used is described in this appendix.

For each possible score on the Cognitive Test of Mathematics, $i \in \{1, 2, 3, \ldots, 24, 25\}$, the proportion of boys who earned that score (p_i^m) was computed. Similarly, the proportion of girls who earned each score was computed (p_i^f). The first set of weights, bringing the women's scores to match the men's math scores, is $w_i^1 = p_i^m/p_i^f$. For example, 8.0 percent of men and 4.6 percent of women score 23. All women with score 23 were weighted by 8.0/4.6 = 1.74, or counted as 1.74 people. Similarly, 3.8 percent of men and 5.2 percent of women score 8, and so women with score 8 were weighted by 0.73.

The mean of a variable (e.g., n observations of the wage) is usually understood to be the sum of all observations divided by the number of observations, or $1/n \sum_{j=1}^{n} wage_j$. The weighted mean is computed as: $1/n \sum_{j=1}^{n} wage_j w^1_{s(j)}$, where $w^1_{s(j)}$ is the weight applied to individual j, who has scored $s(j)$. Note that the mean of $w^1_{s(j)}$ over all j is 1.

To create the second set of weights, we computed the proportion of male college graduates in each college major, M^m_K, where $K \in$ {biology, business, computer science, education, engineering, health, math, physical science, other}. We then computed the proportion of female college graduates in each college major, M^f_K, after applying the first set of weights. For individuals who did not graduate from college, the second set of weights is equal to the first ($w^2_i = w^1_i$). For the college graduates, $w^2_{i,K} = w^1_i M^m_K/M^f_K$.

A third and fourth set of weights were also created, using additional information about SAT-M (SAT mathematics) scores for those students who took the SAT exam (about one-third of all students). Where the SAT-M score was available, the first weight was replaced by the ratio of the proportion of men to the proportion of women with SAT-M scores in the same 50-point range. (These proportions were taken from Paglin and Rufolo 1990, table 4, column 7). For example, women with scores between 700 and 750 were weighted by 2.97. Using this additional information permits greater differentiation at higher levels of math scores. The fourth set of weights was computed in the same way as the second but with college major distributions computed after applying the third, rather than the first, set of weights. The analysis using SAT-M-based weights had almost the same results, which are not reported in the tables. The estimated percentage of women who would be scientists and engineers and average hourly earnings both fell slightly. Among college graduates, simulated hourly earnings rose very slightly, from \$12.60 to \$12.65, when SAT-M-based weights were used.

Note: the weights described in this technical appendix are, in fact, multiplied by the weights described in the preceding data appendix—a detail omitted to simplify the explanation.

Notes

This chapter was written while the author was a National Academy of Education Spencer Postdoctoral Fellow. The very early stages of this research were funded by a grant from the American Educational Research Association. I would like to thank Shirley Alvord-Shepherd, Rani Bush, Noah Friedkin, Mary King, Peter Kuhn, John Mohr, Krista Paulsen, John Sonquist, Lisa Torres, and Sonia Utt for insightful comments on earlier drafts of this chapter.

1. In 1982 23 percent of Hispanic, 26 percent of African American, 41 percent of white, and 55 percent of Asian American high school seniors had completed algebra II. By 1992 these figures had increased and converged substantially, to 47 percent of Hispanic, 41 percent of African American, 59 percent of white,

and 61 percent of Asian American high school seniors (NCES 1995). Similarly, in 1982 only 33 percent of seniors with high school–educated parents completed algebra II, compared with 53 percent of those with college-educated parents. By 1992, the figures were far more equitable: 55 percent of those with high school–educated parents and 59 percent of those with college-educated parents (NCES 1995). These increases in participation are particularly dramatic given that they occurred during a period of falling dropout rates for students of all ethnic groups (NCES 1997, 1999).

2. The average weekly earnings of women employed full-time in these technical occupations are $985 for pharmacists, $966 for doctors, $859 in computer occupations, and $831 for engineers (U.S. Bureau of Labor Statistics 1999).

3. This study estimated the effect of math coursework with and without careful controls for family and personal characteristics that might affect later earnings, including cognitive test scores.

4. Unpublished work by Ackerman (1999) suggests that better controls for the type of math classes and whether they were successfully completed (rather than the number of classes enrolled in) would lead to a somewhat higher estimate of the effect of math education on earnings.

5. Earnings are for individuals aged 35–44 with a bachelor's degree and no higher degree. Occupations are listed in order of descending median annual earnings. Note that physics would probably also be listed for women, except that the number of women is too small to make a reliable estimate. This example draws on median annual earnings listed in Hecker (1995).

6. For discussion of the data and methods used in Examples 1–3, see the data appendix and the technical appendix at the end of this chapter. A more detailed discussion of Example 1 can be found in Weinberger (1999c).

7. The "highly skilled professional" category is constructed in Weinberger (1999c). It contains the following occupations: accountant, actor, author, economist, editor or reporter, lawyer, librarian, psychologist, researcher, urban planner. Average high school math scores are high in each of these occupations.

8. The same holds for a younger sample—among 1980 seniors 8 percent of women with very high math test scores, compared to only 2 percent of the full cohort, were schoolteachers in 1986 (Weinberger 1999c).

9. See table 11.2. The high scoring men in sales, clerical, craft, unskilled labor, or service occupations averaged $13.60 per hour, 18 percent more than an average scoring man with no college degree. These high scoring men in lower-status occupations earned as much as high scoring women or low scoring men in higher-status occupations. In contrast, the average hourly earnings of high scoring women employed full-time in sales, clerical, craft, unskilled labor, or service occupations are only $8.60 per hour, only 2 percent more than those of an average scoring woman with no college degree.

10. This procedure is used in Duleep and Regets (1997).

11. The number of people who benefit from improved scores on civil service or military entrance exams might be too small to be noticed in this analysis.

12. A "cohort" is a group of people who were born (or, in this case, who finished high school) at about the same time. Usually, we can just call a group born earlier the "older" group. That would be confusing here, since we are looking at each group at age 32.

13. The entry of women into health diagnosing and sales occupations was greater during the later period.

14. This example was taken from an article in *Working Woman* magazine.

15. For example, Grogger and Eide (1995) found that demand for technical college graduates rose faster than the supply during the early 1980s. During this period, both supply and wages rose—but wages probably did not rise as much as they would have without the increase in supply.

References

Ackerman, Deena. 1999. "Do the Math: High School Mathematics Classes and the Lifetime Earnings of Men." Manuscript, University of Wisconsin. (Work is in progress on a similar study of women.)

American Association of University Women (AAUW). 1991. *Shortchanging Girls, Shortchanging America: A Call to Action.* Washington, DC: American Association of University Women.

———. 1999. *Gender Gaps: Where Schools Still Fail Our Children.* New York: Marlowe.

Angoff, William, and Eugene Johnson. 1990. "The Differential Impact of Curriculum on Aptitude Test Scores." *Journal of Educational Measurement* 27:291–305.

Arnold, Karen. 1994. *Lives of Promise.* San Francisco: Jossey-Bass.

Aronson, Joshua, Michael J. Lustina, Catherine Good, Kelli Keough, Claude M. Steele, and Joseph Brown. 1999. "When White Men Can't Do Math: Necessary and Sufficient Factors in Stereotype Threat." *Journal of Experimental Social Psychology* 35:29–46.

Badgett, M. V. Lee, and Nancy Folbre. 1999. "Job Gendering: Occupational Choice and the Marriage Market." Manuscript, University of Massachussetts, Amherst.

Bellas, Marcia L. 1994. "Comparable Worth in Academia: The Effects on Faculty Salaries of the Sex Composition and Labor Market Conditions of Academic Disciplines." *American Sociological Review* 59:807–21.

———. 1997. "Disciplinary Differences in Faculty Salaries: Does Gender Play a Role?" *Journal of Higher Education* 68:299–321.

Benbow, Camilla, and Julian Stanley. 1980. "Sex Differences in Mathematical Ability: Fact or Artifact?" *Science* 210 (December) :1262–64.

———. 1982. "Consequences in High School and College of Sex Differences in Mathematical Reasoning Ability: A Longitudinal Perspective." *American Educational Research Journal* 19:598–622.

Betz, Nancy E. 1997. "What Stops Women and Minorities from Choosing and Completing Majors in Science and Engineering?" In *Minorities and Girls in School,* edited by David Johnson, 105–40. Thousand Oaks, CA: Sage Publications.

Betz, Nancy E., and Gail Hackett. 1981. "The Relationship of Career-Related Self-Efficacy Expectations to Perceived Career Options in College Women and Men." *Journal of Counseling Psychology* 28:399–410.

———. 1983. "The Relationship of Mathematics Self-Efficacy Expectations to the Selection of Science-Based College Majors." *Journal of Vocational Behavior* 23:329–45.

Bielby, William. 1992. "Sex Differences in Careers: Is Science a Special Case?" In *The Outer Circle,* edited by Harriet Zuckerman, Jonathan R. Cole, and John T. Bruer, 171–87. New Haven, CT: Yale University Press.

Bishop, John. 1992. "The Impact of Academic Competencies on Wages, Unemployment, and Job Performance." *Carnegie-Rochester Conference Series on Public Policy* 37:127–94.

Blakemore, Arthur E., and Stuart A. Low. 1984. "Sex Differences in Occupational Selection: The Case of College Majors." *Review of Economics and Statistics* 66 (February): 157–63.

Bridgeman, Brent, and Cathy Wendler. 1991. "Gender Differences in Predictors of College Mathematics Performance and in College Mathematics Course Grades." *Journal of Educational Psychology* 83, no. 2:275–84.

Brown, Charles, and Mary Corcoran. 1997. "Sex-Based Differences in School Content and the Male-Female Wage Gap." *Journal of Labor Economics* 15:431–65.

Byrnes, James P., and Sayuri Takahira. 1993. "Explaining Gender Differences on SAT-Math Items." *Developmental Psychology* 29:805–10.

Cohn, Samuel. 1985. *The Process of Occupational Sex-Typing: The Feminization of Clerical Labor in Great Britain.* Philadelphia: Temple University Press.

Davies, Margery. 1982. *Woman's Place Is at the Typewriter: Office Work and Office Workers, 1870–1930.* Philadelphia: Temple University Press.

Daymont, Thomas, and Paul Andrisani. 1984. "Job Preferences, College Major, and the Gender Gap in Earnings." *Journal of Human Resources* 19 (summer): 408–28.

Donato, Katharine M. 1990. "Programming for Change? The Growing Demand for Women Systems Analysts." In *Job Queues, Gender Queues,* edited by Barbara Reskin and Patricia Roos, 167–82. Philadelphia: Temple University Press.

Duleep, Harriet Orcutt, and Mark C. Regets. 1997. "Measuring Immigrant Wage Growth Using Matched CPS Files." *Demography* 34:239–49.

Eccles, Jaquelynne. 1987. "Gender Roles and Women's Achievement-Related Decisions." *Psychology of Women Quarterly* 11:135–72.

———. 1997. "User-Friendly Science and Math." In *Minorities and Girls in School,* edited by David Johnson, 65–104. Thousand Oaks, CA: Sage Publications.

Eide, Eric. 1994. "College Major and Changes in the Gender Wage Gap." *Contemporary Economic Policy* 12 (April): 55–64.

England, Paula, and Nancy Folbre. 1999. "The Cost of Caring." *Annals of the American Academy of Political and Social Science* 561:39–51.

England, Paula, Melissa A. Herbert, Barbara Kilbourne, Lori Reid, and Lori McCreary Megdal. 1994. "The Gendered Valuation of Occupations and Skills: Earnings in 1980 Census Occupations." *Social Forces* 73:65–99.

Ferber, Marianne, and Betty Kordick. 1978. "Sex Differences in the Earnings of Ph.D.'s." *Industrial and Labor Relations Review* 31:227–38.

Ferree, Myra Marx, and Julia McQuillan. 1998. "Gender-Based Pay Gaps: Methodological and Policy Issues in University Salary Studies." *Gender and Society* 12, no. 1:7–39.

Fiorito, Jack, and Robert Dauffenbach. 1982. "Market and Nonmarket Influences on Curriculum Choice by College Students." *Industrial and Labor Relations Review* 36, no. 1:88–101.

Friedan, Betty. 1983. *The Feminine Mystique.* With a new introduction and epilogue by the author. New York: Dell Publishing.

Goldhaber, Daniel, and Dominic Brewer. 1997. "Why Don't Schools and Teachers Seem to Matter? Assessing the Impact of Unobservables on Educational Productivity." *Journal of Human Resources* 32, no. 3:505–23.

Grogger, Jeff, and Eric Eide. 1995. "Changes in College Skills and the Rise in the College Wage Premium." *Journal of Human Resources* 30:280–310.

Haberfeld, Yitchak, and Yehouda Shenhav. 1990. "Are Women and Blacks Closing the Gap? Salary Discrimination in American Science during the 1970's and 1980's." *Industrial and Labor Relations Review* 44:68–82.

Hall, Roberta, and Bernice Sandler. 1982. *The Classroom Climate: A Chilly One for Women?* Project on the Status and Education of Women. Washington, DC: Association of American Colleges.

Hampton, Mary B., and John S. Heywood. 1993. "Do Workers Accurately Perceive Gender Wage Discrimination?" *Industrial and Labor Relations Review* 47, no. 1:36–49.

Hanson, Sandra. 1996. *Lost Talent: Women in the Sciences.* Philadelphia: Temple University Press.

Hanushek, Eric, and Richard Pace. 1994. "Understanding Entry into the Teaching Profession." In *Choices and Consequences: Contemporary Policy Issues in Education,* edited by Ronald G. Ehrenberg, 12–28. Ithaca, NY: ILR Press.

Hecker, Daniel. 1995. "Earnings of College Graduates, 1993." *Monthly Labor Review* 118 (December): 3–17.

———. 1998. "Earnings of College Graduates: Women Compared to Men." *Monthly Labor Review* 121 (March): 62–71.

Hedges, Larry V., and Amy Nowell. 1995. "Sex Differences in Mental Test Scores, Variability, and Numbers of High-Scoring Individuals." *Science* 269:41–45.

Hyde, Janet. 1997. "Gender Differences in Math Performance: Not Big, Not Biological." In *Women, Men and Gender: Ongoing Debates,* edited by Mary Roth Walsh, 283–87. New Haven, CT: Yale University Press.

Hyde, Janet, Elizabeth Fennema, and Susan Lamon. 1990. "Gender Differences in Mathematics Performance: A Meta-Analysis." *Psychological Bulletin* 107:139–55.

Jagacinski, Carolyn M. 1987. "Engineering Careers: Women in a Male-Dominated Field." *Psychology of Women Quarterly* 11, no. 1:97–110.

Jones, Lyle V. 1984. "White-Black Achievement Differences: The Narrowing Gap." *American Psychologist* 39, no. 11:1207–13.

———. 1987. "The Influence on Mathematics Test Scores, by Ethnicity and Sex, of Prior Achievement and High School Mathematics Courses." *Journal for Research in Mathematics Education* 18, no. 3:180–86.

Kilbourne, Barbara, Paula England, Kurt Beron, and Dorothea Weir. 1994. "Returns to Skill, Compensating Differentials, and Gender Bias: Effects of Occupational Characteristics on the Wages of White Women and Men." *American Journal of Sociology* 100:689–719.

Kimball, Meredith. 1989. "A New Perspective on Women's Math Achievement." *Psychological Bulletin* 105:198–214.

Lapan, Richard T., Peter Shaughnessy, and Kathleen Boggs. 1996. "Efficacy Expectations and Vocational Interests as Mediators between Sex and Choice of Math/Science College Majors: A Longitudinal Study." *Journal of Vocational Behavior* 49:277–91.

Leslie, Larry L., Gregory T. McClure, and Ronald Oaxaca. 1998. "Women and Minorities in Science and Engineering: A Life Sequence Analysis." *Journal of Higher Education* 69, no. 3:239–76.

Levine, Phillip B., and David J. Zimmerman. 1995. "The Benefits of Additional High-School Math and Science Classes for Young Men and Women." *Journal of Business and Economic Statistics* 13:137–49.

Lunneborg, Patricia W. 1982. "Role Model Influences of Nontraditional Professional Women." *Journal of Vocational Behavior* 20, no. 3:276–81.

Manski, Charles. 1987. "Academic Ability, Earnings, and the Decision to Become a Teacher: Evidence from the NLS-72." In *Public Sector Payrolls,* edited by David A. Wise, 291–312. Chicago: University of Chicago Press.

Matthews, Frank. 1997. "Working with What Works, An Interview with Dr. Vinetta C. Jones." *Black Issues in Higher Education* 13 (February 20): 31.

McIlwee, Judith S., and J. Gregg Robinson. 1992. *Women in Engineering: Gender, Power, and Workplace Culture.* Albany, NY: State University of New York Press.

Monk, David H. 1994. "Subject Area Preparation of Secondary Mathematics and Science Teachers and Student Achievement." *Economics of Education Review* 13, no. 2:125–45.

Murnane, Richard J., and Frank Levy. 1996. *Teaching the New Basic Skills: Principles for Educating Children to Thrive in a Changing Economy.* New York: Free Press.

Murnane, Richard J., John B. Willet, and Frank Levy. 1995. "The Growing Importance of Cognitive Skills in Wage Determination." *Review of Economics and Statistics* 77 (May): 251–66.

National Center for Education Statistics (NCES). 1994. *NAEP 1994 Trends in Academic Progress.* Washington, DC: U.S. Department of Education.

———. 1995. *Trends among High School Seniors, 1972–1992.* Washington, DC: U.S. Department of Education.

———. 1997. *The Condition of Education, 1997.* Washington, DC: U.S. Department of Education.

———. 1999. *Digest of Education Statistics 1998.* Washington, DC: U.S. Department of Education.

———. n.d. *National Longitudinal Study of the Class of 1972.* Ann Arbor, MI: Interuniversity Consortium for Political and Social Research.

Oakes, Jeannie. 1990. *Multiplying Inequalities: The Effects of Race, Social Class, and Tracking on Opportunities to Learn Mathematics and Science.* Santa Monica, CA: Rand Corporation.

Paglin, Morton, and Anthony M. Rufolo. 1990. "Heterogeneous Human Capital, Occupational Choice, and Male-Female Earnings Differences." *Journal of Labor Economics* 8 (January): 123–44.

Park, Shelley M. 1996. "Research, Teaching, and Service." *Journal of Higher Education* 67, no. 1:46–84.

Polachek, Solomon. 1978. "Sex Differences in College Major." *Industrial and Labor Relations Review* 31 (July): 498–508.

———. 1981. "Occupational Self-Selection: A Human Capital Approach to Sex Differences in Occupational Structure." *Review of Economics and Statistics* 63 (February): 60–69.

Reskin, Barbara, and Irene Padavic. 1994. *Women and Men at Work*. Thousand Oaks, CA: Pine Forge Press.

Reskin, Barbara, and Patricia Roos. 1990. *Job Queues, Gender Queues*. Philadelphia: Temple University Press.

Rosser, Phyllis. 1989. *The SAT Gender Gap: Identifying the Causes*. Washington, DC: Center for Women's Policy Studies.

Rumberger, Russell W., and Scott Thomas. 1993. "The Economic Returns to College Major, Quality, and Performance: A Multilevel Analysis of Recent Graduates." *Economics of Education Review* 12 (March): 1–19.

Schlechty, Phillip, and Victor Vance. 1982. "The Distribution of Academic Ability in the Teaching Force: Policy Implications." *Phi Delta Kappan* 64:22–27.

Schiebinger, Londa. 1999. *Has Feminism Changed Science?* Cambridge, MA: Harvard University Press.

Seymour, Elaine, and Nancy Hewitt. 1994. "Talking about Leaving: Factors Contributing to High Attrition Rates among Science, Mathematics, and Engineering Undergraduate Majors." Bureau of Sociological Research, University of Colorado, Boulder, CO.

Sells, Lucy W. 1978. "Mathematics—A Critical Filter." *Science Teacher* 45, no. 2:28–29.

Shauman, Kimberlee A., and Yu Xie. 2000. "Gender Differences in the Attainment of a Science/Engineering Bachelor's Degree." Manuscript. University of California, Davis.

Sorensen, Elaine. 1989. "Measuring the Pay Disparity between Typically Female Occupations and Other Jobs: A Bivariate Selectivity Approach." *Industrial and Labor Relations Review* 42, no. 4:624–39.

Spencer, Steven J., Claude M. Steele, and Diane M. Quinn. 1999. "Stereotype Threat and Women's Math Performance." *Journal of Experimental Social Psychology* 35:4–28.

Steele, Claude M. 1997. "A Threat in the Air: How Stereotypes Shape Intellectual Identity and Performance." *American Psychologist* 52:613–29.

Steele, Claude M., and Joshua Aronson. 1995. "Stereotype Threat and the Intellectual Test Performance of African-Americans." *Journal of Personality and Social Psychology* 69:797–811.

Strober, Myra, and Carolyn L. Arnold. 1987a. "Integrated Circuits/Segregated Labor: Women in Computer-Related Occupations and High-Tech Industries." In *Computer Chips and Paper Clips: Technology and Women's Employment*, edited by Heidi Hartmann, 2:136–82. Washington, DC: National Academy Press.

———. 1987b. "The Dynamics of Occupational Segregation among Bank Tellers." In *Gender in the Workplace*, edited by Claire Brown and Joseph Pechman, 107–48. Washington, DC: Brookings Institution.

Tack, Martha, and Carol Patitu. 1992. *Faculty Job Satisfaction: Women and Minorities in Peril*. Washington, DC: School of Education and Human Development, George Washington University.

Tannen, Deborah. 1994. *Talking from Nine to Five: How Women's and Men's Conversational Styles Affect Who Gets Heard, Who Gets Credit, and What Gets Done at Work*. New York: W. Morrow.

Tobias, Sheila. 1978. *Overcoming Math Anxiety*. Boston: Houghton Mifflin.

———. 1990. *They're Not Dumb, They're Different: Stalking the Second Tier.* Tucson, AZ: Research Corporation.

Treiman, Donald J., and Heidi Hartmann. 1981. *Women, Work, and Wages: Equal Pay for Jobs of Equal Value.* Washington, DC: National Academy Press.

U.S. Bureau of Labor Statistics. 1999. *Employment and Earnings,* table 39: "Median Usual Weekly Earnings of Full-Time Wage and Salary Workers by Detailed Occupation and Sex." Available at <http://stats.bls.gov/cpsaatab.htm>.

Vetter, Betty. 1979. *Labor Force Participation of Women Trained in Science and Engineering and Factors Affecting Their Participation.* Final Technical Report, ED 177016. Washington, DC: Scientific Manpower Commission.

Ware, Norma, and Valerie Lee. 1988. "Sex Differences in Choice of College Science Majors." *American Educational Research Journal* 25, no. 4:593–614.

Weaver, W. Timothy. 1983. *America's Teacher Quality Problem: Alternatives for Reform.* New York: Praeger.

Weinberger, Catherine J. 1998. "Race and Gender Wage Gaps in the Market for Recent College Graduates." *Industrial Relations* 37, no. 1:67–84.

———. 1999a. "Mathematics Test Scores, Gender, Race, Ethnicity, and the Science and Engineering Workforce." Manuscript, University of California, Santa Barbara.

———. 1999b. "Mathematical College Majors and the Gender Gap in Wages." *Industrial Relations* 38, no. 3:407–13.

———. 1999c. "Allocation of a Scarce Resource: Occupational Outcomes of Young Men and Women with Very Strong High School Math Scores." Manuscript, University of California, Santa Barbara.

Wise, Lauress L., Lauri Steel, and C. MacDonald. 1979. *Origins and Career Consequences of Sex Differences in High School Mathematics Achievement.* ED180846. Palo Alto, CA: American Institutes for Research.

Zuckerman, Harriet. 1992. "The Careers of Male and Female Scientists: A Review of Current Research." In *The Outer Circle,* edited by Harriet Zuckerman, Jonathan R. Cole, and John T. Bruer, 27–56. New Haven, CT: Yale University Press.

PART 4

Conclusion

A Policy Agenda to Raise Women's Incomes in the United States

MARY C. KING

In 1997, three decades after the emergence of the modern women's movement, American women's incomes were only a bit more than half of men's, on average. This huge disparity results from three related factors: women are disproportionately held responsible for the unpaid work of child rearing, housework, and elder care; women are concentrated in paid work that is undervalued because it is "women's work"; and women are infrequently found in well-paid jobs. U.S. institutions and policies either serve to perpetuate these situations or have failed to significantly change them.

Some may think that women's low incomes are natural, the inevitable result of the differences in male and female biology. Yet to hold this position requires that one overlook the tremendous differences across countries, resulting from institutions created by people. Is it more natural that 47 percent of earned income in Tanzania accrues to women or that in Saudi Arabia women earn 10 percent of earned income? Among industrialized countries the range is almost as wide; 45 percent of Swedish earned income goes to women, but only 26 percent of Irish earned income does (United Nations Human Development Programme 1999).

Others may believe that these are conservative times, that little can be gained for women at this moment in U.S. political history. But we have the examples before us of people who have accomplished much in more difficult situations. Ken Burns, when being interviewed about his documentary on Elizabeth Cady Stanton and Susan B. Anthony, pointed out, "When they were born, women could not speak in public, they could not attend college, they couldn't testify in court, they couldn't serve on a jury, they had no rights to keep their earnings, they couldn't inherit property. They had less rights than an insane person in an asylum, and the vote which might have changed that was denied to them. But when these women died, all these things—with the exception of the vote—had been achieved for women" (McCollum 1999).

Now women have the vote. And women are not a minority. Yet millions of American women are seriously disadvantaged by low incomes. Many more millions of children, women, and men would be better off if more women had more money. A policy agenda to substantially raise women's incomes should generate significant political support.

Achieving policy changes to raise women's incomes will require political coalitions among different groups of women, as well as coalitions with organizations other than "women's groups," such as unions, civil rights organizations, and groups focused on the needs of children and the elderly. Creating and promoting a women's economic agenda also requires the recognition that women's experiences and priorities are not all identical. Women are distinguished—but hopefully need not be always divided—by class, race, ethnicity, religion, age, and sexual orientation.

Perhaps the best way to galvanize all of the groups that stand to benefit from economic equality for women is to pursue many strategies at the same time, rather than to attempt to unite everyone on one single best strategy. Barbara Bergmann has frequently asserted that there are three ways to achieve equality for women.

1. Ending gender specialization by integrating men into family work and women into market work, with family-friendly policies at the workplace;
2. Completely commodifying family work, so that we pay for cleaning, cooking, and child care, while women join the paid labor force; and
3. Valuing "women's work" at home financially in some way (Saunders and King 2000).

Women have probably made most progress along the lines of strategy two, commodifying family work while women join the paid labor force on terms similar to those under which men work. Many children, the ill, and the elderly are being cared for at least in part by paid personnel; lots of prepared food is available in grocery stores and fast food restaurants; and a huge range of personal services is available to those who can pay for them. American women's paid labor force participation rates have soared. One reason may be that this strategy can be pursued by women individually, without much change required in government policies or men's work lives. To fully accomplish economic equality between women and men using strategy two we might pursue any and all of the policies considered in this book to raise the pay in "women's jobs" and to move women into higher-paying jobs.

Many of us would prefer to pursue strategy one, to diminish gender roles and reach for fuller human development for everyone. Many women would like to participate in the workforce as men's equals, share more equally both the drudgery and joys of family work with their partners, and provide their families with personal care. The attainment of this strategy would require not only the types of policies considered in earlier chapters but also for men to take on far larger roles at home and for employers to stop expecting their employees to behave as if they all—women and men—had wives at home. We have to abolish what Randy Albelda has termed "jobs with wives," jobs that are structured with the assumption that an employee lives with a full-time housewife and is therefore completely free of family responsibilities; some employers presume even further, that an employee's spouse will entertain or take on other roles to support the firm (Albelda, Drago, and Shulman 1997).

Both aspects of strategy one—that women participate equally in the workforce while men participate equally at home—can be encouraged by policy initiatives. Paid parental leave specifically for fathers is one example being pursued in Sweden. Just as taxes and regulations have reduced industrial pollution, taxes and regulations can be used to motivate employers to implement more substantive family-friendly programs than most offer now—including shorter workweeks, well-paid and responsible part-time work, and on-site child care.

There are also many people who would like to see greater recognition and remuneration for the unpaid work that women have traditionally performed in the home, strategy three. By focusing only on the paid economy we miss—at our peril—much of what is really happening, especially for women and children (e.g., Waring 1988). Again, different policies could provide for compensation to those who rear children, both at the time and in old age. We could measure the unpaid resources being spent on families in the home so we know when children gain or lose resources devoted to their care or if girls are overworked at home, to the detriment of their schooling and future opportunities.

Effective policies to raise women's incomes relative to men's can be found that fit into each of the three overall strategies Bergmann identified. Several initiatives, such as expanding publicly subsidized child care, serve more than one of these strategies.

This means that policies to raise women's incomes can supported by the entire U.S. political spectrum. The potential for a political coalition between feminists and "family values conservatives" is a potent possibility. Conservatives should appreciate the need to reward parents for raising children at home, as otherwise the incentives of our market economy push everyone into the paid labor force. Liberals should appreciate policies to support families that will at the same time significantly reduce poverty. Feminists of all stripes should appreciate policies both to improve women's access to better paid, more responsible employment and to increase the economic security of mothers. There is no need to narrowly focus on one aspect of an agenda to raise women's incomes; a pluralist agenda supports the freedom of choice that allows people to act according to their own values and interests at any particular time in their lives.

Each of the policies discussed in the previous chapters can be thought about in terms of its ability to raise women's incomes, its place in the three overall strategies outlined previously, and its capacity to mobilize effective political coalitions that would support its implementation. The preceding chapters have assessed the potential effectiveness of different strategies to raise women's incomes; this chapter asks who should support each of the different policies.

Political Potential of Policy Strategies

Reducing the Negative Impact of
Child Rearing on Women's Incomes

It is easy to justify increasing public support for parents, whether paying parents some type of child benefit as the Europeans do, passing "real welfare reform," subsidizing child care nationwide, or changing Social Security so that parenting is better rewarded. Parents are creating the most vital ingredient in our economic future—healthy, socialized, engaged young people ready to be trained and educated for productive work as adults. Economists have come to credit "human capital," or the human capability that results from the investment of time, care, and training of young people, with most of economic development.

Several researchers have attempted to estimate the value produced by unpaid work in the household, including child rearing. An Australian, Duncan Ironmonger, has measured what he calls "gross household product" as roughly equal to the value produced by the market economy. Of the time spent creating Australia's gross household product in 1992, about one-half involved child care (Ironmonger 1996).

Now our economic institutions penalize anyone who takes time out of the paid labor force to nurture children, a reality even the most devoted parent has to face. As a nation, we will have to provide incentives for people to spend more time with children, if this is something that we value. These incentives would benefit the middle class, as well as the poor and working class.

Other nations have far more developed family policies than we do. One consequence of these policies is to significantly reduce the number of children and parents in poverty. Having children in the household significantly increases a household's likelihood of poverty in the United States and elsewhere, because children earn no money, require financial outlays, and take the time of adults who otherwise could be working for pay. People who spend much of their adult lives caring for children are also vulnerable to poverty in old age, because they are less likely to have accumulated credit with Social Security, claim on a pension, or savings.

The United States has exceptionally high poverty rates among the economically advanced nations. This is primarily due to our weak antipoverty and family support programs, rather than to any peculiarity of the U.S. labor market or population. While many nations would have poverty rates comparable to ours in the absence of government programs, none actually has poverty rates—particularly child poverty rates—nearly as high as ours. For example, in the early 1990s French antipoverty programs brought child poverty rates down from 27 percent to 7 percent, while U.S. policies reduced child poverty only from 29 percent to 25 percent (Smeeding 1997). In fact, during the 1980s our tax and transfer system pushed more nonelderly households with children into poverty than it lifted out of poverty. This means that the taxes levied on near-poor families pushed more families below the poverty line than our antipoverty programs lifted above the poverty line (McFate, Smeeding, and Rainwater 1995).

Our antipoverty programs leave over 50 percent of U.S. single mothers in poverty, whereas the comparable rate for single mothers in Sweden is 5.5 percent and the rate in the Netherlands is 7.5 percent (McFate, Smeeding, and Rainwater 1995, 53). Sweden and the Netherlands take quite different tacks to support single mothers. Swedish policies encourage mothers to work for pay, while Dutch programs focus on supporting mothers at home. Why shouldn't we do both? The fact that both approaches work means that we can, to some extent, craft a pluralistic, pro-family policy in this country in accordance with the range of values held by Americans.

Increasing public support for parents would clearly benefit women at risk of poverty, a category that includes single mothers, women married to young men, women of color, and women with health problems. We will all be better off in the future if poor parents are able now to provide their children with love, caring, and time, rather than leaving them in poor care to work long hours in badly paid, menial, and only marginally productive jobs (Burggraf 1997). Because our long history of racial discrimination has left so many people of color with lower levels of education and income, increased public support for parents would be particularly helpful to minority communities. Most forms of support for parents should reduce poverty rates among elderly women, who pay in old age for having spent their time raising children.

Better support for parents would also benefit middle- and upper-class women who are stay-at-home mothers. They and their families would be more economically secure, both now and in retirement. These women would gain more power in their families and communities if they were perceived as bringing in their own money and making an important social contribution. Mothers could more easily leave abusive marriages, knowing that they could continue to expect public support. Divorcees and widows would not experience the drop in their living standards they now do. Other middle-income women—and men— might feel that their lives were improved if they were able to reduce their work hours to part-time while their children are young, to spend more time at home.

Alternatively, subsidizing child care would give women of all classes who wanted to work the ability to stay in the labor force or to improve their education, giving them greater personal and financial independence throughout their lives. Subsidies, combined with regulation, should improve the quality of child care available to the large numbers of American children in care.

Increased public support for parents would not be unfair to lesbians or gay men, as many are parents or would like to be parents. Indeed lesbian mothers as a group would particularly benefit from better family policies as they are generally raising children without access to the higher wages and better fringe benefits received by men.

In sum, reducing the negative impact of child rearing on women's incomes would benefit millions of women and their families. Benefits to improve the lives of parents should appeal to antipoverty groups, children's advocacy groups, civil rights groups, and organizations concerned with the situation of the elderly. Smaller constituencies that stand to gain from these policies include child-care workers, who could expect better pay and career opportunities if child care were expanded and subsidized. Our schools would be better if fewer children lived in the chaos that frequently accompanies poverty. Providers of services for the elderly would appreciate the expanded market created by improving the status of older women, and the producers of a gamut of goods and services from housing to breakfast cereal would be happy to supply the wants of lower-income women and families with more money to spend.

"Who's Going to Pay for All This?" Anyone who proposes social programs in the United States—such as pay for parents, a more adequate welfare program, subsidized child care, or better Social Security for older women—is invariably met with the refrain, "Well, that sounds great, but who is going to pay for it?" But this is the wrong way to think about it, as if these social programs were an expensive charity. In fact, increasing support for American parents is an important investment in our future that will pay off for all of us. We will all be better off if the children who are poor today fill our universities, rather than our jails, tomorrow. We must pay now, or we will surely pay later.

We understand that as a nation we need to invest in physical infrastructure, including roads, airports, and telecommunications systems, if we are to leave our children a strong economic foundation upon which to build. We have learned that investment in public education is one of the best we can make, as shown, for example, by the tremendous increase in the productivity of the labor force as a result of the G.I. Bill. Investment in our children is at least as important. Subsidized, high-quality child care and support for caring parents at home will help children enter school prepared to succeed. Additionally, if women bring more money into their households, U.S. businesses will profit from bigger markets, and women working more because of subsidized child care will pay more taxes. Standards of living are very high in the European countries where public support for parents is most developed. And, as all of our industrialized competitors are already paying far more on social expenditures, we will hardly price ourselves out of the global business competition by joining them.

Finally, it is not as if we are not paying already for women's low incomes. We are paying in the unnecessarily circumscribed lives of women and their families. Those paying the highest price are the families in poverty resulting from women's low wages and heavy unpaid responsibilities; and the families living with violence because of women's limited options. But we all pay now—and will continue to pay in the future—the price of a large group of children grown to adulthood deprived of a childhood that could have nurtured productive habits and skills, as well as the outlook of citizens rather than of the dispossessed.

Raising the Pay for Women's Jobs

Raising the minimum wage, pushing through comparable worth pay adjustments, and increasing the proportion of women represented by unions all represent strategies that can raise the pay for "women's jobs," for which a large proportion of women are still trained and which they are currently performing. Lack of these policies is a significant part of the explanation for the relatively large gap between women's and men's pay in the United States, as compared with the majority of other economically advanced nations. American women are more educated, spend more years in the labor force, and are more likely to work full-time than most women elsewhere, but they still suffer from a relatively large pay gap (Blau and Kahn 1996). The reason is that the wage structure in the United States is much more unequal than in the rest of the industrialized world; by international standards our lowest wages are quite low and our highest wages extremely high. All around the world women are concentrated in lower-wage jobs, but in the United States that puts women further below men than it does abroad.

The relative weakness of the U.S. labor movement is one of the reasons for our extreme wage inequality. The legal obstacles to labor organizing are significant in the United States and have been for a long time, with the brief exception of the years during World War II. Consequently the highest proportion of U.S. workers to have been organized in unions was 36 percent in 1945, a peak from which the numbers have declined so that today only 14 percent of U.S. workers are represented by a labor union (Kaufman 1994; AFL-CIO 1999). These compare with proportions in Europe up to 90 percent in Sweden. We need to reduce the legal hurdles to unionization in this country.

The stronger labor movements of Europe and Australia have consistently pushed for a "solidarity wage policy," which means keeping wages up at the bottom and reducing wage inequality. Women, overrepresented at the bottom everywhere, have benefited from these policies, even where labor leaders have held to relatively sexist philosophies. Raising the minimum wage is probably the simplest, most proven way to raise women's wages.

Without an effective advocate in a powerful labor movement or labor party, the minimum wage in the United States has been allowed to fall considerably in its purchasing power over the last twenty-five years, as discussed by Deborah Figart in chapter 6. Historically, wages in the United States were much higher than elsewhere; now the poorest-paid American men earn wages with just half the purchasing power as the poorest-paid men in Italy, Norway, and Germany (Freeman 1994, 13).

Clearly young families are struggling, as are many women, because adult women comprise the majority of minimum wage and near minimum wage workers (Mishel, Bernstein, and Schmitt 1999, 190). Women—and men—of color are overrepresented in the lower rungs of the wage structure, where they stand to benefit from increases in the minimum wage and any ripple effect that increases would set off in wages close to the minimum. These people together represent millions who would benefit from working in a coalition to implement the strategies that will raise women's incomes.

Pay equity policies designed to end the devaluation of "women's work" would significantly raise women's incomes (Figart and Lapidus 1995). As Margaret Hallock points out in chapter 7, pay equity efforts in the United States have been bogged down by the gargantuan task of taking on each workplace individually. However, there are simpler and more effective means to achieve pay equity. In Australia, for example, pay equity has been relatively successfully implemented. Because the Australians set national minimum wages for all occupations, modifying these was relatively easy. Although we do not have the occupational minimum wages that Australia does, we are not without potentially effective national strategies. The U.S. Department of Labor or the National Academy of Sciences could develop wage guidelines for the most common occupations to fairly compensate people for their qualifications, skills, responsibilities, effort, and working conditions

(Bergmann 1986). The federal government and contractors to the federal government could be required to follow these guidelines, while advocates for pay equity nationwide could push for their implementation in their own workplaces, rather than attempting the difficult—and repetitive—task of job evaluation for every firm in the country (Bergmann 1986).

Pay equity would be particularly helpful in raising wages for women of color and for some men as well. Black women are even more concentrated in "women's jobs" than are white women, and educated black men are more likely than white men to work in the female-dominated "helping professions," so both stand to benefit from pay adjustments that correct the devaluation of women's work (Malveaux 1984). Further, African Americans are concentrated in jobs that disproportionately employ other African Americans; pay equity campaigns that include the jobs of people of color that are devalued in comparison with "white jobs" should result in higher pay for women and men of color (Malveaux 1985/86; King 1998; Lapidus and Figart 1998). Civil rights organizations should support pay equity efforts.

Also pay equity would disproportionately benefit women in the most poorly paid positions, as so many of these involve the female skills of "emotional labor," taking care of people in occupations such as child care and health care (Steinberg and Figart 1999). For this reason, antipoverty groups should support the implementation of pay equity.

Unionization is generally positive for women, as the wages of women in unions are closer to men's and union contracts include both more fringe benefits and more opportunities to work out workplace grievances, such as sexual harassment or discrimination. While the labor movement historically excluded women from many unions and did little to organize workers in women's occupations, it has emerged in recent decades as an active champion of the causes of working women. Pay equity campaigns in the United States have all been led by unions. Unions pushed hard for family medical leave. Unions are currently the biggest organized force for raising the minimum wage. Recent union organizing successes have disproportionately involved poorly paid women, often women of color.

So unions are now taking an active interest in the fight to raise the pay for women's jobs. They would be more effective in coalition with civil rights groups and immigrants' organizations, which also represent many people paid too little. Advocates for children and antipoverty organizations should recognize that higher pay for women, particularly those at the bottom, would go a long way to reduce poverty rates. And feminists should support policies to make labor organizing easier.

Business organizations, particularly small business groups, will fight minimum wage increases, pay equity adjustments, and union organizing as they always have, saying that they cannot afford to pay women higher wages. And it is true that higher wages will have to come out of corporate profits or the now astronomical salaries of U.S. upper management. However, American women should not be expected to sacrifice themselves and their families to subsidize business profits or managerial salaries.

Businesses that cannot afford to pay decently need to find a strategy that does not require cheap labor. Reformers calling for the initial establishment of the minimum wage in this country called low-wage employers "parasitic industries," to dramatize the fact that these businesses subsist at the expense of both their workers and the larger community that must too often step in to help with public medical care, food aid, and other charities (Power 1999). Finally, raising women's incomes will be good for the economy overall, if uncomfortable for some businesses, as other firms realize how many more automobiles, appliances, and shoes can be sold to women with more money. Even businesses that operate with minimum wage workers may be able to both raise their prices and sell more if the purchasing power of all workers is higher.

Moving Women into Higher Paying Work

Social scientists continue to find that a substantial part of the pay differences between women and men results from the fact that they are employed in different jobs, even when they have similar qualifications. Raising the minimum wage, gaining pay equity for "women's jobs," and getting union contracts are all routes to raising the wages for jobs that women already hold. The complementary strategy is to help women move into jobs with better pay, into jobs that are currently dominated by men. Affirmative action, helping women enter the skilled trades, and increasing women's mathematical education are all aimed at bringing down the barriers to women attempting to move out of the female ghetto in the workplace.

What each of the chapters in part 3 of this book showed was that these strategies can be and are useful for individual women. Affirmative action—including the particularly tough case of opening the construction trades to women—appears to hold out greater promise for raising women's incomes as a group than does increasing girls' mathematical education. Catherine Weinberger has shown in chapter II that many women with high math aptitude and strong math skills continue to enter traditionally female—and low-paying—occupations. While we should certainly push for all areas of endeavor to be hospitable to women, including the math-based professions, it does not appear that focusing on math education can significantly raise women's incomes without a reduction in occupational segregation and increased valuation of "women's jobs."

Affirmative action, on the other hand, has been shown to produce results when enforced. The case studies examined by Lee Badgett and Jeannette Lim demonstrate the strides that can be made when affirmative action is pursued vigorously. And women in all areas stand to benefit from affirmative action, not only those who hope to work as firefighters and carpenters. Women could be selling cars, rather than cosmetics; serving fine wine, rather than hash browns; and running meetings rather than taking notes.

In the absence of strong enforcement of affirmative action, we see the persistence of "business as usual," despite ever-present rhetoric to the contrary. This is made abundantly clear by Barbara Byrd in chapter 10, in which she discusses women in the skilled trades. It is ridiculous that women entering construction trades still face the same harassment and sabotage that they did thirty-five years ago when affirmative action and antidiscrimination legislation were written (Eisenberg 1998). It is absurd that private businesses claim not to be able to find any qualified women to promote to senior management positions when they lag far behind the public and nonprofit sectors, where affirmative action is taken more seriously. If monitoring and enforcement of existing civil rights legislation had been serious, enough women would now work in those jobs to provide support for new entrants, now eternal pioneers.

Affirmative action, opening the skilled trades, and diversifying the math-based professions are in the interests of men of color as well, who have also been shut out of the best-paid occupations. Antipoverty and civil rights organizations should support these strategies, in coalition with women's groups.

However, many activists are feeling that the backlash against these policies has not been worth the limited results gained by their half-hearted enforcement, particularly under the Reagan and Bush administrations. On the other hand, to give up on compensatory strategies, to accept the notion that they are unfair, and to ignore the legacy of a long history of affirmative action for white men while the playing field has been only partially leveled is to accept that sexual and ethnic inequality will decline only very, very slowly.

Catherine Weinberger also asked a harder question, can affirmative action really work to help women integrate "men's jobs," or will it merely create new "women's jobs"? We continue to see jobs tip from men's to women's work, while the pay falls. Historical examples are teaching, clerical work, and bank teller positions; current examples include pharmacy, journalism, and marketing (Strober and Arnold 1987; Reskin and Roos 1990). New occupations, using new technologies, seem to become instantly defined as male or female and paid accordingly. The "feminization" of an occupation—and its pay scale—results from the social devaluation of women and their work. Perhaps true integration will only be possible when mothering is valued and the pay for "women's jobs" is raised. Perhaps in the end we will need to pursue all three of Bergmann's three strategies to attain full economic equality for women.

Conclusion

In the meanwhile, we can raise women's incomes in the United States by implementing the policies considered in this book. While these policies would particularly benefit women as a group, they will also benefit children, the elderly, communities of color, the poor, and families with low and medium incomes. The political constituency that stands to benefit from policies to raise women's incomes is huge.

Women cannot continue to subsidize those who "cannot afford" to pay women for the full value of their time and contributions—the price is too high. And, as Peter Donohue's account in chapter 8 of the Silverton nurses' campaign reminds us, often those who claim that they cannot afford to pay women more simply prefer not to. We have to push for fair incomes for women, rather than continue to accept second-class status. Implementing policies to raise women's incomes will improve the lives of millions of American women and their families, strengthen our economy, reduce poverty, and diminish inequality.

Perhaps most important, with greater financial clout women can become full citizens. Women's voices will be heard, in our homes, in our local communities, in businesses looking for new markets, and in our national government.

References

AFL-CIO. 1999. Available at <http://www.aflcio.org/publ/press99/pr0125.htm>. Accessed on November 15.

Albelda, Randy, Robert Drago, and Steven Shulman. 1997. *Unlevel Playing Fields.* New York: McGraw-Hill.

Bergmann, Barbara R. 1986. *The Economic Emergence of Women.* New York: Basic Books.

Blau, Francine D., and Lawrence M. Kahn. 1996. "Wage Structure and Gender Earnings Differentials: An International Comparison." *Economica* 63, no. 250 (supplement): S29–S62.

Burggraf, Shirley. 1997. *The Feminine Economy and Economic Man: Reviving the Role of Family in the Post-Industrial Age.* Reading, MA: Addison-Wesley.

Eisenberg, Susan. 1998. "Still Building the Foundation: Women in the Construction Trades." *Working USA* (May/June 1998): 23–35.

Figart, Deborah M., and June Lapidus. 1995. "A Gender Analysis of Labor Market Policies for the Working Poor." *Feminist Economics* 1, no. 3:60–81.

Freeman, Richard B. 1994. "How Labor Fares in Advanced Economies." In *Working under Different Rules,* edited by Richard B. Freeman. New York: Russell Sage Foundation.

Ironmonger, Duncan. 1996. "Counting Outputs, Capital Inputs, and Caring Labor: Estimating Gross Household Product." *Feminist Economics* 2, no. 3:37–64.

Kaufman, Bruce E. 1994. *The Economics of Labor Markets.* Fort Worth: Dryden Press.

King, Mary C. 1998. "Are African Americans Losing Their Footholds in Better Jobs?" *Journal of Economic Issues* 32, no. 3:641–68.

Lapidus, June, and Deborah M. Figart. 1998. "Remedying 'Unfair Acts': U.S. Pay Equity by Race and Gender." *Feminist Economics* 4, no. 3:7–28.

Malveaux, Julianne. 1984. "Low Wage Black Women: Occupational Descriptions, Strategies for Change." Paper prepared for the NAACP Legal Defense and Educational Fund.

———. 1985–86. "Comparable Worth and Its Impact on Black Women." *Review of Black Political Economy.* 14, no. 2/3:47–62.

McCollum, Charlie. 1999. "Burns Tackles Forgotten Era in Compelling 'Not for Ourselves Alone'." *Oregonian,* November 5, p. E8.

McFate, Katherine, Timothy Smeeding, and Lee Rainwater. 1995. "Markets and States: Poverty Trends and Transfer System Effectiveness in the 1980s." In *Poverty, Inequality, and the Future of Social Policy: Western States in the New World Order,* edited by Katherine McFate, Roger Lawson, and William Julius Wilson, 29–66. New York: Russell Sage Foundation.

Mishel, Lawrence, Jared Bernstein, and John Schmitt. 1999. *The State of Working America, 1998–99.* Armonk, NY: M. E. Sharpe.

Power, Marilyn. 1999. "Parasitic-Industries Analysis and Arguments for a Living Wage for Women in the Early Twentieth-Century United States." *Feminist Economics* 5, no. 1:61–78.

Reskin, Barbara F., and Patricia A. Roos. 1990. *Job Queues, Gender Queues: Explaining Women's Inroads into Male Occupations.* Philadelphia: Temple University Press.

Saunders, Lisa F., and Mary C. King. 2000. "An Interview with Barbara Bergmann: Leading Feminist Economist." *Review of Political Economy* 12, no. 3.

Smeeding, Timothy M. 1997. "Financial Poverty in Developed Countries: The Evidence from LIS." Cited in Lawrence Mishel, Jared Bernstein, and John Schmitt, *The State of Working America, 1998–99* (Armonk, NY: M. E. Sharpe, 1999).

Steinberg, Ronnie, and Deborah M. Figart, eds. 1999. *Emotional Labor in the Service Economy.* Annals of the American Academy of Political and Social Scientists, vol. 561. Thousand Oaks, CA: Sage Publications.

Strober, Myra H., and Carolyn Arnold. 1987. "The Dynamics of Occupational Segregation among Bank Tellers." In *Gender in the Workplace,* edited by Clair Brown and Joseph Pechman. Washington, DC: Brookings Institution.

United Nations Human Development Programme. 1999. "Gender Related Development Index." In *Statistics from the 1998 Human Development Report.* Available at <http://www.undp.org/hdro/98gdi.htm>. Accessed on November 12.

Waring, Marilyn. 1988. *If Women Counted: A New Feminist Economics.* New York: Harper.

Contributors

Randy Albelda is professor of economics at the University of Massachusetts in Boston. She received her B.A. from Smith and her Ph.D. in economics from the University of Massachusetts, Amherst, in 1983. Professor Albelda's research and teaching focus on poverty, women's economic status, labor markets, and state and local finance. She is the author of *Economics and Feminism: Disturbances in the Field* (New York: Twayne Publishers) and coauthor of the books *The War on the Poor: A Defense Manual* (with Nancy Folbre; New York: New Press), and *Glass Ceilings and Bottomless Pits: Women's Work, Women's Poverty* (with Chris Tilly; Boston: South End Press). She is an active participant in legislative and educational efforts to improve policies and our understanding of welfare and employment polices that affect low-income women and their families.

M. V. Lee Badgett is a labor economist at the University of Massachusetts, Amherst. She is also the president and acting executive director of the Institute for Gay and Lesbian Strategic Studies. Professor Badgett received her B.A. in economics from the University of Chicago and her Ph.D. from the University of California, Berkeley, in 1990. Her research focuses on race, gender, and sexual orientation discrimination in the workplace and on gay family issues. Her current project is a book on the economic lives of lesbians and gay men. She has taught at Yale University and the University of Maryland and has served as a research analyst for the National Commission for Employment Policy.

Barbara R. Bergmann is professor emerita of economics at the University of Maryland and at American University in Washington, DC. She earned her B.A. at Cornell in 1948 in mathematics and economics and an M.A. and a Ph.D. in economics at Harvard in 1959. Professor Bergmann has written extensively on welfare, child care, women's place in the economy and the family, and the labor market problems of women and African Americans. She is currently working on two books, one on child-care policy and the other a cartoon book on Social Security. Her previous books include *In Defense of Affirmative Action* (HarperCollins: Basic Books), *Saving Our Children from Poverty: What the United States Can Learn from France* (New York: Russell Sage Foundation), and *The Economic Emergence of Women* (HarperCollins: Basic Books). She has served as president of the International Association for Feminist Economics, the Eastern Economic Association, the Society for the Advancement of Socio-Economics, and the American Association of University Professors.

Barbara Byrd is on the faculty of the University of Oregon's Labor Education and Research Center (LERC). She received her B.A. in sociology from Rice University in Houston; her master's degree in labor studies from the University of Massachusetts, Amherst; and her Ph.D. in adult education from the University of Texas. Dr. Byrd coordinates activities out of LERC's Portland office, including program development and training with unions and research on workplace policy issues. She also works with union apprenticeship programs and community organizations in Oregon, assisting with research on women in trades. She has been a labor educator for over twenty years. She is a member of the American Federation of Teachers, Local 8035.

Peter Donohue heads PBI Associates in Portland, Oregon, which assists unions and community groups in organizing, bargaining, and public policymaking. He received his B.A. in economics from Columbia University, his master's degree in labor studies from the University of Massachusetts, Amherst, and his Ph.D. in economics from the University of Texas at Austin. Dr. Donohue has taught at San Francisco State University; the University of California, Berkeley; and the University of Missouri-Columbia.

Deborah M. Figart is professor of economics at Richard Stockton College. She received her B.A. from Wheaton College and her Ph.D. in economics from American University. Professor Figart is coauthor of *Contesting the Market: Pay Equity and the Politics of Economic Restructuring* (Detroit: Wayne State University Press), coeditor of *Emotional Labor in the Service Economy* (Thousand Oaks, CA: Sage Publications), and associate editor of the *Encyclopedia of Political*

Economy (New York: Routledge). Her research interests include work time policies, minimum and living wages, labor market discrimination, and poverty. Her work has been published in numerous social science journals, and she is currently writing a book on wage policies in the twentieth-century United States.

Nancy Folbre is professor of economics at the University of Massachusetts and a staff economist with the Center for Popular Economics. She earned her B.A. and M.A. from the University of Texas and her Ph.D. from the University of Massachusetts. Professor Folbre's research interests focus on the interface between political economy and feminist theory, with a particular interest in the provision of caring labor. An associate editor of the journal *Feminist Economics,* she is also the recent recipient of a MacArthur Foundation Five-Year Fellowship.

Margaret Hallock is the director of the University of Oregon's Labor Education and Research Center. Professor Hallock received her Ph.D. in economics from Claremont Graduate School in 1974. As an economist, she has specialized in women and work. She has consulted internationally on pay equity, and she led the Oregon pay equity commission in the 1980s. Professor Hallock has written papers on women and unions and other topics in labor economics. She also directs the Wayne Morse Chair of Law and Politics at the University of Oregon.

Catherine Hill is the study director for the Social Security Project, Institute for Women's Policy Research (IWPR). She has recently coauthored two reports for IWPR entitled *Why Privatizing Social Security Would Hurt Women: A Response to the Cato Institute's Proposal for Individual Accounts* and *Strengthening Social Security for Women.* Dr. Hill has a Ph.D. in planning and policy development from Rutgers University, a master's degree in city and regional planning, and a bachelor's degree from Cornell University. She has published in *Economic Development Quarterly,* the *Journal of Planning Education and Research,* and the *Berkeley Planning Journal.*

Mary C. King is associate professor of economics at Portland State University and an associate editor for the journal *Feminist Economics.* Professor King earned a B.A. in economics at Stanford in 1979; studied industrial relations as a Rhodes scholar at Oxford University; and received her Ph.D. in economics from the University of California, Berkeley, in 1991. Her research focuses on the dynamics of gender and ethnicity operating in the U.S. labor market and economy. She is currently working on a project on the role of violence in the maintenance of racial and sexual economic inequality in the United States.

Jeannette Lim is an economics doctoral student at the University of Massachusetts at Amherst. She is also a staff economist for the Center for Popular Economics, a nonprofit collective of political economists. She has worked as a research assistant at the Economic Policy Institute and is currently doing research on gender norms. Her research interests include discrimination in the labor market and economic inequality in the United States. Before beginning her doctoral program she worked at the Labor Education and Research Project in Detroit and the Institute for Social Research at the University of Michigan, Ann Arbor.

Lois B. Shaw is currently employed as a senior consulting economist at the Institute for Women's Policy Research in Washington, DC. She received her B.A. from the University of California, Berkeley; and her Ph.D. in economics from the University of Michigan. Dr. Shaw's past employment includes research positions at the Center for Human Resource Research at Ohio State University and at the U.S. General Accounting Office. She has written extensively on issues concerning women's employment and retirement. She recently completed a report under a grant from the Social Security Administration on elderly women and poverty.

Chris Tilly, University Professor of Regional Economic and Social Development at the University of Massachusetts, Lowell, is author or coauthor of *Half a Job: Bad and Good Part-Time Jobs in a Changing Labor Market, Work under Capitalism,* and *Glass Ceilings and Bottomless Pits: Women's Work, Women's Poverty;* his new book *Stories Employers Tell: Race, Skill, and Hiring in America* will appear in January 2001. He serves on the editorial collective of *Dollars and Sense* magazine and has been active in a variety of campaigns on labor and welfare rights. Professor Tilly received his Ph.D. in economics from M.I.T.

Catherine J. Weinberger first met Mary King and Lee Badgett in 1985, while teaching them mathematical economic theory in graduate school. Since 1989, Cathy has been at home, raising two boys, supporting her husband's career as a research scientist, and doing economics research. She has recently published on the relationships between education and earnings inequality and on mathematical models of bargaining. During the 1999–2001 academic years, Dr. Weinberger's research is being supported by a National Academy of Education Spencer Postdoctoral Fellowship. Dr. Weinberger earned her B.S. in mathematics from the University of Wisconsin, Madison; and her M.A. in mathematics and Ph.D. in economics from the University of California, Berkeley.

Index